Literatur und Recht

Band 15

Series Editor

Klaus Stierstorfer, Münster, Germany

Die Reihe „Literatur und Recht“ bietet eine Publikationsplattform für Forschungen im interdisziplinären Gebiet zwischen Literatur und Recht. In Monographien und thematisch integrierten Sammelbänden erscheinen hier Arbeiten in deutscher Sprache, die dieses hoch aktuelle und sehr produktive Feld bearbeiten, erweitern oder neu vermessen wollen.

Wie bereits im Reihentitel angedeutet, liegt der Schwerpunkt nicht nur auf rechtstheoretischen, rechtssoziologischen oder rechtskulturellen Arbeiten, die die Rolle von Literatur im Rechtsdiskurs und dessen ‚Humanisierung‘ erkunden. Diese Form von Arbeiten, die v.a. im Nachgang des amerikanischen Law and Literature Movement seit den 1970er Jahren entstanden sind, wird durch eine neue Akzentsetzung weiterentwickelt. Hier treffen sich die beiden Disziplinen von Literatur- und Rechtswissenschaft auf Augenhöhe ohne monodirektionale Voreinstellung inhaltlicher, theoretischer, politischer oder ideologischer Art. Grundlagenforschung im interdisziplinären Bereich steht neben Einzelstudien zu einschlägigen Spezialthemen. Darüber hinaus soll die Reihe zwar zum einen Literatur und Recht im europäischen Kontext vertieft erkunden, zum anderen aber auch den Blick weiten auf rechtskulturelle und literarische Kontexte, die durch die traditionelle Recht- und Literatur-Forschung noch wenig erschlossen sind, namentlich in Osteuropa, Asien und Afrika.

Klaus Stierstorfer
Editor

Law and Literature in Europe and Beyond

J.B. METZLER

Editor
Klaus Stierstorfer
SFB 1385 Recht und Literatur Universität
Münster
Münster, Germany

ISSN 2730-7085 ISSN 2730-7093 (electronic)
Literatur und Recht
ISBN 978-3-662-69850-1 ISBN 978-3-662-69851-8 (eBook)
https://doi.org/10.1007/978-3-662-69851-8

Titelbild: Franz Kafka: „Mann, eingezäunt" (um 1905); Skizze zum Roman „Der Prozeß" © Archiv K. Wagenbach / akg-images / picture alliance

This J.B. Metzler imprint is published by the registered company Springer-Verlag GmbH, DE, part of Springer Nature.
The registered company address is: Heidelberger Platz 3, 14197 Berlin, Germany

Law and Literature in Europe and Beyond: Introduction

The process of Europeanisation that has happened in political, social, cultural and especially legal form over the last few decades, may duly be considered one of the most important and powerful changes within Europe, but also beyond. The process of instituting and developing a European internal market as a catalyst did not only lead to the transition of important sovereign rights from individual states to the European union, but also contributed to the latter's political regulation and standing. Such processes of European integration are simultaneously embedded in and countered by tendencies towards legal, political and cultural regionalisation and re-nationalisation, thereby enabling not only a Europewide resurgence of right-wing national parties and factions, but also leading to the erosion of constitutional premises in terms of the separation of powers and the freedom of the press. Further elements, such as the Yugoslav Wars of the 1990s, the global financial crisis of 2008 or the refugee crisis of 2015, have contributed significantly to the conflictual positioning between European integration and disintegration. Brexit and climate change, as well as worldwide digitalisation, also signal towards the need of the integration of Europe and its political borders.

National literatures both on the Continent and in Britain have reflected these disintegrating crises critically, but they have also focused on periods of European integration in less critical times (e.g. Robert Menasse, Ian McEwan, Michel Houellebecq). Consequently, there are obvious processes of how law and literature connect each other as well as insights into the reasons why the legalisation processes in Europe have not been accompanied by a similar cultural and literary integration on a European level—although the institutionalisation and legal guarantee of translations supports the phenomenon of European bestsellers.

At the same time, such processes of Europeanisation and European integration need to be considered in their historical dimension, as scholars across Europe during the Enlightenment, for instance, also saw themselves as one community and acted as such. Questions of natural law as well as the importance of literature for the developing Enlightenment necessarily focused specifically on a European context, which can be seen in Gotthold Ephraim Lessing's position on tolerance as represented in *Nathan der Weise*, for instance, since Lessing conceived of such considerations in an imagined dialogue with theorists such as John Locke and Voltaire. Even tendencies towards nationalisation in the nineteenth and twentieth centuries reflect critically on the political and economic internationalisation of law and literature.

This volume seeks to contribute to the understanding of processes where law and literature combine to achieve European significance. This can happen with regard to a) crucial national and local issues with wider ramifications or exemplary functions, b) with regard to themes linking European nations with each other or c) even pointing beyond the confines of Europe where European concepts of law and literature have impacted other cultures worldwide.

In Chap. 1, Shulamit Almog's "Athena as Initiator of the Judicial Role" discusses Athena as a foundational figure of European concepts of the law and justice. Appropriately opening these explorations, Almog's contribution demonstrates how much of the ensuing European legal debates and literary negotiations of them are already present in Aeschylus' characterization of that Greek goddess. One such legal debate running through large tracts of European legal and cultural history is on the question of equity or, on the perceived and ingrained need for complementarity of a different kind in legislative and judiciary systems. This issue is treated in Chap. 2 by Rabea Conrad in her contribution on equity in Shakespeare's *Titus Andronicus*. Franziska Quabeck's reading of *A Tale of Two Cities* by Charles Dickens in Chap. 3 similarly addresses shortcomings in legal systems, here in the comparison between the French (Continental) and English ones, with a view to the right to prisoner's counsel. Onyebuchi James Ile and Sister Adaoma Igwedibia in Chap. 4 revisit the question of state censorship around the well-known case of D.H. Lawrence's *Lady Chatterley's Lover*. Their analysis is innovative not least because it comes from an African perspective. Jan Gordon's "'Vox Populi' v. Codified Law", in Chap. 5, could be read as a summary consideration of the law in need of a wider, cultural contextualization in his interpretation of novels from America, Britain and Germany where he sees the re-valuation of individual voices otherwise repressed in the systemic structures of the law, but now pointing back to the foundational change emblematized by Thomas Hobbes's *Leviathan*.

Ralph Grüttemeier Lotte van den Bosch and Lina L. Blank, in Chaps. 6, 7 and 8, then examine the legal status of literature, with a specific focus on the Netherlands. Using high court archives both in Germany and the Netherlands, they investigate the jurisdiction on works of literature in the two countries, paying special attention to the *exceptio artis* and its position in high court judgements.

Alina Wolski, in Chap. 9, interrogates Juli Zeh's novels, notably her early Adler und Engel, as to their European narratives, as Europe, in its conceptualization, as perceived as the result of narrations. Piotr Pilarczyk widens the view to Poland when he offers an explanation for the absence of legal issues in Polish Romantic literature. This stark contrast to other European literatures opens up an explanatory context for and inferences on the general preconditions of the occurrence of legal themes in literature in general. Chapters 11 and 12, finally lead further afield, with Owojecho Omoha's readings of legal aspects in Wole Soyinka's poetry, which remains tied back to European concerns both on a theoretical as well as legal level, and Cassandra Sharp's comparative look at narratives in social media during the Corona Pandemic in Australia and Germany.

The seeds for this volume were planted at a conference on Law and Literature in Europe, convened by the Collaborative Research Centre 1385 "Law and Literature" at the University of Münster, Germany, in October 2022. The book project would therefore have been impossible without the funding provided by the German Research Foundation (DFG) and the support, both intellectual and administrative, from the CRC. Svea Türlings, Münster, has given invaluable help in bringing the volume together and into print. All remaining shortcomings are of course the editor's responsibility.

Klaus Stierstorfer

Contents

Contributors

Shulamit Almog is a Full Professor in the Faculty of Law at the University of Haifa. She is Presidential Advisor on Gender Equity and Co-Director of the Center of Law, Gender and Policy at the University. She is the founder of Law and Literature research in Israel. She has published numerous books and articles in US, Canadian, European, and Israeli law reviews. Her recent book, published in De Gruyter Law and Literature series is "The Origins of the Law in Homer".

Lina L. Blank is currently doing her doctorate in a DFG project on sociological literary studies focusing on literary concepts of Dutch political elites at the Carl von Ossietzky University of Oldenburg. She completed her Master's degree in Dutch, English and Art and Media Studies at the University of Oldenburg in 2020 and furthermore studied at the University of Groningen (Netherlands) and the University of Gent (Belgium). She wrote her master's thesis in preparation for her PhD on the freedom of art in parliamentary debates in Belgium and Germany. She received several awards during her studies and presented her work on the reception of literary adaptations in comics at the annual conference of the *Comic Studies Society* in Toronto in 2019. Currently she is focussing on the application of Digital Humanities on the intersection of politics and literature.

Lotte van den Bosch is currently writing a literary dissertation within the Deutsche Forschungsgemeinschaft project "A Country of Mediocre Literature. Literary Concepts of the Legal and Political Elites in the Netherlands in the 20th Century" at the Carl von Ossietzky Universität in Oldenburg. She also works as a researcher and teacher at the Department of Constitutional and Administrative Law at Leiden University. This essay is largely based on a chapter from her dissertation-in-progress.

Rabea Conrad studied German Literature and Philosophy at the Ludwig-Maximilians-Universität in Munich. In her master thesis, "Political Female Sacrifice and the Tragic of Order", she examined the notion of purity in Shakespeare's *Titus Andronicus*. Since 2021, she is a research assistant at the Chair of Modern German Literature and Media at the LMU Munich. Her dissertation project focuses on 'sisterhood' as an apolitical utopia in Germanophone literature since Goethe and Hegel, with a special focus on texts by Thomas Bernhard and Ingeborg Bachmann. Her other research and teaching interests include poetics and political theory, postcolonialism, and deconstruction. Since 2023 she is co-editor of the online journal *Medienobservationen*.

Jan B. Gordon With advanced degrees from Princeton, Jan B. Gordon was among six foreign, full-time Professors hired by national universities in Japan when the law was changed in 1983. He is an Emeritus Professor of Anglo-American Studies at Tokyo University of Foreign Studies and author of *Gossip and Subversion in Nineteenth-Century British Literature: Echo's Economies* (Macmillan and St. Martin's, 1996) and more recently *The Politics of Public Opinion in the Novels of Anthony Trollope: A Tenth Muse* (Anthem, 2023). Several of his essays have been reprinted in Harold Bloom (ed), *Chelsea House Series* (Yale Univ. Press). He was an academic witness in the federal pornography case, *Attica State Prisoners Association v. State of New York* and a U.S. State Dept.-sponsored guest lecturer on American culture in various countries in Southeast Asia between 1975–1981.

Ralf Grüttemeier is professor of Dutch literature at the Carl von Ossietzky Universität Oldenburg. He studied Dutch, German and History in Aachen, Cologne and Amsterdam. He took his PhD in Amsterdam (1994) and has taught at the universities of Cologne, Amsterdam and Ankara. Since 1997 he holds the chair at Oldenburg University, where he was dean from 2005–2007 and from 2019–2021. His research focuses on 20th Dutch literature, theoretical questions as intentionality in interpretation and the relation between law and literature. He was and is member of several national and international committees and boards in the humanities, among which member of the CULT-2 panel of Flemish research organization FWO (2010–2015, 2023-present). He was a Research Fellow of the Netherlands Institute of Advanced Study (NIAS) in 2008/9, co-editor (2003–2009) and editor in chief (2009–2012) of the journal Internationale Neerlandistiek and co-editor of the journal Spiegel der Letteren (2013–2022).

Rev. Sr. Dr. Eugenia Adaoma Igwedibia is an Associate Professor in the Department of English Language and Literature, Nnamdi Azikiwe University, Awka, Nigeria. She teaches Pragmatics, African Diaspora Literature, African/African American literature, Caribbean Literature and Semiotics. She is supervising undergraduate and postgraduate students. She has worked in different secondary schools, Colleges of Education and universities in Nigeria. She has presented papers at several local and international conferences. Sr. Adaoma has published numerous articles in both national and international journals. She has English textbook and Literary Pragmatics textbook to her credit. She has numerous book chapter contributions.

Onyebuchi James Ile was the former Head of English Studies and Associate Professor of literature and critical/strategic thinking and development, Nile University of Nigeria, Abuja. He is also currently Associate Professor of Literature and Critical Strategic Thinking and Development, Nnamdi Azikiwe University, Awka. He was a visiting scholar at the English Department of the University of Münster, Germany, where he taught Home and Belonging in Nigerian Diaspora Literature. He holds a BA/MA in English/American studies and political science, Heinrich Heine Universität Düsseldorf, and a PhD in English literature and political science, University of Münster. His expertise covers all areas of literary theory and criticism, African Literature, American and English literature. His research interests are in the area of literature, cultural and social development.

Owojecho Omoha's PhD, at University of Jos, Nigeria, was in poetic madness. He invented the literary model Capture Theory, using cognitive approach to literary studies. Omoha's inventive essay "Capture Theory: Battling with Tropes in T.S. Eliot's The Waste Land" was published by *Arizona Quarterly: A Journal of American Literature, Culture & Theory* in 2019. His research interests are in memory, emotion, attention, madness studies, law and literature. He is a professor in poetry and psychoanalytic studies at the Department of English, University of Abuja, Nigeria.

Piotr Miłosz Pilarczyk is lawyer and historian, university professor at the Faculty of Law and Administration of Adam Mickiewicz University in Poznań. He has published, among others, *The origins of the government budget in Poland* and *The judiciary adopted by the Treasury Commission of the Grand Duchy of Lithuania in fiscal cases (1765–1794)*. He conducts research in the field of legal history, fiscal history and *law and literature*. Member of the Board of the Polish Society for the Legal History.

Dr Cassandra Sharp is a Professor of Law at the University of Wollongong, Australia. Her research is based in cultural legal studies and focuses on interdisciplinary explorations of law as it is constructed in the public imagination through popular texts. Most recently this has involved drawing on cultural studies, linguistic theory, psychology, and legal theory to interrogate public interaction with the law, as manifested within the use of social media responses to terrorism and social crises. The application of this research methodology has been recently applied to the discourses of social media, as illustrated in her latest book: *Hashtag Jurisprudence: Terror and Legality on Twitter* (Edward Elgar, 2022). She is also the co-editor of *Cultural Legal Studies: Law's Popular Cultures and the Metamorphosis of Law* (Routledge, 2015) (with Marett Leiboff, UOW). She was Managing Editor of *Law Text Culture* from 2016–2020 and is currently serving on its Editorial Board.

Alina Wolski is a lecturer at both the law and philology faculties in Bochum and a research assistant at the chair for civil law, international private law, and comparative law, commercial and business law. She holds degrees in general and comparative literature, history, and national and European business law from Ruhr University Bochum, Germany, and Université de Tours, France. In her doctoral thesis, she examines the law and literature movement in the twenty-first century.

Athena as Initiator of the Judicial Role

Shulamit Almog

Introduction

This paper proposes that ancient narratives of Greek Mythology shed light on the intricate nature of the judicial role, manifested by the figure of the goddess Athena. Athena, as depicted in the *Oresteia*, the Aeschylean tragedy, is the founder of the court and of the judicial role. Another layer of Athena's role is her depiction in Homer's *Odyssey* as well as in the *Oresteia* as a mediator and conciliator who promotes multi-party deliberation in order to obtain a long-term solution, optimal to the public good. In this sense, Athena's acts of mediation and conciliation highlight the limitations of formal institutional judging, and signal how to enrich it. In contemporary terms, in her acts of judging Athena integrates elements of alternative dispute resolution.

In the following, the character of Athena in the *Odyssey* and in the *Oresteia* will be presented as crystalizing expectations and hopes related to judgment, as well as the failures inherent in the phenomena of law and judicial ruling. Athena, as will be elaborated, denotes a sort of zero point of the judicial role, as embodying, since antiquity, the challenging sides and the redeeming traits of the phenomena of law.

S. Almog (✉)
Faculty of Law, University of Haifa, Haifa, Israel

K. Stierstorfer (ed.), *Law and Literature in Europe and Beyond*, Literatur und Recht 15, https://doi.org/10.1007/978-3-662-69851-8_1

Athena as a Mediator and Conciliator

Let me commence with two seminal stories set in a period known as Heroic or Mycenaean in the history of Greece.[1] The main event of the heroic period was the Trojan War which according to the myth, lasted about ten years and took place, perhaps, in the twelfth century BC.[2] At the end of the war, the Greek heroes turn home.

In the first story Agamemnon, the leader of the army, returns to Argos, to be immediately slain by his wife and her lover. Orestes, his son, takes revenge by killing both murderers. The goddesses of vengeance seek to exercise their duty to take his life. At this point, Athena intervenes and for the first time in Western history, a court is established by her. Orestes is put on trial and acquitted (Aeschylus 1970a).[3] The intervention of Athena solved not only the specific conflict, but also put an end to the chain of blood that had plagued society are generations. It also established a new regime—from now on conflicts will be dealt with in courts. According to the second story, ten years after Agamemnon's ill-fated return to Argos, Odysseus arrives back in Ithaca, where insolent suitors have been harassing his wife Penelope, aiming to take over his court and murder his son. After Odysseus kills them all, the families seek revenge. In this case, too, Athena intervenes. She asks for Zeus's help, and he makes the family members forget the killing of the sons and brothers. Later, assuming the appearance and voice of Mentor, Athena acts to achieve an alliance between all for the time to come (Homer 2001b).

The first story is told in Aeschylus' (458 BCE) *Oresteia* and is considered a foundational story of the establishment law and formal judgment. The second story is told in Homer's *Odyssey*, written centuries earlier (around the eighth century BC). In both cases, Athena stands at the center of the conflict, and in both it is she who brings it to an end by means of active intervention, motivated, as we are told, by her wish to help the two heroes, Odysseus and Orestes. Her intervention, which in both cases combines elements of coercion and intimidation with elements of rhetoric, conciliation and persuasion, does indeed resolve the two conflicts. There are, however, significant differences between her modes of action in the two stories. Athena plans ahead how to assist Odysseus' return, and to support his revenge on the suitors. On Orestes' behalf she operates *ex post*, only after he decided to take revenge, and fled to her temple. Following, Athena

---

[1] The Heroic Age comes after the Bronze Age and prior to the Iron Age, according to Hesiod (1959, 15–117).

[2] The myths about the Trojan War, the wrath of Achilles, Hector's death, and Odysseus' prolonged return to Ithaca had passed from generation to generation even before Homer recorded them. See Almog (2022, 3).

[3] *The Libation Bearers* recounts how Orestes, Agamemnon's and Clytemnestra's son, murdered his mother and her lover to avenge his father's death, after which the Erinyes arrive and Orestes flees (Aeschylus, 1970c). *The Eumenides* tells how Orestes stands before a court established by Athena (Aeschylus 1970b).

establishes a new institution—a court—which is harnessed to solve Orestes' predicament (Almog 2022, 41). The difference in the way the two creators, Homer and Aeschylus, chose to describe Athena's modes of action could be attributed to the social and political changes in Greece during the centuries that separate the works (31, 32).

Aeschylus' drama reflects a transformation in the course of which the judicial roles and procedures, already present before,[4] shifted from the preservation of patriarchal rituals into pursuing civil justice in the name of the polis.[5] Interestingly, however, Athena's character in *The Eumenides* retains prominent themes that connect to the Homeric Athena. First, in both narratives Athena appears to know that power alone does not yield a sustainable solution in a complex social environment, whether that power is executed as a judicial act, or an act of violence. In both narratives, Athena employs other tools besides power, in order to advance a long-term agreement.

In the *Odyssey* the conflict is finally ended only after Athena employs conciliatory speech. Instead of imposing a coercive resolution, she strives to achieve an agreed one. After Orestes' acquittal, the enraged Furies threaten to send a plague upon Athens. Athena reminds the Furies of the menacing power of Zeus' lightning, and the advantages to be gained if they yield to the verdict:

> You are not dishonored; do not with excessive wrath blight the land of mortals, goddesses that you are! I, for my part, have trust in Zeus, and—why need I speak of it?—I alone among the gods know the keys of the house wherein is sealed the lightning. But there is no need of it; let me persuade you, and do not discharge upon this land the words of an idle tongue so as to cause all things that bear fruit no more to prosper. Lull to repose the bitter force of your black wave of anger, since you shall be honored and revered and dwell with me! (Aeschylus 1970b, 824–833)

Turning to the Athenians, Athena tries to convince them of the advantages of the new way to resolve disputes that she intends to institute from now onwards:

> Such is the object of awe that you must justly dread, and so you shall have a bulwark of the land and a protector of the city such as none of human kind possesses, neither among the Scythians nor in the domains of Pelops. (Aeschylus 1970b, 700–703)

The Furies and the Athenians are won by Athena's arguments. Eventually, it's Athena's mediatory effort and not the acquittal or the divine force that leads to a resolution of the conflict in both cases.[6] Despite Athena's ability to impose on the

[4] The judicial-like scene engraved upon the shield of Achilles is of central importance in this context, illustrating the norms that already existed at the time to control the urge of vengeance (Homer 2001a, 18.580–18.592). For elaboration of the shield scene, see Westbrook (1992, 76).

[5] Aeschylus' tragedies reflect historic changes that diminished the authority of the patriarchal family and subordinated it to the authority of the polis (Kuhns 1962, 66, 67).

[6] On Athena as mediator, see Gagarin (1986, 42).

parties a rigid decision from above that they are obliged to submit themselves to, she strives for an agreed solution, and achieves a long-term pact.

The common element of the closures that Athena is responsible for in these two works is that in both of them the creators depicted Athena as not satisfied with only one tool as she moved away from a formalistic conception of a judicial role, and acts out of what appears to be a recognition that the best interest of society requires wide agreements. In both works, Athena is described as a mediator and conciliator who conducts a multiparty discourse that is lively, dynamic and sensitive to the needs of all sides to the dispute, in order to arrive at a long-term solution beneficial to society as a whole. In the context of the *Odyssey*, Athena's act of mediation and conciliation seems to acknowledge the limitations of power and its inability to provide sustainable solutions to intricate conflicts. In the context of the *Oresteia*, Athena's mediation and conciliation seems to highlight the limitations of formal institutional judging. In contemporary terms, in her formal judging Athena also integrates elements of alternative dispute resolution (Almog 2022, 45). As both the *Odyssey* and the *Oresteia* exemplify, a sustainable resolution is achieved only after recognizing the interests of all sides (Kuhns 1962, 66).

Athena as a Flawed Judge

The duality of the figure of Athena—which perhaps resonates with the profound duality, pointed out by Nietzsche, at the heart of Aeschylus' drama in general[7]—is revealed in yet another context: the conspicuous flaws in the judicial procedure she establishes. 'The triumph of law' in the *Oresteia* is flawed, as various critical readings—Marxist, feminist, and others—suggest.[8]

A number of problems that characterize the judicial procedure described in the *Oresteia*, most of them relating to Athena, are multiple and contradicting roles. The moment Athena becomes the founder of criminal justice; she harnesses the new social instrument that she is establishing, the rule of law, to the service of men:

> For there is no mother who gave birth to me
> and I approve the male principle in all things and with all my heart –
> except in the matter of marriage, and am very much my father's child
> (Aeschylus 1970b, 736–738)

Athena's statement is the gist of the *Oresteia*. Orestes' acquittal of his mother's murder, primarily because the victim was a woman, becomes the primary representation of judicial action on which the rule of law is predicated:

[7] See Nietzsche (2000 [1872], 67).

[8] For elaboration see Goldhill (2004, 30–33).

> […] and I belong altogether to my father. Therefore I shall not give greater weight to the death of a woman, one who slew her husband, the watcher of the house; Orestes is the winner, even should the votes be equal. (Aeschylus 1970b, 738–741)

Thus, from its original formation by Athena, the rule of law is designed as a tool serving the superiority and privileged status of the patriarchal elite. Athena adamantly declares her support for the defendant due to his gender, regardless of the specific matter at hand: "I vouch myself the champion of the man, not of the woman, yea, with all my soul" (Aeschylus 1970b, 737, 738). The way the legal procedure is constructed and conducted reinforces the sense of favoritism. Aeschylus describes the course of the trial with brevity. Athena allows Apollo—who by his own account serves as a witness, as an attorney, and as the one who counseled Orestes to kill his mother—to present his arguments in Orestes' favor (Aeschylus 1970b, 574–580). After Apollo does so at some length, the Erinyes make no response and there is no discussion of the questions that arise. The trial ends in no decision. It is then that Athena casts her deciding vote. Against this background, the Erinyes' frustration and rage is understandable, though they are incapable to label it with tags that developed in later stages of the rule of law such as "bias," "prejudice" or "conflict of interests." When Athena realizes that the judicial outcome cannot stand alone, she takes upon herself the task of conciliating the Erinyes, which is accomplished successfully. And yet, the way Athena functions in the *Oresteia* makes it challenging to reconcile her actions with any conception of procedural or substantial justice associated with the rule of law (Almog 2022, 45).

Athena as a Judge and the 'Literature Alongside Law Paradigm'

The constitutive moment described in *The Eumenides* is of immense importance. Once it was presented, even if the judicial model presented by Athena is imperfect, flawed and blemished, women and men could no longer do without it. The 'literature alongside law paradigm' (Almog 2001, 53–65) is useful for delineation of the intricate juxtaposing between the essentiality of law, its imminent failures and the eternal quest to address them and strive for better law.

The 'literature alongside law paradigm' involves two stages. The first emphasizes the fact that law is vital, alongside its inherently flawed nature. This duality is embedded in the generative narrative pertaining to the establisher of criminal justice in the *Oresteia*. As described, Athena accentuates that the new social instrument that she is establishing—the rule of law through formal courts—is primarily designed to serve male interests. Patriarchal domination becomes a constituting principle of the new legal system. Orestes' acquittal is openly based upon the fact that he killed a woman, and not a man. Thus, literature depicts law from its inception as a tool serving men and failing women. Consequently, the story Aeschylus recounts in the *Oresteia* is not a story of the triumph of justice, equity, or human dignity. It is primarily a story about achieving social stability, and, more specifically, it is the formative story of this new tool, the rule of law, and its instrumental role in perpetuating the dominance of upper-class men (Almog 2022, 17).

Here enters the second stage of the 'literature alongside law paradigm'. Identifying the limits of law is important for developing and shaping remedies. Once the failures and flaws of existing law have been identified, the next step is to imagine putting things right, to achieving equilibrium between law, human needs, and human limitations. This second stage uses narratives that derive from imagination to suggest possible reforms. For example, narratives focusing upon the plight of individuals enhance sensitivity and attentiveness to others. Imagination embedded in literary narratives supports the eternal effort to improve law (Almog 2022, 16).

As the paradigm of 'literature alongside law' proclaims, establishing the rule of law is a tremendous human accomplishment. It reflects the most sophisticated aspects of human social existence. The law is also prone to mistakes and failures, yet these can be addressed. It is capable of protecting and perpetuating social order but can be instrumental in its destruction. History after the *Oresteia* will reveal that law is a constantly evolving mechanism. The continuous flow of 'literature alongside law' supports the unremitting hope of bettering the law (Almog 2022, 17).

Conclusion

The Athena of the *Odyssey* and the Athena of the *Oresteia* are surrounded by many other Athenas that co-exist in the cultural imagination, each of them resonating with historical developments and shifts in the way the character of the Greek goddess was perceived by those who passed on the stories about her from one generation to the next.[9] This paper's focus was on the Athena of the *Odyssey* and the Athena of the *Oresteia* as a figure that embodies the complexity of the judicial role, apparent already in ancient generative narratives relating to its origin. As was described, through the figure of Athena, the act of judgment emerges as a practice that represents the essentiality of law, alongside its failures and the constant hope to achieve better law. Judgment is also presented as a practice that in actual fact leans on deliberation and mediation. Athena, a powerful female character, combining sagacity, shrewd strategizing, and inventiveness, represents all these. Whithin the ancient narratives on her actions, the sources of the complexity of the judicial role can be traced; despite the centuries and massive transformations that separate their authors, both the Homeric epic and the Aeschylean tragedy place at the heart of the narrative the figure of a goddess whose acts represent landmarks along the road to the rule of law (Almog 2022, 126, 127).

As would become clear over the course of generations, law is part of a constantly developing human endeavor, loaded with the ability to protect the social order and the capacity to undermine it. Still, as the 'paradigm of literature

[9] For an instructive review of the history of the development of the use of Athena's character and the abundance of cultural contexts in which it appears, see Deacy (2008, 122–156).

alongside law' asserts, law is indispensable. The artistic works discussed here reveal the arbitrary-delusionary basis of the legal sphere, and at the same time re-establish the law as part of a tremendous human achievement. Law is linked to vision, and achievement, and also deemed to produce mistakes, failures, and disappointments, yet it can never be abandoned. The continuous flow of literature alongside law supports the everlasting hope of bettering the law.

References

Aeschylus. 1970a. *Agamemnon*. Trans. Hugh Lloyd-Jones. Englewood Cliffs, N.J.: Prentice-Hall.

Aeschylus. 1970b. *The Eumenides*. Trans. Hugh Lloyd-Jones. Englewood Cliffs, N.J.: Prentice-Hall.

Aeschylus. 1970c. *The Libation Bearers*. Trans. Hugh Lloyd-Jones. Englewood Cliffs, N.J.: Prentice-Hall.

Almog, Shulamit. 2001. Literature alongside law as a contemporary paradigm. *Cultural Dynamics* 13(1).

Almog, Shulamit. 2022. *The Origins of the Law in Homer*. Berlin, Boston: De Gruyter, 2022.

Deacy, Susan. 2008. *Athena*. London: Routledge.

Gagarin, Michael. 1986. *Early Greek Law*. Berkeley, CA: University of California Press.

Goldhill, Simon. 2004. *Aeschylus, the Oresteia*. 2nd ed. Cambridge, England; New York: Cambridge University Press.

Hesiod. 1959. *The Works and Days: Theogony. The Shield of Herakles*. Trans. Richmond Lattimore. Ann Arbor: University of Michigan Press.

Homer. 2001a. *The Iliad*. Trans. Robert Fagles. London: The Folio Society.

Homer. 2001b. *The Odyssey*. Trans. Robert Fagles. London: The Folio Society.

Kuhns, Richard. 1962. *The House, the City, and the Judge: The Growth of Moral Awareness in the Oresteia*. Indianapolis: Bobbs-Merrill.

Nietzsche, Friedrich Wilhelm. 2000 [1872]. *The Birth of Tragedy*. Trans. Smith Douglas. Oxford; New York: Oxford University Press.

Westbrook, Raymond. 1992. The Trial Scene in the Iliad. *Harvard Studies in Classical Philology* 94: 53–76.

Titus's Rome and Shakespeare's England: The 'Tragic Conflict' Between Law and Equity in *Titus Andronicus*

Rabea Conrad

Titus Andronicus is probably Shakespeare's bloodiest play. It portrays the fall and restitution of an imaginary Rome. The drama's intertexts are numerous: the *Aeneid*[1]; the *Metamorphoses*[2]; but especially the legends of Virginia and Lucretia from the *Roman History* by Titus Livius.[3] In both stories, a virgin woman is raped or threatened with rape by a tyrant, and then sacrificed to restore order to the Roman state. By referring to them, Shakespeare inherits a long Western tradition and goes back to the (imaginary) origin of both Roman state and law as well as the origin of European civilization *in* Rome. In his play, the story of the pious Roman Titus and his family runs parallel to the fate of the state, too.[4] Both family and state are ruined following an initial act of desecration: in the first instance, the victim is the virgin daughter, in the second instance it is the ritual-legal order of

[1] Patrick Gray has interpreted Shakespeare's relationship to this intertext as a postcolonial reading avant la lettre: Shakespeare does not join in Virgil's praise of the Roman empire, but refers to the "missing element, the cost of the imperium": compassion (Gray 2016, 57).

[2] The story of the nymph Philomela is another important intertext for many (feminist) readings of Shakespeare which focus on the 'wilderness' as opposed to the state order of Rome. Nature in *Titus* is both: barbaric and female (see for example Kahn 1997; Miola 1981; Tricomi 1976, Wynne-Davies 1991).

[3] The story of Lucrecia is found in Livius' *Ab Urbe Condita* in Book 1, Sects. 57–59, that of Virginia in Book 3, Sects. 44–48.

[4] Janette Dillon underlines the political dimension of the tragedy in her Introduction: "Titus Andronicus is not the tragedy of one man or even one family, but of Rome" (Dillon 2010, 38).

R. Conrad (✉)
Institut für Deutsche Philologie, Ludwig-Maximilians-Universität München, München, Germany
e-mail: rabea.conrad@germanistik.uni-muenchen.de

K. Stierstorfer (ed.), *Law and Literature in Europe and Beyond*, Literatur und Recht 15, https://doi.org/10.1007/978-3-662-69851-8_2

Rome which is violated. The question usually raised with respect to Rome's self-perception as a civilised state is the following: Who are the barbarians that penetrate from outside into the heart of one's own power, one's own law? Or, in other words: Who rapes the order? I would like to show that in Shakespeare, the question of Rome's legacy is complicated and fragmented. It appears to be not so easy to determine, who are the barbarians here. This affects us even today, and challenges us to question our claim to be just by following the letter of European laws.

Barbarous Romans

At the beginning of the play, General Titus just won the war against the Goths and is now after his return to Rome referred to as "surnamed Pius" (Shakespeare 2021, 1.1.23). In the first scene, his son Lucius asks his father for a sacrifice for his fallen brothers by citing the formula "*Ad manes fratrum*" (1.1.101). In accordance with Roman law and rite, Alarbus is chosen, the eldest son of the Gothic queen Tamora, who has just entered the stage as a prisoner of war in the entourage of Titus. Tamora—as a mother—pleads Titus to save her son's life—as a father:

Tamora Stay, Roman brethren! Gracious conqueror,
Victorious Titus, rue the tears I shed,
A mother's tears in passion for her son!
And if thy sons were ever dear to thee,
O, think my son to be as dear to me. [...]
O, if to fight for king and commonweal
Were piety in thine, it is in these.
Andronicus, stain not thy tomb with blood:
Wilt thou draw near the nature of the gods?
Draw near them then in being merciful.
Sweet mercy is nobility's true badge:
Thrice noble Titus, spare my first-born son. (1.1.107–123)

In her rhetorically demanding speech, Tamora specifically addresses her tears as well as the principal equality of the love of a mother and a father. Ronald Broude (1970) calls her speech "an eloquent plea for mercy" (31) and Virginia Richter (2012) takes her "artful rhetoric [as] a badge of high civilisation in both Roman literature and Renaissance humanism"[5] (190). Therefore, by demonstrating the *humanity* of the Goths through rhetoric, Tamora arouses pity and makes her request seem humanly justified. At the same time, she suggests that the Goths are equal to the—seemingly—more civilized, 'pious' Romans. The parallel she draws is problematic, because it makes the recent war appear as one between equals, equals with respect to their degree of civilization. All of a sudden, it becomes

[5] My translation, R.C. The original quote reads: "Da kunstvolle Rhetorik sowohl in der römischen Literatur als auch im Humanismus der Renaissance ein Ausweis hoher Zivilisation ist, ist Tamoras Rede doppelt effektiv." (Richter 2012, 190).

ambiguous whether the war was a 'rightful war' against barbarians, which is the subtext of all previous action and dialogue. This ambiguity brings about the conflict of the play and the eventual escalation of violence. The sacrifice of Alarbus, which is meant to bring peace, fails precisely because Tamora's plea implicitly questions the constitutive difference between Romans and Goths, between friend and foe.[6] As a result, what seems to be a civilized act of pure and purifying sacrifice, is all of a sudden perceived as a horrific act of violence. Therefore, the attribute 'barbarian', originally attributed to the Goths, can now be attributed to the Roman side (Richter 2012, 194). Paradoxically, it is the strict form, the purity of ritual and Roman law itself, that unleashes the violence in the first place and leads to Rome's downfall. The problem is to be found *within* the Roman order. This also becomes visible at another point in the first scene: in the decision of who will get to marry Lavinia, Titus's daughter.

After Titus declines the rule of the empire that is offered to him, he uses the power of his popularity to promote the unpopular Saturnine to the throne. The latter returns the favour by choosing Lavinia as his bride and empress. Titus gladly accepts the offer, although she is already engaged to Bassianus, Saturnine's brother and rival to the throne. This sets off a discussion on legal rights: Bassianus insists on his "right" and "reason" (Shakespeare 2021, 1.1.283) and is supported by Marcus: "*Suum cuique* is our Roman justice: / This prince in justice seizeth but his own" (1.1.284–285). Lucius also leaps to Bassianus's defense. Nevertheless, Titus remains convinced of his right to make a decision about Lavinia's fate. He is outraged: "Treason, my lord—Lavinia is surpris'd." (1.1.288) Notably, Titus later chooses the same expression—to be 'surprised'—after he has learned of his daughter's rape by Chiron and Demetrius. This parallelism shows how the violation of the legally defined patriarchal right of control over women is doubled in Shakespeare's play: Even before Lavinia is physically raped, Titus has, in his eyes, been robbed of his domestic power over her—a power that is, legally, his. This is equivalent to desecration in that he himself is no longer in control of the "intactness of the daughter's hymen"[7]—which can be read as in the legends of Virginia and Lucretia as a symbol of the intactness of the Roman state and its order (Koschorke et al. 2007, 38). The word 'rape' also draws attention to this

[6] I here refer to Carl Schmitt's concept of the political, which is defined by the distinction between friend and foe: "Die spezifisch politische Unterscheidung, auf welches ich die politischen Handlungen und Motive zurückführen lassen, ist die Unterscheidung von *Freund* und *Feind*" (Schmitt 2015, 25). My translation: "The specifically political distinction to which political actions and motives can be traced is the distinction between friend and foe."

[7] This phrase comes from Koschorke et al.: The author's collective speaks of the "Intaktheit des töchterlichen Hymens" (Koschorke et al. 2007, 44), which is relevant to the legends of Virginia and Lucretia and their political symbolism of their raped virginity: "die Polis selbst, obwohl sie doch nur aus männlichen Subjekten besteht, [spiegelt] sich in Bildern des unversehrten weiblichen Geschlechtskörpers" (Koschorke et al. 2007, 38). My translation: "the polis itself, although it consists only of male subjects, is reflected in images of the 'intact' female body".

double—physical and legal—desecration of Lavinia when it is used in connection with Bassianus' 'bride-stealing':

Saturninus Traitor, if Rome have law or we have power,
Thou and thy faction shall repent this rape.
Bassianus 'Rape' call you it, my lord, to seize my own,
My true betrothed love, and now my wife?
But let the laws of Rome determine all
Meanwhile am I possessed of that is mine. (1.1.408–413)

Bassianus refers to the laws of Rome and thus declares the dispute over Lavinia a legal dispute. He confidently offers his brother a judicial solution, but whether the law is really on his side, Shakespeare leaves unanswered. The formal phrase *suum cuique* as a principle to which both parties ultimately refer remains ambivalent here: the future husband on the one hand, and the father on the other, embody a dilemma of patriarchal Roman law. If the legal claim itself is no longer obvious, neither the barbarian 'rapists' nor a tyrannical ruler can be clearly identified as the cause of state disorder. It turns out that the problem is no longer a simple violation of the law. Instead, in *Titus Andronicus*, law itself becomes problematic, since an appeal to Roman law in its formal purity is no longer plausible, and no longer possible. How could one remain 'pious' to a legal system that is inconclusive?

Titus's Tragic Guilt and the Logic of Roman Law

Paradoxically, by constantly invoking Roman law and the observance of it, Titus becomes guilty several times: he insists on the cruel ritual of the human sacrifice of Alarbus; he helps the future tyrant Saturninus to the throne because he blindly defends the right of the elder. Over the course of the legal dispute over Lavinia, he murders, or 'slays' (Shakespeare 2021, 1.1.298), one of his own sons. This all happens in the first scene; Titus's understanding of law leaves his family and Rome shattered. Faced with the shambles, when Titus does not even want to receive his son's body into the family tomb, his brother Lucius admonishes him: "Thou art a Roman; be not barbarous" (1.1.383). But it is too late. Pious Titus already got caught in the tragic spiral of revenge; he can no longer count on the pity of others, which he himself refused. Over the course of the play, he is caught up with and haunted by the violence triggered by his legal literalism.[8]

[8] Heather James identifies Titus' culpability with the deadly logic of patriarchy: "Titus' religious, patriotic, and familial observances conform to the letter rather than the spirit of the law. Titus' obsession with form is emblematically entwined with death, to judge by the Andronici's prominently displayed 500-year-old tomb." Her argument connects the sinister motif of the family tomb as a symbol of the order to which Titus is committed with his formal legal obedience (James 1991, 125).

In Act 3, when it comes to the show trial against Titus's remaining sons Mutius and Quintus, who are to be framed for the murder of Bassianus (Act 2), he begs the Roman tribunes for pity:

Titus Hear me, grave fathers; noble tribunes, stay!
For pity of mine age, whose youth was spent
In dangerous wars whilst you securely slept;
For all my blood in Rome's great quarrel shed,
For all the frosty nights that I have watched,
And for these bitter tears, which now you see
Filling the aged wrinkles in my cheeks,
Be pitiful to my condemned sons,
Whose souls is not corrupted as 'tis thought. (3.1.1–9)

Although Titus still refers to his own piety, to his own merit for Rome, he already seems to be aware that he is crying and pleading in vain; he now has insight into the merciless connection between Roman piety and pitiless harshness, which made him guilty in the first place. It is the pious, but pitiless consequence or 'consequentiality' which is fatal.

Yet despite this insight, towards the end of the play, this original error returns as the virtue of the new sovereign, who establishes a new order with a new claim of piety that forbids pity in certain cases. Lucius imposes a ban on compassion on the Black servant Aaron: "If any one relieves or pities him, / For the offence he dies. This is our doom" (Shakespeare 2021, 5.3.180–181), and also makes a cruel example of Tamora's body:

Lucius As for that ravenous tiger, Tamora,
No funeral rite, nor man in mourning weed,
No mournful bell shall ring her burial,
But throw her forth to beasts and birds to prey:
Her life was beastly and devoid of pity,
And being dead, let birds on her take pity. (5.3.194–199)

This brutal ending to Shakespeare's revenge tragedy raises many questions: How can the spiral of violence be broken if the new order is also already faced with the problem of pity versus piety? Further, a law that is to be taken seriously needs to be able to be enforced, no matter what. What would be the alternative?

Because Titus paradoxically becomes guilty by strictly adhering to Roman law, his *hamartia*, his tragic guilt, raises the question of the connection between pity and piety, law and violence. I want to show that this dramatic conflict illustrates a certain repetitive dynamic inherent in English legal history as well as the problem of legal philosophy that is inscribed in this dynamic. In the Elizabethan age, the English legal system was a dual system, consisting of both law and equity. The law went back to all the precedents that were ever admitted as 'writs' before the royal court (Buhofer 2007, 721). A 'common' law for the whole kingdom had already developed in England in the twelfth and thirteenth centuries—unlike in continental Europe. This was not primarily the result of a reception of Roman law, but based on a combination of various "local customary laws" (Potter 2015, 46). In the rest of Europe, the civil law was structured 'top-down', based on the Roman model and "rights were formed into directly applicable, abstract concepts"[9] (Buhofer 2007, 730). The more inductive English law was, in contrast, based on individual cases: The function of the writs "was not that of abstract legal concepts"[10] (712) and they were "subject to change and new forms could be created"[11] (711).

So, unlike the strongly formalized and clearly structured civil law, English common law at the time of Shakespeare developed from a Germanic case law (Buhofer 2007, 710). Furthermore, it was oriented towards the type of solution ('remedy'), and not strictly organized according to the type of conflict (722). The common law "unfolded along practical needs"[12] (719, 720). Towards this background, the common law—with its orientation towards concrete individual cases—could be described as 'fairer' than the Roman civil law, which, due to its abstractness, was more indifferent to the individual. The 'barbaric' English law appears to be the more humane. Harry Potter (2015) pathetically underlines this ability of English law to assert pity in his *Brief History of Common Law*: "Equity stitched a tear in the fabric of justice" (100).

Given that Shakespeare was familiar with English law—as derived from Germanic case law—, the friendly or even civilized portrayal of the 'barbarian Goths' and the emphasis on pity as a human virtue in *Titus Andronicus* is understandable. For Shakespeare, this humanity could be found in the barbarians, of all people, and the Roman legal system would prove harsh and inhumane. This interpretation is shared by Ronald Broude (1970), who argues that—due to a Protestant self-image—the distinction between the supposedly uncivilized Germanic Goths and the supposedly civilized Romans was not as self-evident for Elizabethan Englishmen as we may assume today (27–29).

There is, however, another story to be told with regard to England's common law. It is about the concept of equity, which was a right of grace of the king that could additionally compensate for injustices of the common law. But why does the common law need an instrument to compensate for unjust hardship? Here, we need to consult the more recent past of Shakespeare's time: the period immediately following the Wars of the Roses. In these times, the old law had to be

---

[9] My translation. The original quotation reads: "direkt anwendbare[], abstrakte[] Konzepte" (Buhofer 2007, 730).

[10] My translation. The original quotation reads: Die Funktion der *writs* war "nicht diejenige abstrakter rechtlicher Konzepte" (Buhofer 2007, 712).

[11] My translation. The original quotation reads: Sie waren "Änderungen unterworfen und neue Formen konnten kreiert werden" (Buhofer 2007, 711).

[12] My translation. The original quotation reads: Das *common law* "entfaltete sich entlang praktischer Bedürfnisse" (Buhofer 2007, 719, 720).

reinstated in a country that had fallen into disarray as a result of the wars, and in order to implement this, a strong royal authority was needed (Potter 2015, 97). The Tudor dynasty made extensive use of their rights of intervention (97). Under Henry VIII, in 1539, the *Statute of Proclamations* was passed, which gave the king extensive legislative power (98). This prominent position of the king held the danger of despotism for future generations and the emerging absolutism (98). At the time, the common law took on a Roman imperialist flavour. One could speak of a Roman 'fall from grace' of the common law, but on closer inspection, the legal development in fifteenth century England shows: The 'Roman evil' can be found even earlier, and in the heart of the common law, and made royal interventions such as equity necessary in the first place.

Stephan Buhofer (2007) has pointed out that despite all 'Germanic' independence, there was already a first, intensive contact with Roman law in the early stages of common law (714). This becomes especially evident in the efforts to create a comprehensive and systematic overview of the writs in order to condense them into a legal order, and thus create a legal system (711–714). Even if this failed in that Roman categories could not be adopted (719), the procedural criterion of the writ system was nevertheless formalized and codified. As a result, the formerly flexible case law had solidified into a narrow legal framework in the fifteenth century (Potter 2015, 98). The law had become "less receptive to foreign ideas" (98) and could not develop further after its initial rapid development: "The law grew rigid, while injustice increased and circumstances changed" (99). The seemingly 'human' English law had become "highly technical" and "legalistic" (99) and proved incapable of recognizing exceptions in the sense of justice.

Interestingly, equity served as an instrument of the ruler to compensate for precisely such injustices and hardships of the law, which derived from its formalization. King James I explained how the king's balancing intervention was used, and addressed the humanistic mission attached to it:

> Laws are ordained as rules of virtuous and social living and not to be snares to trap good subjects; and therefore the law must be interpreted according to the meaning and not to the literal sense. (as cited in Potter 2015, 100)

What could quickly transform into an arbitrary and despotic intervention due to the suspension of the established law, was initially supposed to enable natural and balancing justice.

Between Despotism and Rigid Strictness: Justice?

Once again there is the idea of 'stitching a tear into the fabric of justice', by incorporating pity into the law. But the attempts at consolidating different approaches to justice cannot be completely absorbed into a legislation which is fully just. The fundamental conflict between the law and equity, piety and pity, is not overcome by new attempts at reform, but perpetuated. There seems to be a dialectic of law that allows no synthesis. The political-legal history, just as its dramatic representation, ends in an aporia. The irresolvable problem is that equity, which was conceived as a way of compensating for the unjust hardships of the common law that had ossified into formalism, in turn generated unjust arbitrariness and was itself seized by an urge to systematize. In *Titus Andronicus*, the *aporia* derives from the impossibility of demanding formal rigor from, and piety to the abstract law, and at the same time, the urge to do justice to the individual human being. Although the action of the play confirms the necessity of pity; at the end of the play, when the order is reinstated, it is precisely the principle of pity which is precluded. This is evident in the exclusion of the 'barbaric' Tamora as well as of the Black character Aaron from the supposedly natural-innocent order of pity and reconciliation.

These aporias, which are inscribed in law and justice, are also addressed by Jacques Derrida in his essay and lecture *Force of Law: The 'Mystical Foundation of Authority'*. In this essay, Derrida presupposes the distinction

> between justice and *droit*, between justice (infinite, incalculable, rebellious to rule and foreign to symmetry, heterogeneous and heterotropic) and the exercise of justice as law or right, legitimacy or legality, stabilizable and statutory, calculable, a system of regulated and coded prescriptions. (Derrida 1992, 22)

Based on this distinction is his description of the aporia of justice: the question of how freedom and calculability are related to one another. According to Derrida, we need to assume the axiom of freedom in order to conceive the possibility of responsibility and just action. However, in order to be able to recognize something as just, it needs to be related to the law in the first place, which in turn, in its pure derivability and calculability, excludes freedom and thus also justice (Derrida 1992, 22, 23). In order for a judge to judge justly, he therefore needs not merely to follow the letter of the law (23). Simply applying the law is insufficient. This is what Titus fails to understand due to his piety. Instead, the judge needs to confirm the law, to reinvent it and, as it were, reinstate it in the act of interpreting it (Derrida 1992, 23). This being the case, the aporia is that a just decision "must, in its proper moment if there is one, be both regulated [in order not to be arbitrary, R.C.] and without regulation [in order to be free, R.C.]" (Derrida 1992, 23).

This aporia of justice suggests that the dynamic of established law and justice, of common law and equity, of Roman piety and human pity, is dialectical and at the same time rules out any kind of synthesis. The infinite claim to justice—whether it is based on the idea of a balancing equity or articulated as a demand for pity—prevents the law from coming to a definite end. Further, the claim to justice implies the possibility that any kind of law, whether sixteenth-century law or contemporary law, may become visible in its 'barbaric' brutality, in its cruel formalism, if an individual human being and a specific case are treated in accordance with, and subsumed under a general rule. As a consequence, the individual would be robbed of its humanity and the case of its uniqueness. The Goth Tamora may be civilized in her plea to the Roman Titus, but he does not recognize her as an equal—or even a human being.[13] Pious Titus becomes guilty because he cannot deviate from his strict interpretation of the law in the decisive moment. Still, he does not become guilty by chance, but necessarily. Since justice can neither be calculated, nor be reduced to right and wrong, it remains undecidable whether someone can actually be considered a just person. Paradoxically, it is Titus's desire to be right, to 'be on the safe side', that makes him guilty; precisely his legal literalism makes his decision unjust. Given that tragic *hamartia* can also be considered a paradox of blameless guilt of the hero, it points to the aporia of justice which even an 'enlightened', modern constitution is unable to eliminate. Shakespeare wrote a modern play, the ambivalent ending of which shows that the phantasm of the pure and just law justifies violence—racist violence in particular.[14]

By tragically staging the contradictions inherent in the Roman law and self-image, *Titus Andronicus* questions not only the authority of Rome as the origin of all culture, but also one of the constitutive narratives of the Western world about itself: that it is civilized merely due to the rule of law. Shakespeare's revenge tragedy thus urges us to critically question ourselves: Are we living up to our own Enlightenment claim of equality and justice today? Or to put it differently: With respect to Europe's refugee policy, maybe we should ask ourselves, who is more barbaric: the cannibalistic Goths coming from outside, raping Roman women, or the pious Romans who insist on their cruel laws demanding human sacrifice?

References

Broude, Ronald. 1970. Roman and Goth in "Titus Andronicus". *Shakespeare Studies* 6: 27–34.

Buhofer, Stephan. 2007. Die Strukturierung eines Rechts. Das Common Law und das römische Institutionensystem. *Schweizerische Zeitschrift für internationales und europäisches Recht* 17(5): 703–736.

Derrida, Jacques. 1992. Force of Law: The "Mystical Foundation of Authority". In *Deconstruction and the Possibility of Justice*, ed. Drucilla Cornell, Michel Rosenfeld, und David Gray Carlson, 3–67. New York, NY: Routledge.

Dillon, Janette. 2010. *The Cambridge Introduction to Shakespeare's Tragedies*. Cambridge: Cambridge University Press.

Gray, Patrick. 2016. Shakespeare and the Other Virgil. Pity and 'Imperium' in "Titus Andronicus". *Shakespeare Survey* 69: 46–57.

[13] According to Derrida (1992), justice is therefore based less on equality than on an absolute inequality, an "absolute dissymmetry" that arises from the absolute particularity and uniqueness of the Other (22).

[14] In the end, the Roman order is restored with the help of an army of Goths. One could understand this as a conciliatory ending, which—after punishing the perpetrators—is able to integrate the Goths into the Roman state after all. However, this happy ending is only possible through the cruel death of Aaron, the only Black figure in Shakespeare's play. It is his sacrifice through which the distinction between friend and foe is reestablished at last, in that he is marked as evil par excellence. Unlike the Goths, his 'Otherness' remains incommensurable, and he needs to be excluded from the order. Finally, it is also a misogynistic ending that once again requires the sacrifice of the violated daughter as in the legends of Virginia and Lucretia.

James, Heather. 1991. Cultural Disintegration in "Titus Andronicus". Mutilating Titus, Vergil, and Rome. In *Violence in Drama*, ed. James Redmond, 123–140. Cambridge: Cambridge University Press.

Kahn, Coppélia. 1997. *Roman Shakespeare. Warriors, Wounds, and Women*. London: Routledge.

Koschorke, Albrecht, Thomas Frank, Ethel Matala de Mazza, and Susanne Lüdemann. 2007. *Der fiktive Staat. Konstruktionen des politischen Körpers in der Geschichte Europas*. Frankfurt am Main: Fischer.

Miola, Robert S. 1981. "Titus Andronicus" and the Mythos of Shakespeare's Rome. *Shakespeare Studies* 14: 85–98.

Potter, Harry. 2015. *Law, Liberty and the Constitution. A Brief History of the Common Law*. Woodbridge, Suffolk: The Boydell Press.

Richter, Virginia. 2012. Geopferte Nachkommen. Transferfigurationen zwischen Krieg und Frieden in Shakespeares "Titus Andronicus" und "Much Ado About Nothing". In *Ästhetik des Opfers. Zeichen/Handlungen in Ritual und Spiel*, ed. Alexander Honold, Anton Bierl, and Valentina Luppi, 183–201. München: Fink.

Schmitt, Carl. 2015. *Der Begriff des Politischen. Text von 1932 mit einem Vorwort und drei Corollarien*. Berlin: Duncker & Humblot.

Shakespeare, William. 2021. Titus Andronicus. In *The Arden Shakespeare Third Series Complete Works*, ed. Richard Proudfoot, Annn Thompson, David Scott Kastan, and H.R. Woudhuysen, 1271–1298. London: Bloomsbury Publishing.

Tricomi, Albert H. 1976. The Mutilated Garden in "Titus Andronicus". *Shakespeare Studies* 9: 89–105.

Wynne-Davies, Marion. 1991. 'The Swallowing Womb'. Consumed and Consuming Women in "Titus Andronicus". In *The Matter of Difference. Materialist Feminist Criticism of Shakespeare*, ed. Valerie Wayne, 129–152. Ithaca, N.Y.: Cornell University Press.

Blood on the Continent or What is a Gentleman?—*A Tale of Two Cities*

Franziska Quabeck

Dickens and the Guillotine

There is blood on the Continent, but there is no blood in Britain. It was the best of times, it was the worst of times and there is no blood in Britain. After all, the blood on the Continent is owing to the barbarity of the French. Presumably, the thirst for blood in Europe is a threatening spectre for Dickens in 1859 still. *A Tale of Two Cities* is one of his two historical novels and he writes the story of the French Revolution not only from a geographical distance, but from a moral distance. This happened 'there'; it did not, could not, would not happen 'here'. England is, after all, not Europe. Europe is the Continent. England is this sceptred isle, this stone set in the silver sea. And there is blood on the Continent. The guillotine looms large over Dickens's novel, a symbol of French barbarity and depravity, the dreadful plaything of the mob:

> A large cask of wine had been dropped and broken, in the street. […] All the people within reach had suspended their business, or their idleness, to run to the spot and drink the wine. […] Some men kneeled down, made scoops of their two hands joined, and sipped, or tried to help women, who bent over their shoulders, to sip, before the wine had all run out between their fingers. Others, men and women, dipped in the puddles with little mugs of mutilated earthenware, or even with handkerchiefs from women's heads, which were squeezed dry into infants' mouths; others made small mud-embankments, to stem the wine as it ran; others, directed by lookers-on up at high windows darted here and there, to cut off little streams of wine that started away in new directions; others devoted themselves to the sodden and lee-dyed pieces of the cask, licking, and even champing the moister wine-rotted fragments with eager relish. (Dickens 2012, 32)

F. Quabeck (✉)
Englisches Seminiar, Münster, Germany
e-mail: fquabeck@uni-muenster.de

K. Stierstorfer (ed.), *Law and Literature in Europe and Beyond*, Literatur und Recht 15, https://doi.org/10.1007/978-3-662-69851-8_3

France is thirsty. Dickens's 'introduction' of the French people is less than subtle, especially when he adds "one tall joker […] scrawled upon the wall with his finger dipped in muddy wine lees—BLOOD" (Dickens 2012, 33). This lack of subtlety in the novel is astounding. It was the best of times, it was the worst of times, there is blood on the Continent, there is no blood in Britain. After all, the gallows are thankfully blood-free. The ground before the guillotine is soaked in blood—the ground before the gallows is bone dry. Hanging is not barbaric after all—or is it?

Dickens's *A Tale of Two Cities* is not only his historical novel, but it is also his European novel. Unfortunately, it is also an inferior novel, which is not only due to the superficial parallelisms that characterize the text from the beginning, but also because such parallelisms, constructed as they are with immodest symbolisms, seem to create a contrast between England and Europe that makes the novel a cautionary tale. As David Marcus (1976) puts it, "Dickens is not content to leave matters at the level of suggestion" (58). The statement itself is a bit of a euphemism. It is fitting, perhaps, that Dickens's lack of subtlety has produced equally orthodox readings of the novel that emphasize a presumed inherent xenophobia and nationalism of the author: "Liberty, Equality, Fraternity, or Death!" (Dickens 2012, 328). Thus, the novel's final struggle between the French and the English mother figures, Madame Defarge and Miss Pross has been read as "a battle between pitiless French savagery and staunch English humanity" (Alter 1969, 139) in Robert Alter's words. The novel seems to express Dickens's fear of mobs, a fear that "is as constant and close to Dickens as his own heartbeat" (141). His fear of moral anarchy may be felt at home too, but, for Dickens, so the story goes, "French rioters are by definition more despicable than English" (Collins 1972, 344). The tale of these two cities would therefore rightly be the tale of "sense and nonsense" (Baumgarten 1983, 173), the tale of a firm placement of rationality in England. If this were a completely precise assessment, one could possibly find more merit in Dickens's overt symbolism and see less ironic detachment in Carton's set-up as a reincarnation of Christ: "I am the resurrection and the life" (Dickens 2012, 371). However, the novel's perceived lack of subtlety and the idea that it may truly express nationalist sentiments then add to a late melodramatic Manicheanism in Dickens that is in fact unusual for the very late 1850s. There must be more behind this troublingly symmetrical novel, and there is.

'Kill All the Lawyers!'

Sydney Carton's Christ-like self-sacrifice, as he marches towards the guillotine in Darnay's stead as if it were the Cross, is supposed to secure law and order for generations of Britons to come. His inner monologue at the end specifically imagines the children that will grow up in a different England. His sacrifice proves English superiority and the willingness to accept great plights and peril for the future welfare of the country that is, after all, an expression of nationalism that may explain why the revolution is remote on the Continent. And yet, two things must be kept in mind: one, none of these characters are characters. They are representatives of a system and the system Dickens is interested in here, once again, is the law. Two, Sydney Carton may be a hero and Sydney Carton may fulfil the ultimate sacrifice, but critical opinion almost exclusively circumvents the fact that Sydney Carton is a lawyer. This poses a greater problem for the novel than all the others. In Shakespeare's *Henry VI, Part 2*, the mob cries "The first thing we do, let's kill all the lawyers!" Not only is Dickens heavily influenced by Shakespeare generally, but throughout his works he seems particularly attuned to this one sentiment. He kills only two lawyers, Mr Tulkinghorn and Sydney Carton—but his use of the lawyer character has always seemed quite subjective—to say the least. J. Hillis Miller (2001) writes:

> Dickens detests lawyers, the legal system, and most legally operative speech acts. He has no confidence in the benign power of the written word in its official, public, legalized form. Lawyers' performatives are, for him, the most infelicitous felicities that could be imagined. They are a pollution of the body politic [...]. (56)

However, Dickens's attitude towards the law is not quite as single-minded and his lawyer characters often provide a clue for greater complexity, as I have argued elsewhere (Quabeck 2021). Thus, the fact that Sydney Carton is a lawyer too, also opens up a different view of the novel. *A Tale of Two Cities* shows that Dickens's criticism of the law is the great equalizer, for the system is just as bad in England as it is on the Continent—in fact, it is worse. Amidst the trite parallelisms and contrasts that seem to simplify the novel's meaning, there are also two legal trials, one in Europe, one in England. As it turns out, it is the trial in England that shows the dreadful erosion of the system and the fatal irresponsibility of the gentlemen of the law.

In France, the jury is indistinguishable from the mob and their thirst for blood fills the courtroom:

> Before that unjust Tribunal, there was little or no order of procedure, ensuring to any accused person any reasonable hearing. [...] A life-thirsting, cannibal-looking, bloody-minded juryman [...]. The whole jury, as a jury of dogs empanelled to try the deer. (Dickens 2012, 372, 373)

The verdict is predictable, the outcome unjust, there is no great surprise here. At home, however, things are worse. Dickens may be afraid of the mob, but he understands the mob. As Cates Baldridge (1990) has pointed out, "an undercurrent of sympathy makes its way into the text" (634). It is not the failure of the law in France that is disturbing for Dickens—it is the failure of the law in England. The English trial in the beginning of the novel runs counter to the French trial at the end. And the English trial is presented to the reader as infinitely more devastating, because this should be the 'shop' for justice. The lack of due process, as it were, both during the time of the Revolution and on the remote French Continent generally, may be presented by the novel as gruesome, but it is not half as terrifying as the legal malpractice Dickens exposes in England.

Dickens's views of the law as they keep turning up in his novels from early to late in his career are complex and never quite as formulaic as they seem, but they have everything to do with the notions of power and agency. The most frightening aspect of the law, its Gothic aspect, as it were, is its power to oppress its subjects to the point of paralysis. It is the overreaching power and oppression of the system that inspires such heart wrenching diatribes as Gridley's in *Bleak House* (1852–1853):

> I am told, on all hands, it's the system. I mustn't look to individuals. It's the system. I mustn't go into Court, and say, 'My Lord, I beg to know this from you—is this right or wrong? Have you the face to tell me I have received justice, and therefore am dismissed?' My Lord knows nothing of it. He sits there to administer the system. I mustn't go to Mr Tulkinghorn, the solicitor in Lincoln's Inn Fields, and say to him when he makes me furious, by being so cool and satisfied—as they all do; for I know they gain by it while I lose, don't I?—I mustn't say to him, I will have something out of someone for my ruin, by fair means or foul! *He* is not responsible. It's the system. (Dickens 2012, 185)

Gridley reiterates a charge that is laid at the doors of all of Dickens's lawyers, which is the unwillingness to take responsibility for their actions. The law is as powerful and oppressive a system, because the individuals acting in and for it are content to hide behind its systemic injustice at the cost of subjects like Gridley and others. Dickens is able to play the conflict for comedy, too, as he does, for instance, in *Oliver Twist* (1836–1838), but mostly, the theme is laid out as a tragic miscarriage of justice that is nurtured by the individual's irresponsibility. The lawyers are hence mostly despicable creatures, because they act in accordance with the system out of the desire to secure their own gain—at the literal and metaphorical cost of all others. Gridley's rant has laid the groundwork for many of the most important interpretations of *Bleak House*, for it could not expose the unconscionable conduct of those who represent the law any clearer: "Chancery practice presents us with a paradigm of the ways in which civilized men are responsible for one another, and fail in that responsibility" (Fradin 1966, 98). The great evil of the portrayal of the legal system lies not in technical, but in institutionalized neglect, what Bruce Robbins (1998) has called "organised, legitimated irresponsibility": "It is by means of their profession that the Chancery lawyers evade the responsibility for their actions, that they shoot their daily arrows in the air without being obliged to consider on whom the arrows are falling" (143, 144). However, the irresponsibility of the law is not confined to the civil courts and takes on a highly more dramatic dimension in the criminal trials of *A Tale of Two Cities*.

Doubles

From its opening sequence, capital punishment looms large in the novel that voices a fear of the arbitrariness inherent in the contemporary execution of the law. Dickens brings the novel's symmetry to its climax through the indistinguishability between Carton and Darnay in order to emphasize how easily the wrong defendant may be unjustly killed. In order to criticize the system's power over the paralysed individual, who is deprived of his own agency in view of the fact that he has no right to prisoners' counsel, Dickens anonymizes the central players in the novel's two trials.[1] The representatives that wish to send Darnay to the gallows and not the guillotine are the irresponsible nameless that sustain an unjust system through manipulation. In England heads might not be rolling dramatically in blood, but they are likely to be taken off unjustly nevertheless:

> Mr Attorney-General had to inform the jury, that the prisoner before them, though young in years, was old in treasonable practices which claimed the forfeit of his life. [...] That, for these reasons, the jury, being a loyal jury (as he knew they were), and being a responsible jury (as they knew they were), must positively find the prisoner Guilty, and make an end of him, whether they liked it or not. That, they never could lay their heads upon their pillows; that, they never could tolerate the idea of their wives laying their heads upon their pillows; [...] in short, that there never more could be, for them or theirs, any laying of heads upon pillows at all, unless the prisoner's head was taken off. (Dickens 2012, 76–78)

The fact that Mr Attorney-General is proficient in the law is made abundantly clear by Dickens. The fact that Mr Attorney-General makes the law what the ruling class wants it to be is also made abundantly clear by Dickens. In short, Mr Attorney-General is not a gentleman.

The laws in England and in France are both after Darnay's head and the systems are so ruthless that there can be no conclusion to the novel until a head rolls. Famously, it is not Darnay's head but Sydney Carton's. What are we to make of the fact that Carton is a hero and a lawyer? For one thing, it is Carton, who understands that the system is arbitrary and that justice is blind—in the bad sense. Darnay's acquittal from the English trial that is based on the argument that he cannot be clearly identified foreshadows the exchange of the prisoner at the end. Darnay's and Carton's physical similarity allows the one to stand in for the other, demonstrating to the reader that the law only requires a head—whose head it is, is tragically immaterial. The fact that Darnay is acquitted in the beginning is worse than the fact that he is condemned in the end. There is no room for truth in the English legal system and Sydney Carton knows this better than anyone. He works in the law, yet refuses to have a career in it. Carton seems to be only half of a character, as many critics have argued, due to the inconsistency of his actions. Carton and Darnay are therefore often considered doubles in that sense that the Victorian novel tends to employ as a narrative strategy: "The novelist who consciously or unconsciously exploits psychological Doubles may either juxtapose or duplicate two characters; the one representing the socially acceptable or conventional personality, the other externalizing the free, uninhibited, often criminal self" (Rosenfield 1967, 314). Consequently, critics read Darnay and Carton as two sides of the same coin that only constitute a fully realized character when put together,

---

[1] I use the masculine single pronoun throughout, for Dickens does only portray men in immediate conflict with the law.

although the caveat is obvious from the first: "'doubling' is too pallid a word to describe adequately what goes on, for such a term still implies two separate identities, two discrete selves, whereas what actually occurs is more properly described as a veritable *merging* of two individuals into one" (Baldridge 1990, 646, 647). Albert Hutter (1978) has argued instead that Dickens simply "divides a single ego into two" (455), but the odd pairing of Darnay and Carton still seems far removed from the double in the Victorian novel that criticism has identified as a literary convention. In fact, the novel's preoccupation with the law reveals that the doubles are not Carton and Darnay, but Carton and Stryver.

Sydney Carton and Stryver form a lawyer duo that can duly be considered a double act, for Stryver acts for Carton in Dickens's possibly subconscious attempt to make Carton a lawyer, but not a real lawyer. Someone has to do the dirty work that Dickens associates with the legal system and while he needs Carton to take responsibility even as a lawyer to make him the hero of his story, his conception of both a gentleman and a hero are diametrically opposed to the character investment he can put into the figure representing this profession. Thus, Carton is presented in court as entirely uninterested. His whole attention "seemed to be concentrated on the ceiling of the court" (Dickens 2012, 71). Sydney is the opposite of a successful lawyer, because he is portrayed as unwilling to comply with 'the system'. He defies its oppressive powers by the ostentatious refusal to carry out his profession that characterizes him throughout the novel. Instead, Dickens creates the 'real' lawyer, Stryver, who acts out Sydney's role as, almost literally, his 'criminal' self. Carton is the opposite of the lawyer 'at it': he openly defies his profession, not the system. In this sense, Stryver is his double: "[H]e has been marginalized, so to speak, by the energy and values embodied in Stryver who, more properly than Darnay, is his alter ego" (Rignall 1984, 581). Dickens makes the parallel unmistakably clear, for he introduces the two wigged gentlemen as exactly the same and yet completely different. While Stryver is 'at it,' Carton refuses to participate, his inaction and inattention expressing a silent protest against the court proceedings. Their professional costumes are supposed to render them indistinguishable representatives of justice, but Carton deliberately confuses the identification with his colleague through his ostentatious indifference to the proceedings in court. These proceedings are at length demonstrated by Dickens to be a fabrication, an arbitrary narration that is as highly ambiguous as the novel itself.

The court proceedings in *A Tale of Two Cities* are Dickens's most elaborate discussion of an actual trial since *The Pickwick Papers*. Even *Bleak House*, which goes to its famous lengths in its condemnation of the judicial system, is not this thorough on the professional execution of the law. Darnay's first trial constitutes a vivid dramatization of the actors and actions in law, but the manner in which the novel presents them is reminiscent of the Dodger's astute assessment that this is not the shop for justice in *Oliver Twist*. Consequently, the attorney-general is Mr Attorney-General, the personified enemy of the unjustly accused, and the jury's preconceived notions determine a trial, which is without evidence. The satire is trenchant, the chapter title "A Disappointment," deeply cynical. The jury, the crowd, the highest representative in the legal order, all act on prejudice and are prone to manipulation. The case is fabricated, the witness is bought; Mr Attorney-General 'spins' the case and bullies the jury. Dickens gives us legal practice at its worst, for now it is not only incompetent and formulaic on paper and the case does not simply end in heaps of discarded documents and massive financial costs, but here, for the first time, the life of an almost unequivocally good character is in danger. The whole system, it seems, rests on lies and fabrication. Accordingly, Carton's trick that introduces the reader to the physical resemblance between the two men—which will later resolve the novel's final conflict—is in itself highly ambiguous. Not only is it doubtful evidence, but it is also treated by Stryver as a fabrication: "That was a rare point, Sydney, that you brought to bear upon the identification. How did you come by it? When did it strike you?" (Dickens 2012, 102) Thus, even the one trick that resolves the whole conflict is not exempt from suspicion, as Frances Ferguson (2005) has pointed out. Dickens "treats this resemblance as one that waxes and wanes" and thereby "raises the possibility that even the observed resemblance is a lawyer's ploy" (67, 68). Although the legal context in the novel is exclusively a sphere of life and death, the arbitrariness within the system is treated no less drastically by Dickens. There is no truth in the law and justice is really blind, if it cannot tell the difference between Carton and Darnay. Thus, Sydney Carton can provide the ultimate twist in the case without seeming to be paying attention. His note, handed to Stryver as Darnay's legal counsel, saves a life, yet seems to be born of utter indifference: "[T]he wigged gentleman who had all this time been looking at the ceiling of the court, wrote a word or two on a little piece of paper, screwed it up, and tossed it to him" (Dickens 2012, 85). The bare minimum of words and an utterly careless handling of them are enough to turn a case of capital punishment on its head.

In such a legal system, a 'striver' is of course a morally ambivalent character. Stryver acts as defense counsel, but his success in court makes him a dishonest man, Dickens suggests with remarkably little restraint. Stryver is marked as professionally and socially oppressive and ungentlemanly, both a bully and a boar:

> Mr Stryver, a man of little more than thirty, but looking twenty years older than he was, stout, loud, red, bluff, and free from any drawback of delicacy, had a pushing way of shouldering himself (morally and physically) into companies and conversations, that augured well for his shouldering his way up in life. (Dickens 2012, 93)

Although he is often overlooked as a character, the creation of Stryver may duly be considered a prejudicial jibe at the lack of education and intellect among the members of the Victorian Bar, which makes him the vulgar person he is. The rivalry Dickens creates between these two different types of lawyers thus emphasizes their apparent difference in terms of class. This difference is also markedly imprinted on the discourse between the two that could be classified as a type of banter with a very serious competitive subtext pursued by Stryver. His insistence that Sydney is too emotional a character thus shines a different light, for he attests an excessive sensibility that is of course a common prejudice against the upper classes—so is the idleness that is Stryver's most explicit reproach of Carton.

On the surface, it seems that Carton lacks an ideal sense of professionalism and earnestness that makes him a worthy representative of the middle classes, but underneath, the text suggests that Carton cannot be a professional man, because of his socially superior station. The hero himself defines this exactly, when he claims that Stryver simply pushed himself into the front rank despite their equal upbringing:

> 'Before Shrewsbury, and at Shrewsbury, and ever since Shrewsbury, [...] you have fallen into your rank, and I have fallen into mine. Even when we were fellow-students in the Quartier Latin, picking up French, and French law, and other French crumbs that we didn't get much good of, you were always somewhere, and I was always—nowhere.' (Dickens 2012, 104)

'Nowhere' in this reading is a position clearly above Stryver's in terms of social rank and the novel makes a consistent point that Carton, unlike the lion, has not only received this education, but that it has also made him intellectually superior, which allows him to decipher legal proceedings that Stryver cannot master. Carton's 'genteel' nature, however, forbids him from truly thriving in the profession, because it is socially and morally beneath him. As John Kucich (1980) has pointed out, Stryver is an example of "what success means" (122) and this is a success that Carton can partake in because of his gentlemanly nature. In Sydney's own words, it sounds as if he was kept from a success that should be rightfully his: "You were always driving and riving and shouldering and pressing, to that restless degree that I had no chance for my life but in rust and repose" (Dickens 2012, 104, 105). Thus, Cates Baldridge (1990) accuses Stryver of unethically profiting from what "should rightly be the labor of a single person," which makes Carton a "victim of alienated labor" (644, 645). While this is true, strictly speaking, the text reveals through Carton's status as a gentleman that such success as Stryver's is not open to him. It becomes his social station much better to spend his time in court seemingly indifferently staring at the ceiling.

Stryver is a brute, whose ethics seem designed for success in the law. Carton, on the other hand, is the legal mastermind, who refuses to act in court and engage in its unethical manipulation. Much has been made of the fact that Sydney Carton is and always has been a popular character. His last words echo persistently in cultural memory: "It is a far, far better thing that I do, than I have ever done" (Dickens 2012, 442). Carton is simply awkwardly placed: he is an honourable man and the idea of an honourable lawyer sits uneasily with Dickens. The contrast between the two characters, who are inextricably linked, suggests that the legal profession allows either success for the vulgar, or failure for the genteel. One 'whole' lawyer is split into these two versions and there is no question with whom the novel sides. Thus, Sydney's retort, "It should be very beneficial to a man in your practice at the bar, to be ashamed of anything," (Dickens 2012, 161) accentuates the ruthlessness and lack of delicacy that success in the profession requires. David Marcus (1976) has suggested that Sydney is "too paralyzed to realise [...] his professional capabilities" (65), but the juxtaposition with Stryver as his alter ego shows that Sydney cannot be a capable professional, if he is supposed to turn out a reformed hero. Thus, John Kucich (1980) has argued that "Carton appeals to us through his freedom from convention and from constraint" (123), which is another way of saying that we like Carton, because he refuses to thrive in a profession that the novel again presents as dishonest, corrupt and vulgar. There is a lawyer in Carton, which is clear enough from his intellectual ability to discern the law and provide Stryver with his successful cases, but the narrative fate that awaits Sydney does not allow him to be identified with the profession. Thus, his talent, "his genius", as John Kucich has it, is far superior to that of a lawyer: "The mark of Carton's genius is this very ability to penetrate to the most important, the most essential levels—to see beyond the limited vision of others, or to say what others dare not say" (Kucich 1980, 123). Carton's innate social station thus gives him an air of superiority over Stryver that is the privilege of the gentleman. All his idleness and indifference can therefore be read not as just characteristic of the typical Dickensian ne'er-do-well, but as discursive markers of the gentleman protagonist. It is easy to see in Carton the "guilty scoundrel" (Hutter 1978, 451), or the rogue (see Cook 2011, 254), or even a clown (Eigner 1983, 149), but since the novel pairs him with Stryver, it clearly suggests that Carton is too much of a gentleman to be a lawyer. Carton is not a dandy like Ned Gowan (see Harvey 1969, 310), but he is not a professional man either, although his intellect would easily allow him to be. As the character says himself to his alter ego, he has too much shame to be a successful lawyer.

A Lawyer and a Gentleman

Technically, a Victorian lawyer was a gentleman and was not a gentleman. By Act of Parliament, he was; by education, he was not. The standard general education in the profession was "abysmally low" (Kirk 1976, 204) and to make matters worse, the level of legal education virtually non-existent, since examinations for the Bar were not compulsory until 1872 (Baker 1979, 149). While this lack of formal education certainly did not speak for the qualification of the profession, from a hierarchical point-of-view it offered another problem as to where to place the lawyer in the social order. After all, without a respectable family tree, only a proper education could enable one to achieve the status of gentleman. Whether or not solicitors, no matter how wealthy, could therefore properly be regarded as gentlemen, was a point of discussion. Formally, they had to be considered gentlemen because of the Act 'for the better Regulation of Attorneys and Solicitors' from 1730:

> Those whose names were admitted to the role of solicitors became officers of the Court of Chancery and enjoyed the same privileges as the attorney who from time immemorial had been regarded as officers of their respective courts. Accordingly they became entitled to call themselves 'gentlemen.' This is the origin of the jibe that solicitors are gentlemen by Act of Parliament. (Birks 1960, 136)

The discrepancy between the ‘formal’ status of gentleman and the ‘ethical’ status of gentleman as a man of good breeding and education seems to lie at the heart of the lawyer’s questionable position in society—and in Dickens. The prejudices and jibes against lawyers—that are, to be fair, common in all cultures since Antiquity—certainly ring through all of Dickens’s novels. Their questionable social rank and their professionally conditioned focus on money lead to characters such as Dodson and Fogg or Mr Tulkinghorn. Thus, Dickens’s attempt to make his hero in *A Tale of Two Cities* a lawyer is necessarily a doomed feat.

Carton is an impossible character, which explains his unconvincing position as a Christ figure. Carton understands the law, yet is unwilling to work within the system. The novel’s own unashamed ambiguity has infiltrated this character: he is a lawyer, he is not lawyer; he is a gentleman, he is not a gentleman. He is, technically, a ‘gentleman of the law’, which, for Dickens, is a contradiction in terms. Thus, he makes Carton a lawyer to make a point about the system and he makes him a heroic gentleman to complete his novel. This inherent, and, possibly, unintentional, ambiguity makes the novel the failure that many have regarded it to be. If we ignore the fact that Carton is lawyer, who has to die because the legal system is determined to see heads roll, we cannot understand that *A Tale of Two Cities* is not about France or England or even about the French Revolution. In this sense, the novel is not a historical novel at all and it is not concerned with the state of things at the end of the eighteenth century. In fact, it is very much concerned with the state of things in 1859. Thus, the bloodthirsty French are harmless compared to the English. Being a gentleman, after all, is not just a social rank, it is an ethical norm. Dickens makes a point against the ruling class and their laws of contradiction, casting doubt, in Linda Colley’s (2012) words, on “the belief that men of land and birth were inherently more suited to the exercise of authority” (153).

Robert Donovan (1962) argues that “justice for Dickens was generally open and palpable. He couldn’t understand why man’s natural emotional response to injustice wasn’t sufficient impulse to lead him to correct it if he could” (179). Carton does the gentlemanly thing that the common lawyer will not do: he takes responsibility into his own hands. Dickens was not a revolutionary, but he took great pains to demonstrate that a revolution in the law was devoutly to be wished—even at the expense of a novel’s success. *A Tale of Two Cities* never seems to be about the law—not like *Bleak House* or *Little Dorrit* are about the law, but at a closer look, it is another Victorian novel that cannot overcome the dire conditions and gross injustice that result when justice is blind. Dickens makes this abundantly clear when he sends a lawyer and a gentleman to the guillotine. “The first thing we do, let’s kill all the lawyers”? Dickens does not kill Carton to be rid of lawyers. He kills him because to die in order to correct an unjust system is the honourable and the gentlemanly thing to do. It may be an extreme solution to the lawyer’s unwillingness to take personal responsibility in answer to the legal system’s unjust oppression, but it provides a solution to the novel nevertheless. Sydney’s act of self-sacrifice saves a new generation. The blood that has been spilt on the Continent may not have been spilt in Britain, but the novel makes unmistakably clear that a new generation is being ushered in that needs a new ethical standard. By saving Darnay's life, Carton ensures a new beginning for the English:

> I see the lives for which I lay down my life, peaceful, useful, prosperous and happy, in that England which I shall see no more. […] I see that child who lay upon her bosom and who bore my name, a man, winning his way up in that path of life which once was mine. I see him winning it so well, that my name is made illustrious there by the light of his. I see the blots I threw upon it, faded away. I see him, foremost of just judges and honoured men … (Dickens 2012, 441, 442)

Carton does not only ensure a new generation for the English. He secures a new generation of lawyers and judges. He has taken responsibility for his failings and has finally defied that all-overpowering system. He envisions a new legal order, which is highly individualized through his eponymous professional heir. Carton sees the end of the anonymization of the law and the end of blood unjustly spilled. He sees gentlemen of the law.

References

Alter, Robert. 1969. The Demons of History in Dickens' *Tale*. *Novel* 2.2: 135–142.
Baker, J. H. 1979. *An Introduction to English Legal History*. London: Butterworths.
Baldridge, Cates. 1990. Alternatives to Bourgeois Individualism in *A Tale of Two Cities*. *SEL* 30: 633–654.
Baumgarten, Murray. 1983. Writing the Revolution. *Dickens Studies Annual* 12: 161–176.
Birks, Michael. 1960. *Gentlemen of the Law*. London: Stevens & Sons Limited.
Colley, Linda. 2012. *Britons. Forging the Nation, 1707–1837*. New Haven and London: Yale University Press.
Collins, Philip. 1972 A Tale of Two Novels: *A Tale of Two Cities* and *Great Expectations* in Dickens' Career. *Dickens Studies Annual* 2: 336–351; 378–380.
Cook, Susan. 2011. Season of Light and Darkness: *A Tale of Two Cities* and the Daguerrean Imagination. *Dickens Studies Annual* 42: 237–260.
Dickens, Charles. 2012. *A Tale of Two Cities*. London: Penguin English Library.
Donovan, Robert A. 1962. Structure and Idea in *Bleak House*. *ELH* 29.2: 175–201.
Eigner, Edwin M. 1983. Charles Darnay and Revolutionary Identity. *Dickens Studies Annual* 12: 147–159.
Ferguson, Frances. 2005. On Terrorism and Morals: Dickens's *A Tale of Two Cities*. *Partial Answers* 3.2 2005: 49–74.
Fradin, Joseph I. 1966. Will and Society in *Bleak House*. *PMLA* 81.1: 95–109.
Harvey, William R. 1969. Charles Dickens and the Byronic Hero. *Nineteenth-Century Fiction* 24.3: 305–316.
Hutter, Albert D. 1978. Nation and Generation in *A Tale of Two Cities*. *PMLA* 93.3: 448–462.
Kirk, Harry, *Portrait of a Profession. A History of the Solicitor's Profession, 1100 to the Present Day*. London: Oyez Publishing, 1976.
Kucich, John. 1980. The Purity of Violence: *A Tale of Two Cities*. *Dickens Studies Annual* 8: 119–137.
Marcus, David. 1976. The Carlylean Vision of *A Tale of Two Cities*. *Studies in the Novel* 8.1: 56–68.
Miller, J. Hillis. 2001. Moments of Decision in *Bleak House*. In *The Cambridge Companion to Charles Dickens*, ed. John O. Jordan. Cambridge: CUP: 49–63.

Quabeck, Franziska. 2021. *The Lawyer in Dickens*. Berlin/New York: Walter de Gruyter.

Rignall, J. M. 1984. Dickens and the Catastrophic Continuum of History in *A Tale of Two Cities*. *ELH* 51.3: 575–587.

Robbins, Bruce. 1998. Telescopic Philanthropy: Professionalism and Responsibility in *Bleak House*. In *Bleak House. Contemporary Critical Essays*, ed. Jeremy Tambling. Basingstoke: Macmillan: 139–162.

Rosenfield, Claire. 1967. The Shadow Within: The Conscious and Unconscious Use of the Double. In *Stories of the Double*, ed. Albert J. Guerard. Philadelphia: J. B. Lippincott.

D.H. *Lawrence's Lady Chatterley's Lover* and The Legal Overreach in Its Ban: A Study of the Implications for Law and Literature

Onyebuchi James Ile and Sr. Adaoma Igwedibia

The law is understood as "a set of rules that are created and are enforceable by social or governmental institutions to regulate behavior" (Robertson 2006, 100). It has been variously described as a science of justice (Núñez Vaquero 2013, 53–81); but it is also seen as an art of justice (Cohen 1992). Obviously, it is the science and art of justice. Indeed, law covers two domains: the domain of public law and the domain of private law. The domain of public law comprises constitutional law, administrative law, and criminal law, while private law "deals with legal disputes between individuals and/or organisations in areas such as contracts, property, torts/delicts and commercial law" (Horowitz 1982, 1423–1428).

Law allows not only for scholarly enquiry into legal history (Gordley 2006, 752–774); but it also provides scholarly enquiry into philosophy (Bor 1974, 539–543). It also provides scholarly enquiry into matters of economics (Rubin 2019), just as it raises important, critical and complex issues regarding equality, fairness, equity and justice (Pound 1914, 195–234).

If any collection of written works involves law books, then law is also literature; it belongs to the sphere of norms—rules of human behavior (Škop 2015, 7). Another marked dimension, which ultimately forms the design of law, is the dimension of ethics. Legal rules include moral contents, values or ideas which society considers correct. Law would make no sense without values; literature, too, embodies values, norms, ideas and ideologies that exist in societies. It is art because of its aesthetic value, and law is also affected by aesthetics. Both law and literature are possible because of language. Therefore, both law and literature are determined by language,

O. J. Ile (✉)
Nnamdi Azikiwe University, Awka, Nigeria
e-mail: oj.ile@unizik.edu.ng

S. A. Igwedibia
Department of English language and Literature, Nnamdi Azikiwe University, Awka, Nigeria

K. Stierstorfer (ed.), *Law and Literature in Europe and Beyond*, Literatur und Recht 15, https://doi.org/10.1007/978-3-662-69851-8_4

especially literary language. Literary language in narratives helps to establish a certain order that follows in a sequence from some starting point (Fitzpatrick 1992, 42). Right from the time a lawyer debriefs his client to the time he prepares his case as well as the time the judge prepares their judgment, law shows itself to embody narratives just as literature itself is narrative. Even in courtrooms law as literature persists because the examination and cross-examination of plaintiffs by the defendant's lawyer or vice versa, as well as the interrogation of witnesses, elicits stories, which are subsequently analyzed and evaluated by judges as a literary critic would analyze and evaluate literary texts (Allison and Norris 2011, 11).

Law is said to have resulted from the will to power and as such is neither moral nor immoral (Nietzsche 1901, 11). It raises important and complex issues concerning equality, fairness, justice and other socio-cultural and economic issues (Pound 1914, 195–234; Sarat 1996, 18, 19). This is actually where law and literature meet, because literature portrays life as lived by human beings. Sometimes, it engages ethical and moral issues with regard to law. It sensitizes us too on issues of justice and injustice, equality and equity, etc. While literature does not pronounce judgment as law would, it allows us to be the judges ourselves. Furthermore, while law aims at delivering justice, literature aims at helping us pursue the ideal, which is also a kind of justice. It is believed that "works of literary art and criticism … may structure discussions of fundamental legal issues" (Weisberg 1986, 473–486), and this is exactly what D.H. Lawrence's text, *Lady Chatterley's Lover* has done; for indeed literary works or "narrative acts lead to passivity in the face of clear injustice or, worse still, to the creation of injustice itself" (Weisberg, 178). One may then ask: how did the narrative act of Lawrence lead to passivity in the case of clear injustice? And how did it create injustice with regard to the text, *Lady Chatterley's Lover*? Maybe in the hurting of sensibilities of some people and maybe by the writer and publisher, as well, taking it for granted that good texts or literature defamiliarize experience by deliberately disfiguring language in order to renew and rekindle awareness in experience; hence, the historical view of the text in some quarters as pornographic, and in other quarters as artistic. In other words, as Aristotle puts it: "Spoken words are the symbols of mental experience and written words are the symbols of spoken words." However, the inability for words to trap fixed meanings in their being gives credence to Derrida's (1967) idea of deconstruction, which was an effort by him to debunk the idea that words and language express fundamental realities of being, a privileging of a kind in Western scientific and philosophical tradition, identified as *logocentrism* by the German Philosopher, Ludwig Klages (Joseph-Storm 2017, 221). Law is indeed nothing but an act of social magic (Bourdieu 1991, 42). However, this social magic is enabled by words, words with magic effect, magic words or a play with words (Škop 2015, 7, 8). A play with words is a kind of quest for their meaning. This is one activity that happens in the domain of law and literature, a deconstructive act.

It is in being deconstructive that law and literature have a meeting point in the pursuit of the ideal or justice; for while it was law, in the obscenity act, that determined why the text, *Lady Chatterley's Lover* should be banned, it was still law, at the court, that argued for the acquittal of the text and its publisher by using arguments that were deconstructive to fault the positions of the government prosecuting team. There is no doubt that literature's aim is to lead to new insights; therefore, countless texts have enabled such insights in legal studies and practice; for example, Shakespeare's *Merchant of Venice*: it is always believed that the law insists on reason or logic or even empirical evidence, which makes it even almost a science in its approach to matters. This is evident in the Venetian court in a case involving Shylock, the Jewish money lender and Antonio, the guarantor to Bassanio, who borrows money from Shylock in order to be able to court Portia. Bassanio is unable to pay back the loan at the appointed time and Antonio's goods are wrecked on the high sea so that as guarantor he is also unable to pay on behalf of Bassanio. The matter goes to court and Shylock, who bears grudges against Antonio for seeing Jews as usurers and for undermining them by lending without interest, demands a pound of Antonio's flesh as agreed at the time he was taking the loan. The logic of the law is demonstrated when Portia, who is disguised as a lawyer, requests that Shylock take his pound of flesh as the law guarantees, but that in taking the pound of flesh, no drop of blood should escape from the flesh as that is not part of the pound of flesh. As Portia puts it:

> This bond doth give thee here no jot of blood. The words expressly are "a pound of flesh." Take then thy bond, take thou thy pound of flesh, But in the cutting of it if thou dost shed One drop of Christian blood, thy lands and goods Are, by the laws of Venice, confiscate. (Shakespeare, 4.1.306–11)

Although the law thrives on logic and seeks evidence or fact, it also seeks equity and justice, hence the demand by Portia that Shylock take his pound of flesh—and it seems the law is aware that his seeking Antonio's pound of flesh is owing to the grudge he bears him—but that in cutting the pound of flesh, no drop of Antonio's blood be spilled. It could be argued that Portia obtained justice fraudulently, yet Shakespeare had to introduce a situation that brings Portia to act as an imposter Judge or Lawyer so that the law could be applied with tact and sensitivity and so the spirit of the law is not sacrificed to the letter of the law (Posner 2009, 107–110).

Law in Literature: *Lady Chatterley's Lover* and Obscenity

The text *Lady Chatterley's Lover* begins thus:

> Ours is a tragic age, so we refuse to take it tragically. The cataclysm has happened, we are among the ruins, we start to build up new little habitats, to have new little hopes. It is rather hard work: there is now no smooth road into the future: but we go round, or scramble over the obstacles. We've got to live, no matter how many skies have fallen. (Lawrence 2003, 5)

The cataclysm that happened refers, obviously, to the First World War; but before then, there had been defining political, cultural and economic moments in

European history, one of which is the modern era, which dates as far back as the Renaissance. It is an era of constant evolution in terms of human, industrial and economic relations. The fact that the Age of Enlightenment was preceded by the scientific age means that developments in mathematics, physics, astronomy, biology, human anatomy and chemistry changed the views of society about nature (Clagett 1961, 218–219, 252–255, 346, 409–416, 547, 576–578, 673–682).

The Age of Enlightenment focused on the value of human happiness, the pursuit of knowledge obtained by means of reason which is the evidence of the capacity of the human mind as well as ideals as liberty, progress, tolerance, fellow-feeling, law, constitutional government and the divorce of the church from the state (Outram 2006, 29 and Zafirovski 2010, 144). From the Age of Enlightenment onward, the English legal system became even more established; so much so that it even looked at things that were considered obscene. The modern English law of obscenity began with the Obscene Publications Act of 1857 (Drake 2003, 470). This is also known as Lord Campbell's Act. Lord Campbell was the Chief Justice of the Queen's Bench and it was he who introduced the bill, which ensured that obscene and pornographic materials were prohibited from being circulated (Bartee 1992, 64, 65). The law also authorized the destruction of obscene books (Robert 1971, 231). In fact, in the case between Regina and Hicklin in 1868, the court ruled that all material with the inclination "to deprave and corrupt those whose minds are open to such immoral influences was obscene, regardless of its artistic or literary merit" (Craig 2008, 540).

A world dedicated to the service of the machine, a world bereft of intuitive and emotional lives would be condemned to inhumanity; therefore, D.H. Lawrence tries in *Lady Chatterley's Lover* to show that reclaiming life from its enslavement to the intellect and by extension to the machine is necessary. He uses physicality of sex as a focal point for his argument, shocking as it may seem. But again, in societies where couples are working class, one sees always the corrosive effect of overindulging the intellect or the exploitation of labour force and the rendering of men impotent as well as making conversations that make reference to the sexual act, according to Lawrence, impossible. He uses the character, Lady Chatterley, to argue that the future will not be defined by science or industrialization, but in the restoration of humanity, in placing value on passion and compassion, intuition and emotional life, in the awakening of the sexual life in order to regain all that was lost to industrial capitalism. Observe what the Game-Keeper, Mellors, Lady Chatterley's lover, says:

> The world is all alike: kill off the human reality, a quid for every foreskin, two quid for each pair of balls. What is cunt but machine-fucking!—it's all alike. Pay 'em money to cut off the world's cock. Pay money, money, money to them that will take spunk out of mankind, and leave 'em all little twiddling machines. (Lawrence 2003, 226)

Here Mellors bemoans the slave man has become to capitalism; however, the narrator uses metaphors to paint a graphic image of the world, which has become female genitalia consistently "fucked" by capitalism, the world's "cock" or penis.

The vulgarity of the language here is palpable even though it is rendered in such a way that it cannot be said to be pornographic; however, "cunt" as used in the text, *Lady Chatterley's Lover*, does not directly refer to the female genitalia but instead is concerned with the concealment of it (Rooke-Lay 2020). According to Mellors, in answering Connie's question on what "cunt" is, "cunt" is "what he gets when he i'side of her" (Lawrence 2003, 178). In other words, it is the pleasure both enjoy in the act of sex. If that is so, why then was it considered obscene in the first place? The etymology of the word was examined in order to find out why it became obscene; obviously, "the word 'obscenity' is etymologically connected to the Latin term 'obscēnus', which means filthy, disgusting and indecent […], that which is culturally deemed to be filthy, disgusting, improper or shameful, and so has to be concealed. The word 'cunt' was considered in the twentieth-century, the context in which Lawrence produced *Fig* and *Lady Chatterley*, to be an obscene term for the female genitalia" (Rooke-Lay 2020). Furthermore, on the one hand, "the etymological roots of "obscene" also convey the sense of matter that is [off-"scene"][,] […] [and] that cannot be shown; obscenity, therefore, signifies that which […] is beyond the accepted codes of public visibility" (Nead 1992, 90); on the other hand, "the etymology of 'cunt' is connected to the prehistoric Indo-European root word 'cu', which is a signifier for the feminine and is also cognate with later terms which refer to the female genitalia. She explains that 'cunt' was only considered to be obscene by the end of the seventeenth-century and then became the most censored word in English language" (Wolf 2012, 247–295). This is exactly what happens with words: there is no end to the meaning they are capable of yielding—what Derrida (1997) occupied himself with in his famous work, *Of Grammatology*, which inaugurated what is today known as deconstruction. It is in the realm of post-structuralism that law and literature share similarities; for sometimes an accused might be guilty of the offense for which they are charged but they might be acquitted based on the technicalities of the law: the meaning of justice sought in prosecuting the accused is never arrived at—even when everyone knows they are guilty. Here the sign, signifier and signified concept of Saussure (1997) with regard to language make sense: the accused being a legal sign whose signified is arbitrarily arrived at; for there is no logical connection between being accused and being guilty: the accused might be guilty in the eyes of the people but not in the eyes of the law. Yet again, it is in that arbitrariness that literature finds a moral subject of discourse, which in turn helps law to better readjust itself in order to attain justice, which is the ideal, and the ideal is also the target of literature. However, Derrida (1965) questions law's possibility of prescribing justice since the idea of justice may never fully be embodied in law, just as the idea of the ideal may never fully be attained in literature, which justifies Hegel's dialectics, and which explains dialectic process towards the ideal as infinite. There are other scenes in the text that may yield to verdicts of obscenity when examined on face value through sheer legality typical of the law; for example, Mellors describes Bertha's genitalia to Connie as "soft down there, like a fig, a beak that rubbed and tore" at him (Lawrence 2003, 201). Furthermore, he tells Connie that it is "as if she had no sensation in her except in the very outside top tip of her beak" (201).

Mellors again would want to obliterate the genitalia of the "Lesbian" women who "go on writhing their loins till they bring themselves off against your thighs" (203). In fact, as the prosecutor in the trial of *Lady Chatterley's Lover* puts it in his opening address of the court: "Let me emphasize it on behalf of the prosecution: Do not approach this matter in any priggish, high-minded, super-correct, mid-Victorian manner. Look at it as we all of us, I hope, look at things today, and then, to go back and re-quote the words of Mr. Justice Devlin. You will have to say, is this book to be tolerated or not?" (Temple 2017). He further argues that the novel is capable of inducing lustful thoughts in the minds of those who read it "sets upon a pedestal promiscuous and adulterous intercourse. It commends, and indeed it sets out to commend, sensuality almost as a virtue. It encourages, and indeed even advocates, coarseness and vulgarity of thought and language" (Temple 2017).

It is on record that Griffith-Jones had asked the court: "would you approve of your young sons, young daughters—because girls can read as well as boys—reading this book? Is it a book that you would have lying around in your own house? Is it a book that you would even wish your wife or your servants to read?" (Temple 2017). By asking that question, Griffith-Jones draws attention to the thirteen "episodes of sexual intercourse" in the book, twelve of these "described in the greatest detail […] leaving nothing to the imagination." (Temple 2017) He says, "the word 'fuck' or 'fucking' appears no less than 30 times […] 'cunt' 14 times; 'balls' 13 times; 'shit' and 'arse' six times apiece; 'cock' four times; 'piss' three times, and so on." (Temple 2017) He submits that it is not the nature of great writing, nor the habit of a great writer to be that vulgar (Temple 2017). Griffith-Jones, thereby, implies that he knows the nature of great writing and the habit of great writers: he literally demonstrates the will to power, the will to privilege an idea over the other: the idea that great writing has a particular nature while a great writer has a particular habit. He attempts to cajole the law into willing to power.

Being that the law results from the will to power as Nietzsche had posited, agents of the law, looking for a long time how to crack down on D.H. Lawrence, may have had an alibi here. Indeed, the text may have yielded to obscenity in all the imageries, evoked to achieve beauty as art, but are they really pornographic? As the judgment of the verdict reads:

> Just as the content of a positive law can be evil, it is possible to find an obscene element in a work of art which we generally accept as valid art. Because pornographic writings usually lack artistic quality. This writing which is truly a valid piece of art is not a pornographic writing, as already established by the decisions since the trial in the first instance. (Case number 1953 (A)1713)

Furthermore, it is the desire to achieve art, first of all, that D.H. Lawrence also wills to power; for metaphors are especially used in order to achieve effect both in law and literature, and sometimes the pronouncements of the law are vague as if it desires not to be trapped so that we have to depend on interpretation to make progress, which also may become no progress at all depending on the interpreting court and judges. It is here again that law and literature meet; for the business of literature is largely that of interpretation; for "[s]tudies in this field recognize that there are fundamental similarities between the problem of interpretation in literature and the problem of interpretation in law" (Ayer 1987, 896).

Obviously, it is, probably, the literariness of the text, *Lady Chatterley's Lover*, which made the prosecution team lose the case against it, because many of the words and expressions in the text are used metaphorically or symbolically. The prosecution relied on the possible impressions such imageries would create in the minds of readers, taking for granted the fact that the writer never used language denotatively but instead connotatively so much so that neither the writer nor the book, nor even the publisher could be held responsible for the way readers interpreted the work or the impressions made in the minds of readers. As it is obvious, "[l]aw is characterized by battles for influence. Various actors try to obtain monopoly over the definition of individual notions and these battles have the nature of battles over language and interpretation" (Škop 2015, 9) These notions by individual lawyers in court are further studied by a judge or the jury in order to make informed judgments. These debates by lawyers in court are also similar to knotty issues a text debates with itself in the characters that populate it. Knotty issues as adultery, which some laws may frown at, are thrown open for critical analysis. For example, must a Connie forgo sexual needs, which is natural, and which her husband cannot satisfy owing to medical conditions as paralysis because civil or religious laws prohibit adultery? Is she not allowed to seek divorce if she desires to do so? Here literature provides space for law to improve itself by raising questions on issues law would, ordinarily, determine based on pure legality; that is, what the law insists on and what is morally justifiable or unjustifiable. It seems, therefore, that the text, Lady Chatterley's Lover, makes us understand that, "life is a work of art" (Ayer 1987, 911), but "the trick is not knowing how to follow the rule," but "knowing how to go on" (Wittgenstein in Holtzmann & C. Leich eds. 2006, 139–242). Therefore:

> In a broader sense, too, the *Chatterley* trial expanded Britain's vision of the future, right at the beginning of the liberalising decade of the 1960s. The verdict was almost certainly a factor in the abolition of the Lord Chamberlain's role as theatre censor in 1968 and the rise of gritty, explicit working-class drama on television. Whether it is directly linked to the liberalisation of laws on divorce, homosexuality and abortion in the same decade is doubtful, but they are all part of the same change in the social contract. (Self 2020)

It is not only Self (2020) that thinks that the trial and eventual acquittal of the text, *Lady Chatterley's Lover* and its publisher, Penguin, led to a new insight into a lot of things as homosexuality, adultery and abortion, but also Baski, who believes that the trial and eventual acquittal "is credited as being a crucial step in liberalising the country's cultural landscape, encouraging frank public discussion of sexual behaviour that meant sex was no longer a taboo in art and entertainment. It also shifted views on major human rights issues including the legalisation of homosexuality and abortion, the abolition of the death penalty and divorce reform" (Baski 2019).

Conclusion

D.H. Lawrence is classified as a modernist writer, and the modern period was a period of industrial and technological progress. It was also the period of the great revolutions. The great progress made in science, technology and industry had great impact in human relations. The prevalent scientific culture robbed humankind of their sexual, emotional and intuitive life. It was as a result of this that romanticism as a movement evolved, and placed emphasis on the intuitive and emotional life. Romanticism was characterized by its emphasis on emotion and individualism, idealization of nature, suspicion of science and industrialization, and glorification of the past with a strong preference for the medieval rather than the classical (Damrosch 1985, 405–424). In fact, it was a reaction to the social and political standards of the age of enlightenment and scientific rationalization of nature (Casey 2009). Using his novel, *Lady Chatterley's Lover*, Lawrence intervened for the age and shone the light on the neglected part of humankind and, thereby, achieved cohesion between the mind and the body, "for body without mind is brutish; mind without body [...] is a running away from our double being" (Hoggart 1973, viii); furthermore, the novel also exposed the issue of class relations in Lawrence's time, for, on the one hand, "Clifford Chatterley was more upper class than Connie. Connie was well-to-do intelligentsia, but he was aristocracy. Not the big sort, but still it. His father was a baronet, and his mother had been a viscount's daughter" (Lawrence 2003, 5); on the other hand, Connie and Mellors belong to different classes—the one aristocratic, the other the lower working class: Connie could either resist his overtures or yield to it, according to Schorer (1993, 17).

Lawrence's art was, however, adjudged pornographic and subsequently banned. The publishers were subjected to prosecution in line with the obscenity act of the law of England. The state failed to prove beyond reasonable doubt that the publisher did wrong in publishing a book with supposedly many pornographic contents. Upon wining the case against the state, the book sold about three million copies on the day the judgment was delivered (Robertson, 2010); therefore, it becomes imperative to use the text to understand the relationship between law and literature. It is a fact that both law and literature derive their being through language; therefore, the relationship between both can be better appreciated through the tool of literary/critical theory. Both strive for the ideal, which could be arrived at through a deconstructive process. Law wills to power; but it also subverts its power in the quest for justice. The subversion is enabled at the courts through debates rife with interpretations by lawyers. The debates are articulated as narratives by judges, who in turn study the narratives as a critic studies texts and passes judgments as critics do.

References

Ayer, D. John. 1987. The Very Idea of "Law and Literature". *Michigan Law Review* 85(5; 6): 895–913.

Baski, Catherine. 2019. Lady Chatterley's Lover. https://www.theguardian.com/law/2019/aug/01/lady-chatterleys-legal-case-how-the-book-changed-the-meaning-of-obscene. Accessed: 3 October 2022.

Bor, L. Fredric. 1974. The Nexus Between Philosophy and Law. *Journal of Legal Education* 26 (4): 539–543.

Bourdieu, Pierre. 1991. *Language and Symbolic Power*. Translated by Raymond Gino and M. Adamson. Cambridge: Polity Press.

Casey, Christopher. 2009. "Grecian Grandeurs and the Rude Wasting of Old Time": Britain, the Elgin Marbles, and Post-Revolutionary Hellenism. *Foundations* 3(1): 31–64.

Clagett, Marshall. 1961. *The Science of Mechanics in the Middle Ages*. Madison, U of Wisconsin P.

Craig R. Ducat. 2008. *Constitutional Interpretation: Rights of the Individual*. Cengage Learning.

Cohen, L. Morris. 1992. *Law: The Art of Justice*. United States: Beaux Arts Editions.

Damrosch, Leopold. 1985. *Adventures in English Literature*. Orlando, Florida: Holt McDougal.

Derrida, Jacques. 1997. *Of Grammatology*. Translated by Gayatri Spivak. Baltimore: John Hopkins U P.

Drake, Miriam. 2003. *Encyclopedia of Library and Information Science*. Vol. Abs-Dec. CRC P.

Fitzpatrick, Peter. 1992. *The Mythology of Modern Law*. London: Routledge.

Gordley, James. 2006. Comparative Law and Legal History. In *The Oxford Handbook of Comparative Law*, ed. Mathias Reimann and Reinhard Zimmermann, 752–774.

Hoggart, Richard. 1973. Introduction. *Lady Chatterley's Lover (2nd ed.)*. Harmondsworth: Penguin.

Holtzman, H. Steven, and M. Christopher Leich. 2006. *Wittgenstein: To Follow a Rule*. Oxon: Routledge.

Horwitz, J. Morton. 1982. The History of the Public/Private Distinction. *University of Pennsylvania Law Review* 130(6): 1423–1428.

Josephson-Storm, Jason Ananda. 2017. *The Myth of Disenchantment: Magic, Modernity, and the Birth of the Human Science*. U of Chicago P.

Judgment Upon Case of Translation and Publication of LADY CHATTERLEY'S LOVER and Article 175 of the PENAL CODE. https://www.courts.go.jp/app/hanrei_en/detail?id=11. Accessed: 15 October 2022.

Lawrence, David Herbert. 2003. *Lady Chatterley's Lover*. London: Penguin Books.

Nead, Lynda. 1992. *The Female Nude*. London: Routledge.

Núñez Vaquero, Álvaro. 2013. Five Models of Legal Science. *Revus. Journal for Constitutional Theory and Philosophy of Law / Revija za ustavno teorijo in filozofijo prava* 19: 53–81.

Outram, Dorinda. 2006. *Panorama of the Enlightenment*. London: Oxford U P.

Posner, A. Richard. 2009. *Law and Literature*. Harvard: Harvard U P.

Pound, Roscoe. 1914. The End of Law as Developed in Legal Rules and Doctrines. *Harvard Law Review* 27(3): 195–234.

Robertson, Geoffrey. 2010. The Trial of Lady Chatterley's Lover. *The Guardian*. https://www.theguardian.com/books/2010/oct/22/dh-lawrence-lady-chatterley-trial. Accessed: 28 August 2023.

Robertson, Geoffrey. 2006. *Crimes Against Humanity*. London: Penguin.

Rooke-Ley, Isabella. 2020. "What is 'Cunt?' She Said": Obscenity, Concealment and Representations of the Vulva in D.H. Lawrence. *Polyphony* 2(1). https://www.polyphonyjournal.com/post/what-is-cunt-she-said-obscenity-concealment-and-representations-of-the-vulva-in-d-h-lawrence. Accessed: 6 October 2022.

Rubin, Paul H. 2019. Law and Economics. *The Library of Economics and Liberty*. Liberty Fund, Inc. https://www.econlib.org/library/Enc/LawandEconomics.html. Accessed: 28 August 2023.

Sarat, Austin, and Thomas R. Kearns, ed. 1996. *Justice and Injustice in Law and Legal Theory*. Michigan: U of Michigan P.

Schorer, Mark. 1993. Introduction. *Lady Chatterley's Lover*. New York: Grover P.

Self, J. 2020. Lady Chatterley's Lover. https://www.penguin.co.uk/articles/2020/10/d-h-lawrence-lady-chatterleys-lover-trial. Accessed: 3 October 2022.

Škop, Martin. 2015. Law and Literature – a Meaningful Connection. *Filozofia Publiczna i Edukacja Demokratyczna* 4(1): 6–20.

Tait, Allison, and Norris, Luke. 2011. Narrative and the Origins of Law. *Law and Humanities* 5(1): 11–22. https://doi.org/10.5235/175214811796219745

Temple, E. 2017. Lady Chatterley's Lover. https://lithub.com/why-exactly-is-this-book-obscene-skip-to-the-dirty-bits/. Accessed: 6 October 2022.

Wolf, Naomi. 2012. *Vagina.* London: Virago Press.

Weisberg, H. Richard. 1986. More Words on *The Failure of the Word*: A Response to Heinzelman and Levison. *Cardozo Law Review* 7(2): 473–488.

Zafirovski, Milan. 2010. *The Enlightenment and Its Effects on Modern Society*. North Texas: Springer.

'Vox Populi' V. Codified Law: An *Amicus Curiae* Brief

Jan B. Gordon

My interest in the relationship between law and literature began with a subpoena at the intersection of the two disciplines in a formal judicial hearing. Law clearly has its literature, both discursive and encoded in canonical libraries of 'case law,' and literature has its own increasingly flexible laws: genres. Both canons have undergone expansion thanks to unforeseeable conditions of production: e.g., Afro-American Literature or post-colonial literature on the one hand and an enhanced range of criminal offenses (e.g., wire fraud, marital rape), on the other. Rigorous policing of both disciplines, make law, literature, and the judgments surrounding them, growth industries. As disciplines, law and literature share an appeal to a formal, but contextually obscured, application of foundational precedents as well as a literacy highly sensitive to the narcissism of nuanced, slight differences.

In 1975 I was subpoenaed to testify in the case of *Attica Prisoners Association* v. *State of New York* in the U.S. Court for the Western District of New York. The ACLU had submitted an *amicus* brief[1] defending the rights of high security prisoners who sought admission to the prison library of what the Office of the State Attorney General thought to be pornography five years after the Attica Prison Uprising. As an alleged academic authority on the subject (a genre that did not exist prior to the nineteenth century), I was to explain the literary merit of "Hustler" and "Playboy," *Last Exit to Brooklyn, The Story of O*, James Baldwin's *Giovanni's Room*, two novels of Samuel Delaney, a novel of J.P. Donleavy,

[1] An *amicus curiae* ("friend of the court") brief is an opinion filed by a third party in an attempt to expand arguments advanced by prosecution and defense in a case that may touch wider interests. Recently chief Justice John Roberts of the U.S. Supreme has suggested that such briefs are in practice "seldom helpful," insofar as they distract from both law and the alleged offense.

J. B. Gordon (✉)
Kyoto, Japan
e-mail: Japangordons@lapis.plala.or.jp

K. Stierstorfer (ed.), *Law and Literature in Europe and Beyond*, Literatur und Recht 15, https://doi.org/10.1007/978-3-662-69851-8_5

The Tropic of Cancer, Roth's *Portnoy's Complaint* and both *My Secret Life* and *The Pearl*. In two confining environments (courtroom and prison), how and what is read becomes of 'compelling community and judicial interest'.

Attorneys advise witnesses to avoid emotion, to answer queries with a scholarly, uninflected voice. Because the 'redeeming social merit' of a work qualified it as art rather than mere pornography in 1975, literary merit had to include social melioration. Filmmakers had long known that 'redeeming social merit' might be earned, as in the film, *Deep Throat*, by choking off the woman of a thousand sex acts: Linda Lovelace meets her end in a gratuitous car accident. Punished by a transcendent Judge, alleged pornography is acquitted.

My academic testimony was going well under cross examination by the Assistant State Attorney General until asked to read aloud from Chapter XIV of the anonymous Victorian novel, *The Pearl*. In that scene an aged couple confined to wheelchairs attempt to become intimate, wheels lock, sexual equipment becomes enmeshed and my academic composure disappeared with explosive laughter. The cross-examination being interrupted, the court recorder was directed to note that the 'distinguished academic witness' had been rendered temporarily 'breathless with laughter'. Great literature of course can be both comic and socially meritorious, but I am a slow thinker: 'I am not laughing at cheap literature Your Honour; I am laughing at my situation now, matching that of aged lovers'. The wheels of justice are at odds with speech, especially speech lacking recuperable, informing precedent. Law and unauthorized *énonciations*, to adopt the nomenclature of Émile Benveniste,[2] have an uneasy, even mutually predatory, relationship. Vocal outbursts lacking determinable intentionality (by severing Frege's relationship between reference and meaning) can be, impossibly, banished to a ban (contempt of court), beyond the law.[3]

This suspension of private utterance in the public interest was foundational in Anglo-American legal history. In Hobbes' *Leviathan* man devised law so as to a) protect himself against nature in such a way as to form stable communities and b) distribute the benefits and shortages of nature to make for more equitable access. Individual speech would be surrendered *a priori* to a Sovereign power in the foundation of this community. This yielding of the individual, free voice would foreclose a necessary relationship between law and morality (which judges individual acts against some standard). Hobbes' account of the history of the law imagines individual voice as a form of hoarding. Philosophically, it shares certain features

[2] Émile Benveniste (1966) suggested that only in the act of enunciation does language embrace its own subjectivity, the fact that it contains the linguistic forms appropriate to its individual expression. Subjectivity would thereby emerge "*en instances discrètes*" (47) including variable discursive contexts, tone, conditions of addressivity, and anticipated interrogations. The silent reader of a book could never realize his emergent subjectivity, one representation of freedom.

[3] Ironically, some judgments 'under the law' banish the accused to a place beyond the domain of the law. If convicted of a felony, the criminal might lose say, the legally guaranteed right to vote. Public opinion, by contrast, cannot conceivably remove someone from further opinion, its relevance and application forever remaining a 'matter of opinion.'

with British logical positivism: notably, the idea that Socratic dialogue is ineffective in arriving at semantically errant legal truths, leaving a legacy of divisiveness rather than harmony. Harmonious community is bought at the price of potentially disruptive individual throats.

In *Leviathan* the inscribed pedigree of a norm alone and the ability to re-petition an historical descent of a particular statute in order to determine its applicability to a specific transgression, is crucial. The "body" of law em*bodies* historical lineage, like other features of British social life, initiated by a conception, the voice of a sovereign: "*Understanding* being nothing else but *conception* caused by *speech*" (Hobbes 1982, I-3, 10). Voice is a fertile organ. Were the speech acts of the sovereign to no longer command belief, Hobbes' would imply that he would no longer be sovereign. To digress, this feature of Hobbes' thought seems remarkably Oriental on two counts: a) the loss of the mandate of heaven would be obvious to all and b) it is a mandate, having nothing whatsoever to do with morality, a constant complaint of the West against cultures which Ruth Benedict long ago termed 'shame cultures' as opposed to Abrahamic 'guilt cultures', more dependent on judicial determination.

Behind the conceiving breath, the foregrounding voice of the sovereign, is an antecedent Sovereign. A vocal component of the law was there from the Beginning, "for if we consider the same Thoeremes [sic] as delivered in the Word of God, that by right commandeth all things, then are they properly called lawes" (Hobbes 1982, I-15, 216, 217). Given the divine right of the Sovereign, obedience to the Creator's Word is synonymous with law. Rights, implying a freedom *from*, could not exist. In forming a commonweal, the individual has exchanged the sovereignty of individual, breathed voice for the advantageous protections and sociality of community.[4] Hobbes uses the concept of "rights" only to denote the absence of external impediments: "Right consists in the liberty to do or forebeare" (Hobbes 1982, I-14, 189, 190). If the determination of the morality of an act depends upon the freedom to act or dissent, there arises a huge gap between the truth of morality (which involves discovery) and that of the law. No such discovery is needed if the legal utterance is regarded as akin to speech acts. In conception, "Let there be light" would not be radically different from "I pronounce thee man and wife." An intention becomes inseparable from the act in enunciation, without need for the circuitous search for antecedence. No wonder that guilt would be acknowledged

[4]Like the Hobbes of *Leviathan*, the early Jürgen Habermas in *The Transformation of the Public Sphere*: *An Inquiry Into a Category of Bourgeois Society* argued that a "public square" conducive to genuinely free and unrestrained, rational discourse, would require the suspension of private interests and inputs including religious belief. More recently during a debate with the former Cardinal Ratzinger, he has altered that position by allowing religion, if "translated" into a rationality accessible to all, to have an important place as a modifying 'normative' needed to prevent excessive (immanent) 'free discourse' that might run the subject off the rails. Such a translation would obviously rob adversarial discourse of charismatic enunciations. See Jürgen Habermas and Joseph Ratzinger (2004, 5–28). The debate, organized by the Bavarian Catholic Academy, had been held on 18 January 2004, in Jürgen Habermas and Joseph Ratzinger, *Les Fondments prépolitiques de l'État démocratique* trans. by J. L. Schlegel, *Esprit* 306 (July 2004), 5–28.

by the same dynamic: the pronounced, oral 'giving up' of the Word that is confession.

There is in *Leviathan* a grammatical restlessness attached to traditional legal disputes. Both nature and man's nature are characterized by an interanimating struggle for dominance. There is no *summum bonum* to which any Law might strive as a just terminal resolution: "I put for a general inclination of all mankind, a perpetual and restless desire of Power after power that ceaseth only in Death" (Hobbes 1982, I-11, 160).

In Hobbes' thought law is both a creative Word and an animating carrier, much as inhaling (breath) precedes enunciation, a beginning before the Beginning. This is surely the space of intention, in which so-called "strict constructionists" of the law presume to find a home, a rest from wandering, conflictual errancy in the maze of legal indeterminacy, extraneous applications, and misreading. Like the orphan-figure of Victorian fiction, the search for some foundational/conceiving moment of antecedent intentionality, resembles another foundational discontinuity. That would be the search for an identifiably inscribable paternity which might lend law the author(ity) of legitimacy, difficult given the unintentional nature of intention surrounding and during all acts of conceptions, even if recuperable.

An interest in the interrogation of the circumstances surrounding initial invocation of a law has its corollary in the rise of the fiction of detection in the second quarter of the nineteenth century. One identifies criminal conception and perpetrators by identifying *a priori* circumstances that initially motivated the criminal to act. And in application, codified law makes distinctions in its schedules of crimes and punishments between, say, first-degree murder (conceived in advance) and third-degree manslaughter (killing a pedestrian in a crosswalk while driving under the influence of alcohol) though death results from both acts. As we study law and the literature of criminal detection we work backwards, from an event to its inception, to a pre-inception, the conception known as motive (a movement before the movement).

The similar search for intentionality bound to an unrecoverable (imaginary) metaphoric interval prior to the law's written presence, yields a 'bad infinity' in which *re*-covery occludes or disguises recovery. This problematic is perhaps denoted in an ellipsis that precedes the initiating conjunction of the first sentence of the first law book: "And God said, 'Let There Be Light'." What deep inhale preceded the conjunctive, "and" as God breathed life into Creation? In Hobbes, the speech of the Sovereign is imagined simultaneously as necessary for creating community *and* as a structured form of dominance by an author(ity) over voluntarily surrendered voices. Traces of Hobbes' binding sovereign voice remain part of a two-track legal system that evolved in Great Britain with its separation of Courts of Common Law and Courts of Equity until incompletely unified in the Judicature Act of 1857. Lacking a written constitution, British Courts of Common Law had recourse only to the application of (presumably commonly shared) custom that came to be historically codified. Hence, for the eighteenth-century jurist William

Blackstone, law was in many instances "in the breast of the judge,"[5] a pulmonary repository, a breath, preceding and informing vocal judgment often irreducible to logical analysis. Courts of Equity, by contrast, were dedicated to the achievement of 'equitable relief' when there was no adequate remedy at law. In practice Courts of Equity were often applied as an injunction or restraining order for the relief of a continuing practice for which no monetary settlement was available.

The eighteenth-century marked a radical attempt to dilute the singular voice in a sovereign 'breast of the judge,' by effectively creating a country *sui generis.* A fictive singular voice was derived from a plurality (*e pluribus unum*) in a speech act: "We hold these truths to be self-evident…" *We* need search for no paternal authority or conceptual intention that would legitimately ground this cry, an outburst from nowhere, a *Declaration* of Independence (by which the written becomes voiced) in evidence, for all is self-evident. Unlike Rousseau's appeal to "natural law," there is no antecedent legal model in the American foundational declaration. In retrospect, it is a document-as-voiced-cry of individuals as a collective "we."

A digression might illustrate how radical this voice was in establishing an inconceivable (in two senses) *a priori* right. It is independent of what can be conferred, endowed, commanded or developed. It is tantamount to the investment of a singularity in each individual. This radical independence is profoundly anti-social, unimaginable in Hobbes' *Leviathan.* No Establishment could either confer or revoke, the rights being inalienable; hence they have the potential to always be in excess. This undefined extra-territorial surplus in Hobbes' contractual relationship will initiate mass exposure to public opinion to become, in the nineteenth century, a law unto itself.

It is in this parasitical relationship between an exhaled voice and its codification, between some allegedly originary, repressed or enjoined, speech and the law, that we locate the foundational novels of three different countries. Hawthorne's *The Scarlet Letter*, though written in 1850 is historically set back to the period between 1664 and 1669 in the Massachusetts Bay Colony of Puritan New England. Set in Salem, Massachusetts, site of the infamous Salem Witch Trials one of whose dissenting judges was John Hathorne, Hawthorne's ancestor.

Hester Prynne is freed from a confinement after confinement where she has been sentenced after giving birth to a natural (author-less) child whose legitimacy would be established only by her voicing the name of the child's father to be inscribed in the church registry. Hester's refusal to name Pearl's father is symbolic of her transgression against the stern Father of Creation of a radically conservative faith. From which, one might add, Hester Prynne seems slightly estranged with her "Oriental complexion" (Hawthorne 1959, 16). When forced to recite from memory her primer, the Westminster Catechism, before Judge Bellingham, Pearl, ever the natural child, is seized by a strange declaration, an oral "perversity"

[5] For a detailed account of the two-tier system which created Courts of Common Law and Courts of Equity in Britain, see William Blackstone (1915, 33–76).

which "*impelled* her to *speak* words amiss," (111) with those voiced Satanic sibilants.

Bellingham, the historical Governor of the Massachusetts Bay Colony who lends his name to two American cities, took as his second wife a woman thirty-two years his junior, by pronouncing himself man and wife in a solitary speech act resembling the country's foundational declaration. There being no distinction between Church and State in Puritan New England, a minister of the faith could marry himself. As punishment for her refusal to name Pearl's father and her child's refusal to embrace the Divine Father's text, Hester is inscribed with another text, the scarlet letter "A": apparel as tattoo. Her refusal to orally name the father, reduces her to an overdetermined text. Even after her release from jail, the Inscribed Law of the Father is unsuccessful in forcing her to *speak* the name. A silent mother has given birth to a child who cannot read and speaks in tongues, a compounded illiteracy.

The failure to evoke a verbal enunciation of the name of the Father is compensated by the transformation of Hester's body to a book (a tattoo?) whose first letter, "A" (adultery), is universally legible. Like her Puritan forebears, like America, she can never be free from the inscribed letter of the law. Physically free, but banished from sociality, she has learned while incarcerated, how to artistically amend the textual "A" with "elaborate embroidery and fantastic flourishes of gold thread [...] against the sumptuary regulations of the authorities" (Hawthorne 1959, 60). Ever the outlaw, she amends to the literal letter of the law a figurative rhetorical dimension, by breathing life into a mark. Her acquired skills enable the slow conversion of an austere community defined by its grey garb, pointed hats, and solemn, restrained behavior, contrasting so noticeably with the colorful American headdresses of neighboring Indians and the suntanned pirates of the main who appear on Election Day, once a holiday in America. Her flourishes transform the iniquity of written law into a commentary on its lifelessness.

The enriched "A" becomes a commercial start-up, creating demand for her products in a community previously critical of anything decorative. She is summoned to sew garments for the newly deceased, swaddling for the newborn, and the lace investiture garments for the newly elected. The object of a community's persecution becomes a self-sustaining capitalist entrepreneur, converting opinion to such an extent that at novel's end both Fathers speak from a scaffold on Election Day. To reread *The Scarlet Letter* is to understand the incomplete transformation of our own Taliban, our puritan "students" of God's law, into a modern, more tolerant entrepreneurial society, with frequent lapses, to be sure. But it is also to read of the necessarily adversarial, yet dependent relationship between an informing, albeit repressed, voice and the written Word with which it shares an agonistic dialectic. Hawthorne's novel is framed as a written manuscript "found" in a "Custom House"—that symbolic nesting place of American independence from British stamp duties. The same custom house was also a bureaucratic prison from which Hawthorne had to free himself (thanks to adverse results on another Election Day) which liberated him as a bureaucratic clerk to become a writer of Hester's declaration of independence from a dominant culture's imprisoning pre-destination.

A spontaneous "voice"—an emergent 'still small voice of humanity,' to borrow from Wordsworth's early, liberal phase—is potentially silenced by an expanding volume of codified affidavits and rejoinders that repress voice (while presuming to represent it) until eruption as Richard Carstone's blood in *Jarndyce vs. Jarndyce* of Dickens' *Bleak House*. If we consult the Oxford English Dictionary (John Murray's Victorian project to discover the original use and successive permutations over time of every word in English), the first entry for "public opinion" dates to 1862. We are in the chronological neighborhood of the utilitarian philosophers associated with the *Westminster Review*.

Did the concept have a longer history, but no appropriate nomenclature? Was Great Britain so ideologically united that a public opinion different from that of accepted opinion was not articulated? In the first quarter of the nineteenth century, critical public opinion was shaped by magazines sponsored and under the editorial supervision of political parties like *The Quarterly Review* (Tory), *Blackwood's Edinburgh Magazine* (Whig), publications of the Church of England and five or six metropolitan journals. In 1819, King George III had created a separation between 'public news' as a textual category—gazettes, shipping information, parliamentary proceedings—and so-called 'newly-published news' which included some opinion, subjecting the latter category to a Stamp Duty. The repeal of the Stamp Duty in 1859 had the effect of inducing the penetration of provincial markets by new newspapers, freed from the domination of metropolitan interests identified with national interests. It must be recalled that Dorothea's uncle, the elder Brooke, in *Middlemarch* (anachronistically in an 1871 novel set back to the eve of the First Reform Bill in 1832), purchases a provincial newspaper to advance his shaky political platform. These new organs were often referred to simultaneously as both "buzzing flies,"[6] but also a self-cancelling (given cacophonous public opinion) machine producing at least potentially a symphonic harmony if the individual parts could be brought under the control of a skillful conductor (Hobbes' sovereign).[7] In operation, and perhaps application, public opinion formation results in a kind of energy force-field which can do incredible social damage or be harnessed to power social harmony.

These competing models of a public 'voice' are precisely the context for John Stuart Mill's *On Liberty* (1859). In Chapter I, having defined civil liberty as a limit to be set on society's power over each individual, Mill raised the problem of the tyranny of a truly participatory, democratically-elected majority, a problem carried to a more disturbing extreme in Bernard Schlink's lovely, *The Reader.* In Chapter II, Mill claims that no voice should be silenced, because a viewpoint's popular acceptance does not necessarily make it true, truth often remaining hidden or appearing illegibly disguised. Even though holding an intolerant, because

[6] "…these things called papers, were bred to grow up and pester society, flitting about for a time with borrowed brilliancy…insidious and fatal." (Anonymous 1857, 5–8).

[7] "The multiplication of newspapers will create a Babel of opinions which will neutralize each other." (Anonymous 1859, 192–194).

a near-monopoly on opinion, the Catholic Church, Mill (2015) reminds us, used a "devil's ad-*vocate*" (23) to give voice to imaginary arguments against a candidate for sainthood.[8]

Later in the chapter, on those occasions when "opposition is absent," Mill suggests that, "though indispensable, but so difficult, to create," *imaginary* opposition must on occasion be conjured (fake news?) much as prescribed in the methodology of the "Socratic dialectics" (Mill 2015, 45). Public opinion, unlike law in democratic societies, which has specific jurisdictions and defined applications to a pre-scribed schedule of transgressions, would come to have a necessary Imaginary component to push boundaries of public acceptance: an Imaginary alloy in the hardening of truth. Its enunciative extra-territoriality endows public opinion with a consensual plurality to cover its singularity with deniability of individual responsibility. Both law and public opinion have designated institutions dedicated to maintaining our attendance as interpellated in it.[9]

For A.V. Dicey, Mill's heir to a more moderate utilitarian posture in his Lecture II of *Lectures on the Relation Between Law and Public Opinion in England During the Nineteenth Century*, the problem was posed as the proverbial issue of 'chicken and egg,' so indeterminable was the question of which came first:

> A *cross-current* of opinion may be described in any body of belief or sentiment which, while strong enough to affect legislation is, yet in a measure *independent of it*, though perhaps not directly opposed to the legislative creed of a particular era. (Dicey 1981, 366, 367)

The metaphoric force fields of opinion are part of what goes into the law-making, but yet somehow preserves independence from the end product. The (on occasion) imaginary (phantom) voice of opinion can be both a marginalizing and marginalized voice. It can inform law-making, be often stifled in the statutes, and yet, unbelievably, after judgment, can become a kind of appellate division of the law: the commentary of a public upon rendered verdicts and judgments. This is a voice that can hold the law as a colony and yet, itself, be colonized, unable to speak (or breathlessly laugh, or scream) in its own voice, by the law.

[8]The devil, in Catholic doctrine, has no material existence, but is a non-substantive "turning away" (perversion) from good. If enough people came to believe in Mill's *imaginary opposition*, initially advanced as merely a transactional tool to situate a space for public opinion formation, then the *Imaginary* could become tyrannical, absent something like Popper's test for eligibility to empirical falsification.

[9]Emmanuel Levinas has argued that though ethical responsibility is anterior to all other questions of responsibility insofar as we "face" and substitute ourselves for the Other, a third party ("Le Trier")—and hence a public politics—raises questions about duties, rights, and what is "owed" to each sharer. The Subject and the Other cannot form a totality; hence they must deal with a neighbor (Other) who exists alongside both. The "third" puts sovereignty into a relationship with a human totality, but not the totality of a unity. He seems an ideological next-of-kin to Mill's positing of an Imaginary. See Emmanuel Levinas (1981, 157).

Anthony Trollope, the most underrated nineteenth-century political novelist, was the first to exploit this unique metaphoric borderland shared by law and the voice of public opinion in his fictive *Barsetshire.* In the first of six novels, *The Warden*, a group of infirm, charity pensioners live under the pastoral care of Warden Harding, a kindly beneficiary of a sinecure supported by the two-hundred-year-old last will and codicil of John Hiram. Given the unforeseeable increase in the price of rents over the years, the interest on the principal amount now exceeds the original gift. The deed initially bequeathed only the title to the land. The distribution of the excess windfall (an imaginary realization)—to the Church of England, the Warden, or equally divided among current pensioners—is a question raised 'pro bono' by the privileged John Bold in behalf of the general public rather than a specific plaintiff, unique in British jurisprudence then. His suit gives those lacking it, incarcerated within an eleemosynary institution, voice. Even the pensioners, some with symptoms of dementia, are divided on the question. The preamble to the proceeding is a letter to the editor of one of the new provincial newspapers, the *Jupiter*, Tom Towers. The paper circulates the story, later applying it to larger questions of church reform and its aging clerics, some of whom enjoy the benefits of multiple livings with long periods of only nominal attendance to duty.

A narrowly-defined law suit for recovery of excess accumulated by a bequest, in the hands of an aggressive press, expands to include the need for reform of an idle clergy that is a partner to an Establishment. Public opinion formation and the law compete as what Pierre Bourdieu designates as capital.[10] In addition, the practice of law is itself in excess, because of the potentially overlapping jurisdictions of Ecclesiastical Courts (maintained by the Church) and Courts of Common Law and Equity (maintained by the State). Public opinion arouses, like crypto-currencies or literary criticism, a dormant investment in competitive speculation.

Although the suit for recovery of indeterminable, accumulated proceeds is ultimately abandoned, the newly 'woke' Warden Harding wrestles during a long night of the soul. He ultimately indicts himself for needing the "clarion voice of public opinion" to stir an inner voice of conscience (Trollope 1984, 154). Harding's sentence, meted out by the touch of public opinion, outside of legal judgment as a consequence of the abandonment of the suit, resembles Weber's model of *rationalization.* He becomes a functional bureaucrat, remote from his previous pastoral care:

> Mr. Harding did *not desert them*: from him they had as much consolation as a dying man may receive from his Christian pastor, but it was the occasional kindness of a *stranger* which ministered to them, not the *constant presence* of a master, a neighbor, and a friend. (182, emphasis mine)

[10] In contradistinction to its common materialist definition, *capital* here acquires the meanings attached to the term by Pierre Bourdieu: 1) a source of power that socially differentiates, like classifications and 2) forms adopted by strategies to accumulate, exchange, co-opt, or displace, often by disguise, one position (type of capital) for another. The theory is perhaps best articulated in Pierre Bourdieu (1977).

There could be no better expression of the alignment between alienation and Weber's rationalization. The warden, even literally a guardian over the disadvantaged, becomes a mere attendant bureaucrat rather than an intimate. The intention of the donor, like the document 'found' in a custom house drawer by Hawthorne's narrator, is historically irrecoverable and the case that had temporarily aroused public opinion is dropped along with both the imaginary intention of the original donor and the equally imaginary voice of a plurality made over by a slight of hand, into a singular authority: public opinion.

Trollope goes to great lengths to show the impossible recovery of an imaginary intention. When Attorney Bold attempts to cajole Editor Towers into returning a "Letter to the Editor" which became part of the outreach to extra-judicial *publicité* (voice) in the case, Towers replies that he cannot return it. Once deposited, the letter loses authorial intention, becoming public domain. The editor publishes ostensible "Letters to the Editor" supposedly written by an anonymous "Veritas" but actually written by Towers himself in the interests of stirring up public opinion, thereby increasing circulation. The strategy is apparently effective, for as we read through twelve novels, the paper evolves from the *Jupiter*, to the *Daily Jupiter* to a *New Jupiter.* Public opinion is becoming more stylishly *au courant*, even on the mastheads of its organs. The "Vox populi" will become in Trollope a constant presence, both immanent and transcendent like a "Tenth Muse," on watchful duty, as a self-appointed court in response mode to a changing summons.[11]

The lack of accessibility to the breath of intention, makes of it a kind of transcendent value resembling nothing so much as the generators of public opinion which even metaphorically, are given a similar autocratic posture in Trollope adjacent to the sacred. In the offices of the *Jupiter*

> reigns a pope, *self-nominated, self-consecrated* ay, and much stronger too—self-believing [...] a pope hitherto afraid of no Luther, a pope who manages his own inquisition. (Trollope 1984, 118, emphasis mine)

In *An Autobiography* Trollope once compared the reading public with a judge and himself to a disciplined law clerk bound to his seat with wax. And in the last of the *Parliamentary Novels*, *The Duke's Children*, an innocent American, anticipating Henry James' Isabel Archer, the commoner Ms. Boncassen, postpones her marriage to the Duke of Silverbridge, until he gets the approval of his friends, family, and fellow toffs. Acceptance by public opinion trumps both affection and submission to God's legal vows of marriage.

Yet, Dicey's notion that there is a reciprocal relation between law, informed by public opinion as part of legislation, and a public opinion that serves as a commentary, even an appellate division, on legal judgments—while both strive to maintain a fragile sovereignty—is everywhere present in Trollope's foundational epic. The discovery by Lawyer Finney that the voice of public opinion (represented by the

[11] For a philosophical elaboration, see Jan B. Gordon (2022, esp. 39–82, "Miming the Law").

Jupiter) is allied with written law brings great joy: "he was beside himself. What? To be engaged on the same side as the *Jupiter*, to have had the views he recommended, seconded, and furthered, and battled for by the *Jupiter*" (161).

The enhanced relationship between public opinion and the law is also evident in an easy elision both spatially—newspaper offices located near Lincoln's Inn—and professional careers. Trollope's own father was a failed barrister. Tom Towers similarly apprentices as a "feeless barrister" before deciding that more people will hear of him if he becomes an editorial writer for an emergent local press. The impoverished Irishman, Phineas Finn, who lends his name to two of the *Parliamentary Novels*—*Phineas Finn* and *Phineas Redux*—initially apprentices under Lawyer Low, before assuming work as a writer for the radical rag, *The Banner*, to support himself. finally abandoning the study of the law altogether in favor for intermittently successful runs for Parliament under the Liberal banner. When indicted for the murder of a parliamentary whip after both depart from a Liberal redoubt, defense Attorney Chaffanbrass describes his task as that of keeping his client alive until public opinion delivers a new context for a re-reading (by re-contextualizing) the crime on appeal. The wily Chaffanbrass, a recurrent presence in other Trollope novels, would concur with one of Trollope's epigraphs in *The Way We Live Now* regarding the sudden fall of the swindler, Auguste Melmotte: "public opinion has its bar as well as the law courts" (Trollope 1982, 117).

The independently dependent, dialectical relationship of law and public opinion exhibits obvious aporias that prevent one from being folded (as etymologically, compliant) within the other, even in application. Insofar as law and public opinion threaten even as they feed off of each other, the relationship seems more parasitical. Public opinion and law attempt to preserve a singular sovereign and independent space, even as they need each other for self-maintenance and propagation, almost like Trollope's Establishment partners: church and state. In the United States, prospective jurors are frequently vetted as to how much they have been unduly influenced by public opinion on a given matter of relevance and subsequently disqualified by plaintiff or defense attorneys. In certain high-profile cases where public opinion is inescapable due to amplified publicity, the trial venue is shifted to another city. Jurors may be sequestered for the duration of a trial, forbidden to watch or read media coverage. In the United Kingdom, indictment and conviction for libel is quite frequent, suggesting that the intrusion of the oral slur, damaging public opinion, is itself a crime in the absence of other transgressions. After indictment, comments by all parties are often covered by a 'gag order,' while the case is considered *sub judice*. Perhaps the greatest difference between proceedings in Britain and the United States, addressed elsewhere, is that 'hear-say' (indirect, third-party oral testimony, i.e., unverified gossip) is admissible as evidence in British courts, but never admissible in any U.S. court.[12] To institutions entrusted with procedural administration of the law, second-hand utterance, like outbursts, is fugitive.

[12] See Jan B. Gordon (2001, 203–218), where the different criteria in the U.S. and the U.K. for the admission of indirect oral testimony is analyzed on a case-specific basis.

The one obvious difference—which grounds many others—might be that public opinion, even when inscribed, functions as if it were an indeterminately sourced, plural voice shared among all classes and occupations and hence functions much like a kind of collective intention. It hence has the patina of a platform for democratic participation in a public square, but given sufficient velocity in circulation, can resemble the rule of the tyrannical 'mob' (mobile voices). It is always an inclusively plural (as opposed to a royal) 'we,' but endows itself with a sovereignty that draws speculative interest, hence constituting a quasi-materiality. It is ontologically both responsive and conducive to, almost inviting, further continuous response among 'likes': the algo-rhythmic 'network effect.' Because, unlike most written literature, it is perpetually unfinished, always *in situ*, public opinion summons only speculative investment or demurral (as belief) of those touched by it: credibility is crucial to the maintenance of credit.

In Trollope's *The Eustace Diamonds*, an ambitious, but indebted young woman, Lizzie Greystock, redeems pawned trinkets, assisted by an antique dealer who becomes her effective partner in capturing the attentions of a young scion of the nobility. Money being necessary to make money, the speculative investment pays off with marriage to Lord Florian Eustace who dies suddenly during their continental honeymoon. Symbolic of the power of the family are the valued brilliants in the necklace with which a noble family has stored a portion of its wealth, but needed for other purpose if the young widow is to remarry advantageously. Long chapters are dedicated to discussions in chambers to determine the conditions under which Lord Florian gave the necklace to his wife. If an heirloom, then the necklace stays with the family assets as a legacy inheritable by an as yet non-existent heir. If, on the other hand, the jewels were given in route, as a gift, the assets are hers outright, and hence alienable in the eyes of the law. A legal difference between an un-economic gift, an investment vehicle, and an historical heirloom drives the plot of a 450+ page novel. What was the intention that preceded presentation of the gift? If she claims to be hers what is actually a familial asset, Lady Eustace is a thief; if a gift, the Eustace Diamonds are hers to dispose of as she wishes, including bait to catch another husband. The conditions under which she has taken possession on the honeymoon are legally indeterminable. When she wears the necklace in public in violation of a court order, potential suitors (and the public) must decide between two antagonistic investments: the wealth represented by the diamonds or Lizzie's questionable reputation as a scheming thief with a co-partner, the antiques dealer who made an investment (by virtue of an enabling loan) early on that the marriage would indeed occur. Were the Eustace Diamonds intended by its donor as a gift outright, an inalienable heirloom to be held in trust, or, given the financing of the marriage by a pawnbroker, a public offering open to investors? Indeterminable intention determines possession of a materiality which in effect, opens materiality to speculation.

Public opinion fills the gap left by a conflict over the legal status of a materiality. The jewels are finally believed to have been stolen or sold, but in any case, broken up as a singularity and alienated—disposed of in fragmentary form 'somewhere' to be remounted, made invisible in circulation. Public opinion is always as divided as the necklace will come to be, in liquidation, while always representing itself as a totalization in Trollope:

> *Opinion* was much *divided* as to Mr. Harding's conduct. The mercantile part of the community, the mayor, and the corporation, and the council, also most of the ladies, were loud in his praise. But the gentry were of a different way of thinking—especially the lawyers and the clergymen. They said such conduct was weak and undignified [...]. (Trollope 1984, 175, emphasis mine)

Whereas the emergent middle classes feel that justice was rendered under the threat of legal suit, the gentry, hitherto above the law that they in large part created as an Establishment, feel victimized by the loss of dignity that results from appeals to, or applications of, the law. Public opinion both informs law-making and is an appellate division of judicial judgments.

Those who enjoy a high status are possessed of an immunity, an *a priori* restraint from a public law that would hold them accountable. Like 'natural rights,' their status confers an inalienability as if the grace of received public opinion were simultaneously transcendent and immanent, miming certain claims of received law. When the Earl of Silverbridge threatens to take his father to court for refusal to accede to his marital choice, the Duke and occasional Prime Minister, Plantagenet Palliser, suggests that going to law will ruin him in public opinion: "Do you recognize no duty but what the laws impose upon you. [...] You should so live as not to come near the law, or to have the law come near you" (Trollope 1983, 485). Exposure to the law, even tangentially as a plaintiff, violates socially privileged status as being above the law. Going to law in a family dispute would threaten the family's historical status, an heirloom for respectful public opinion. One should perhaps now take note of the fluid terms in our dialectic: public opinion can constitute an appellate division of legally-rendered judgments; can force the termination of a legal case; or can serve as an immunizing mechanism against the social illness of legal exposure to which the privileged classes are vulnerable while parasitically miming certain features of the procedural dynamics of the law. Hobbes' attempt to reduce private opinion in the interests of shared commitment to a commonwealth creates an anonymous public opinion that disguises its private investors.

What shapes public opinion often cannot be read or resists an internally consistent reading. If public opinion is in fact another kind of capital a la Bourdieu to which we make (often disguised) investments, withdrawals, and assists in circulation, then it metaphorically resembles a kind of reservoir waiting to be filled with new information. People bring a variety of personal prejudices in evaluations which can be self-serving in the competition for Bourdieu's capital. A virtual cottage industry exists in Trollope criticism dedicated to the determination (or acquittal) of Trollope as an Anti-Semite,[13] even though positive ethnic identification is unreadably indeterminate, given the efficacy of cosmopolitan disguises.

[13] See Bryan Cheyette (1986, 34–71). Also, Ann Marlow (2015) and in a slightly different context, Ronald Berman (1998, 57–67).

Squercum, an aggressive attorney on behalf of his clients, is assumed to be Jewish, though another character adds to the uncertainty by remarking that he is known to ride to the hounds on the sabbath. The swindling financier Auguste Melmotte, is characterized throughout *The Way We Live Now* as a speculative Jewish *arriviste* with successful dealings in the City and eventual election as an M.P. One has to be a careful reader of the novel to learn post mortem, that he was the son of one Irishman named Melmody, a notorious "coiner" (counterfeiter) (Trollope 1982, 449). Madame Goesler, assumed to be a central European Jewish divorcee who finances and later marries Phineas Finn, has the facial appearance, dark hair and long nose of a central European Jew, but the novel continually questions the mystery of her beliefs, partially because independent wealth and sophisticated parties and taste varnishes her putative Jewishness, enabling social assimilation. In Trollope, the Jew is characterized as being consistently *unreadable* with any certainty by the majority of the population. In other words, the inability to read—both tactical and literal—may enable assimilation. Ethnic identity, like genuine political identification and loyalty in the *Parliamentary Novels*, is transactional because it cannot be *read* with certainty, given disguises, tactical conversions, collaborators and the varnishing by religious conversion or wealth (Mealyus of *The Eustace Diamonds*/Disraeli) or "new" (unlanded) money (Madame Goesler/Baron de Rothschild). This resistance to being consistently and univocally read is characteristic of law, public opinion, and ethnicity—as in Hester Prynne's "Oriental complexion"—all of which are characterized by some foundational *errancy*: the potential for misreading. If read allegorically, the Jew (as heir to the "Old Law" prior to the New Dispensation) cannot be consistently read.

John Stuart Mill's curious, posited *Imaginary* in the absence of an opposition, should not be conceived of as an emptiness, but crucial to creating the *faux transparency*, necessary to create a competitive field, crucial to public opinion formation. We would dwell in it not as a formalism, but in ready response to unforeseeable demands and pressures. It would have a deniable collective/composite voice, but one not fully articulated or comprehensible. Public opinion would be independent of the law, yet activated by the law and vice-versa to create an exchange system with a variety of entry points. A present or imaginary *vox populi* would be, like and unlike the law, a circulating breath or lifeblood interrogating us as we interrogate its exchange-and-acceptance systems, like other "currencies"[14]. As did Jurgen Habermas (1991) U.S. Federal Reserve Chairman Ben Bernak with the need for a consistent flow of public opinion, former Federal Reserve Chairman Ben Bernanke at the outset of the financial crisis in an interview with CNN (January 12, 2009) stated that liquidity--now frozen--was the lifeblood of the economy, citing Bagehot's (2014 [1873]) „Lombard Street" as his source:

[14] During the 2008 financial crisis in the United States, the then Chairman of the U.S. Federal Reserve, Ben Bernanke, actually referred to the banking system as the "lifeblood" of any economy as justification for a massive government transfusion. He actually cited his source, a contemporary of Trollope, Walter Bagehot, who used the phrase in his analysis of a panic caused by a run on the banks as "life blood" turned to "sugar water" in his novel, *Lombard Street: A Description of the Money Market* (1873).

> [...] it is because this universal has no necessary body and no necessary content; different groups, instead, compete between themselves to *temporarily give to their particularities* a function of universal representation. Society generates a whole vocabulary of empty signifiers whose *temporary signifieds* are the result of political competition. (Laclau 2004, 35, emphasis mine)

Laclau's "empty signifiers" would be entirely compatible (from the perceiver's stance) with invisibility, transparency, or a willed illegibility. This paradoxically opens (whatever) to a perpetually competitive revaluation and re-denomination to endow empty signifiers with a changing valence. Like the action of public opinion in Trollope, 'character' is under continuous interpellation, as if under a revaluating sur-veillance.[15] But this peculiar signifier might also melt or be dissolved into a general 'effect' that obscures its occasions of intercession. On what occasions and conditions does 'Jew-ish' assume variable, even antagonistic values?

Bernard Schlink ends *The Reader* (1997) with a rationalization, the coda to a novel that had begun with an exchange system, making "desire an entry in a strange moral accounting" (17): a ledger, like that of the early New England puritans, that had sought to balance the columns of grace and faith. Most mystery stories begin with some disappeared object: a father (Hawthorne); life (Conan Doyle); a purloined letter (Poe); a diamond necklace (Trollope); Hanna Schmitz (Schlink). If only we know where to look or how to read (in a certain way, of course, as with all accounting), the answer is often "elementary." Schlink's *The Reader* (1997) imagines a secondary elimination or occlusion of narrative spawned by a historical Disappearance, the Shoah:

> Thus, there are many different stories in addition to the one I have written. The guarantee that the *written* one is the right one lies in the fact that I wrote it and not the other versions. The *written version wanted to be written*, the many others *did not*. (215, emphasis mine)

The law's determinate power lies in its having been handed down, inscribed as historically privileged, by virtue of legibility, and hence presumptive intentionality, whereas we remain illiterate of the "many others." Yet, in a retrospectively-written novel, the future jurist and first-person narrator, Michael Berg, here lends to the written word what it can never possess: wants. Only writers, not words, have intentions that resist access. Because writers lose sovereignty in the act of dispatch, intention can only be a presumption—in the middle-ages, a cardinal sin of imagining (Mill's Imaginary writ large?) yourself as Divine!

---

[15] The publication of the *Black Notebooks*, and its confirmation of the ways in which Heidegger's being-historical interpretation of race belongs to the context of the unfolding narrative of the history of Being, has strengthened accusations of his persistent Anti-Semitism. Emmanuel Faye has proposed a legally-mandated illiteracy ("you cannot read it") toward Heidegger's work: that all should be removed from the philosophy section of libraries, like alleged pornography from the Attica State Prison Library. See Peter Trawny (2016). Ironically, for Heidegger, it would be only in Being-Towards-Death, the realized consciousness of her mortality, that would enable Schlink's illiterate Hanna to become the authentic person she really *is*.

Commonly referred to as authorial intention, any recovery of the *Ding an sich*, is further made uncertain by "geological labors of our lives" (215). As time and layers of sediment obscure our access to the earth's foundational moments, so layers of legal and historical commentary obscure the recovery of any original intention demanded of "strict-constructionist" legal scholars.[16] Given the necessary loss over time of full foundational context, we remain illiterate wanderers in the dark, probing contaminated evidence in search of some impossible *arché*. As any intelligent respondent to public opinion knows, but omniscient narrators forget, 'there are always other stories to be told.' Schlink's Michael reads our moral issues, specifically those confronting post-war German citizens, as differences in reading skills that confront all readers, invariably blind to something.

The Reader commences with a reading/story telling club: an inverse *Arabian Nights*. The adolescent Michael assumes the role of the fabulist, Scheherazade, to choose a new story to be read aloud each night as a necessary prelude to love-making. The relationship begins when Hanna Schmidt tends to him after a bout of nausea in front of her apartment house, triggered by hepatitis, an illness whose antigens remain in the blood throughout life, so that its victims can never be entirely cured. As full citizenship was tied to blood in the Third Reich, as it formerly was among Jews, the malady seems initially to freeze Schlink's tale into a (too) easy allegorical reading. The sterile post-war 'art brut' apartment house with its faux-Gothic façade is home to a transient population of renters, anonymous residents seldom seen by its adolescent visitor: an economic diaspora with no landed stake in Germany's miraculous economic recovery. The relationship between sovereignty and nativity is interrogated in Hanna's childhood spent, significantly, in a German-speaking enclave in Romania. She is party to the Hegelian historical partitions crucial to Central European history.

Their exchange economy, oral discourse for intercourse and the comparable anticipation of more, threatens the 'kid's' progression from the Fifth Form toward admission to and completion of a degree in legal jurisprudence to which Hanna urges his dilatory attendance. The author's surrogate no more understands Hanna's incessant need for oral stories as foreplay, than Scheherazade understood the peculiar attentiveness of Shah Shahryar who has pledged to kill a new 'bride' each night before she survives an earlier Holocaust of her sisters in the tales originally comprising the *Hazar Afsaneh*, literally, *A Thousand Stories*. Survival is enabled by creative story-telling whose interruption brings death.

Their relationship moves from a therapeutically custodial beginning, to shared oral discourse, to something beyond a flirtation from which the author's first-person persona can neither fully commit nor extract himself. "Flirtation" is surely an

[16] The noted American jurist, Richard Posner, has suggested that strict constructionists dedicated to the recovery of original intention behind laws are using *formalism* to mask conservative, *status quo* opinions, *Ad hoc* considerations of the "external complexity" of the real world would bring judging closer to public opinion. See Richard A. Posner (2013, 81).

appropriate trope by, which some might understand the mysterious attractions of the Third Reich. Their shared "breaths" are a literal afternoon conspiracy (even etymologically, "breathing together") against the study of the law in which he has been indoctrinated by a father, a well-known academic, teaching German Idealist philosophers. If the reader of *The* Reader responds similarly, Schlink's novel must be read as foundational. The curriculum, with its emphasis upon "voices" in drama, is heavy with *burgerlichtes Trauerspiel*: *Emilia Galotti* and Schiller's *Kabale und Liebe*. Both plays deal with the contrast between the arbitrary law of an aristocracy and a different "enlightenment" morality attached to emergent bourgeois love.

The narrator cannot recall from a memory stratified by time, what initially attracted him to Frau Schmitz. It is "as if she had withdrawn into her own body, and left it to itself" (Schlink 1997, 14), her face rather expressionless. She is remembered in fact as a perfumed anonymity committed to cleanliness and frequent bathing, as if wanting to rid herself of some stain. The absence of facial expression and ritualized bathing gives her a certain resemblance to the anonymous figures of *porne*, (an illegible, facelessness) of traditional pornography, not unlike "O" in Pauline Reage's *L'Histoire d'O*. Her Hebrew name, shared with Hannah Arendt, was the (initially) sterile mother of the Biblical Solomon, the last judge among the Jewish prophets. Otherwise, Hanna's past history, and until later in the novel, her secret, remains similarly a blank slate. Never a driver, she supports herself as a conductor on a public tram, with its historical resonance in the rail platforms which greeted doomed arrivals at internment camps and but also the redeemed of the 'Kindertransport' program. But once again, the critic always has 'a posteriori' literacy, informed by layers of built-up association: a special way of reading.

Her refusal to accept his invitation to read to him or her failure while they are on a "lost weekend" to heed a written note asking her to wait for him, should have been read by Michael. His illiteracy is a failure to read her inability to read, which affects some readers of *The Reader*. Their relationship ends on a curious day at a public swimming pool frequented by the "reader" and the joyous voices of his adolescent friends, a setting she previously avoided: bathing in the light of day. An anonymous presence, "her face turned towards me, but with an expression, *I cannot read at all*" (79, emphasis mine)—a deduction arrived at only much later—but denoting a universalizing illiteracy and silence. Figural moral blindness and political silence has a resonance in Otto Dix's 1948 lithograph series, "Rothaariges Mädchen," wherein a youngish woman with vacuously empty eyes and mouth is framed by ghostly, marginal shadows (Fig. 1).

Hanna then disappears, is arrested and charged as a Nazi collaborator for her wartime role as guard for female prisoners in an internment camp, an occupation requiring no literacy. Awaiting trial, she is denied release from prison on her own recognizance—as demanded under the *habeas corpus* statutes imposed by the Occupying Powers—regarded as a flight risk given her failure to answer a series of (written) summons. Illiteracy compounds the offense.

Fig. 1 Otto Dix 1948 signed lithograph (4/30), "Rothaariges Mädchen", owned by Jan B. Gordon

To say that our moral failures result from real or strategic illiteracy, 'We never knew because the camps were in restricted areas' or the interrogative, 'How could we have known?', is often used by collaborators in Nazi Germany in self-defense, but rings hollow to much of the outside world. Metaphorically strategic illiteracy, shared with Pearl, can both abet assimilation and exclude one from social judgment. George Steiner has suggested that a certain kind of writing (and therefore a certain kind of reading?) is impossible after the Shoah.[17] Is this willing 'turning away' from reading (and the re-reading crucial to self-reflection), in fact an inwardness rivalling illiteracy, shared with Schlink's Hanna? Is moral blindness analogous to willed illiteracy? Is this shared 'blindness,' to borrow from Paul De Man, our collective "insight"?

Hanna Schmidt is convicted largely by the conflicted testimony of a then-child who survived the Holocaust in the confusing days near war's end, and sentenced. Her role in rescuing or not the children under her guard from a fire and what her orders were, is indeterminate. She has confessed by signing the written charges

[17] In a blurb for the rear cover of paperbound Weidenfeld and Nicolson edition of *The Reader* (2017), adapted from a review in the *Observer*, Steiner addressed the "masterly work" with the ironic comment: "the reviewer's privileged function is to say, as loudly as he is able, 'Read this' and 'read it again.'" Even in his praise, the distinction between voice, reading, and re-reading is maintained.

even though she is illiterate. Her former lover, Michael Berg, collaborates in her punishment by never speaking to the court of her illiteracy. Hanna is a scapegoat for a systemic failure which Schlink suggests, is one of the "charges" of the law: to hold someone sacrificially re-sponsible who could never have possibly been in a position of obedience, but is nevertheless indicted by *post facto vox populi* demands. Neither plaintiff nor defendant can be identified with certainty. Written law and the voice of public opinion dialectically abet and threaten the sovereignty of the other.

After acquiring modest literacy while incarcerated, Hanna hangs herself a day before she is to be released and accompanied by her former lover, Michael Berg, to be rehabilitated (like Germany) to everyday life. She belatedly joins, by some accounts, 10.000 Germans who committed suicide in the three months after World War II. Ironically, her modest savings are donated—given the absence of family—to a charity promoting literacy in Israel. Does German guilt create a Jewish state? The extra-territorial 'reparation' for guilt, determined by Levinas' infamous third, "Le Trier," enhances a historically significant language—by which the Old Law was handed down by a Creative Judge—but a written language of which 95% of secular Jews in the diaspora (including your speaker) are illiterate: 'I can't read it.'

Nathaniel Hawthorne, Anthony Trollope, and Bernard Schlink are foundational novelists: their achievements narrate a shared inflection point, when a country at a certain gestational phase came into a Being that acknowledges problematics in its existence. In some sense, all the countries live in a peculiar judicial ontology, perhaps most literally in the suicide by hanging of Hanna Schmidt, a literally suspended sentence. Perhaps not coincidentally, the authors of all three novels have some connection, by ancestry or occupation, with the procedures of codified law and its relationship to the power of circulating public opinion, with an interest in how a repressed *vox populi* impacts legal judgments that it has also informed. All three authors had careers as public servants, as a prelude to literary ambitions, and in Schlink's case a distinguished career as a Professor of Law at NYU and a noted German jurist. Trollope was the inventor of an everyday convenience, the pillar post box system, wherein private writing was deposited into a convenient repository, an institutional mouth, for efficient circulation.

In *The Theory of the Novel*, Georg Lukács suggested that only when the novel depicted the unfolding of lives in *real time* can life impose its own form rather than having imposed upon it some external forms (laws) like genre (Lukács 1971, 46). The Hungarian critic's embrace of a lost, but recoverable, orality of the epic would be a dream of collectively-shared voices ('curiae'), lost when mechanically-applied forms created bourgeois narrative space. Like the oral epic, the *voice(s)* of public opinion render judgments in real time, adapting to Judge Posner's "complexities" of real life, most recently with so-called "victim" or "community-impact" oral statements prior to sentencing. Rendered continuous by victims' words, the law comes closer to *methexis*, the oral *currency* of (harmoniously responsive) public opinion: the Greek chorus.

In conclusion, let us now collectively, inhale, pause, suspend breathing for twenty seconds, then exhale: *tief durchatmen*. We are alive in its pre-*scriptive* sound; yet, potentially in a violation of law, represented as con-spiracy ("to breathe together"). But, this kind of breathing is a two-way street. Walter Benjamin in his ill-fated postdoctoral project, *The Origins of Tragic German Drama*, (many of which are on Michael Berg and Hanna Schmidt's reading list) compared acute moments of perception to a de-allegorization in which associations are eliminated in the preservation of a singularity. Benjamin compared the experience with holding your breath, a collective Hobbesian suspension of breathed voice:

> This can be likened to a *pause for breath*, after which thought can be totally and unhurriedly concentrated on the minutest object without the slightest inhibition. [...] In the act of true contemplation [...] the abandoning of deductive methods is combined with an ever wider-ranging, an ever more intense reappraisal of phenomena, which are, however, never in danger of remaining the objects of vague wonder. As long as representation of them is also representation of ideas, for it is here that individuality is preserved. (Benjamin 1977, 37, emphasis mine)

In a familiar instance of the return of the repressed, law periodically re-enacts its Hobbesian origins by suspending rhythmical breathing. Holding one's breath grounds both intention (the commencement of voice) and Benjamin's interrogation of a temporary suspension of breath as an escape from deductive reasoning and into meditative concentration, as yoga practitioners profess. A witness' breathless laughter, my 'petite mort' in a Buffalo, New York courtroom, that earned a legal objection; Pearl's breathless shrieks in *The Scarlet Letter*; Hanna Schmidt's suspension of breath in hanging herself prior to release—all conform to the model. No wonder recent world public opinion was collectively aghast at the last utterance of a man with the knee of the law upon his neck, sharing a gasping, last breath: "I can't breathe."

References

Anonymous. 1857. The Newspaper Press by a Quarterly Reviewer. *Quarterly Review*.

Anonymous. 1859. Popular Literature—The Periodical Press. *Blackwood's Edinburgh Magazine*.

Bagehot, Walter. 2014 [1873]. *Lombard Street: A Description of the Money Market.* New York: Charles Scribner & Sons.

Benjamin, Walter. 1977. *The Origins of Tragic German Drama.* Translated by J. Osborne. London: New Left Books.

Benveniste, Émile. 1966. *Problèmes lingusitique générale,* Paris: Galimard.

Berman, Ronald. 1998. Jews in the Nineteenth-Century Novel. *Journal of Aesthetic Education* 32(2): 57–67.

Bernanke, Benjamin. 2009. Interview with CNN January 14 2009.

Blackstone, William. 1915 [1765]. *Commentaries on the Laws of England I and II*, ed. William C. Jones. San Francisco: Bancroft & Whitney.

Bourdieu, Pierre. 1977. *Outline of a Theory of Practice.* Translated by Richard Nice. Cambridge: Cambridge University Press.

Cheyette, Bryan. 1986. *An Overwhelming Question*: *Jewish Stereotyping in English Fiction and Society 1875–1914.* Unpublished PhD Dissertation, Sheffield University.

Dicey, A.V. 1981 [1914]. *Lectures on the Relation Between Law and Public Opinion in England During the Nineteenth Century.* Introduced by Richard A. Cosgrove. New Brunswick and London: Transaction.

Gordon, Jan B. 2001. Hearsay Booked: Fugitive Talk Brought to Justice. In *TalkTalkTalk: The Cultural Life of Everyday Conversation*, ed. Shelley Salamensky. London and New York: Routledge.

Gordon, Jan B. 2022. *The Politics of Public Opinion in the Novels of Anthony Trollope: A 'Tenth Muse.'* London and New York: Anthem.

Habermas, Jürgen. 1991. *The Transformation of the Public Sphere: An Inquiry Into a Category of Bourgeois Society.* Translated by Thomas Burger and Frederick Lawrence. Cambridge, MA: MIT Press.

Habermas, Jürgen and Ratzinger, Joseph. 2004. *Les Fondments prépolitiques de l'État démocratique* trans. J. L. Schlegel. *Esprit* 306 (July), 5–28.

Hawthorne, Nathaniel. 1959. *The Scarlet Letter.* Introduction by Leo Marx. New York: Signet.

Hobbes, Thomas. 1982. *Leviathan,* ed. C.B. Macpherson. Harmondsworth: Penguin.

Laclau, Ernesto. 2004. *Emancipation(s).* London and New York: Verso.

Levinas, Emmanuel. 1981. *Otherwise than Being, or Beyond Essence.* Translated by Alphonse Lingis. Pittsburgh: Duquesne University Press.

Lukács, Georg. 1971. *The Theory of the Novel.* Translated by A. Bostock. London: Merlin.

Marlow, Ann. 2015. Why Anthony Trollope is the Most Jewish of the Great English Novelists. *Tablet Magazine.*

Mill, John Stuart. 2015. *On Liberty, Utilitarianism, and Other Essays*, ed. Mark Philp and Frederick Rosen. Oxford: Oxford University Press.

Posner, Richard A. 2013. *Reflections on Judging.* Cambridge and London: Harvard University Press.

Schlink, Bernard. 1997. *The Reader.* Translated by Carol Brown Janeway. London: Weidenfeld & Nicolson.

Trawny, Peter. 2016. *Heidegger and the Myth of a Jewish World Conspiracy*. Chicago and London: U of Chicago P.

Trollope, Anthony. 1983. *The Duke's Children*, ed. Hermione Lee. Oxford: Oxford University Press, 1983.

Trollope, Anthony. 1984. *The Warden*, ed. Robin Gilmour. Harmondsworth: Penguin.

Trollope, Anthony. 1982. *The Way We Live Now*, ed. John Sutherland. Oxford: Oxford University Press.

Mapping Literary Trials. What Judicial Archives Can and Cannot Do About the Dearth of Evidence

Ralf Grüttemeier

Historical and comparative contextualisation of national and transnational legal practices and theories is key for most relevant questions in the field of Law and Literature (Hiebaum et al. 2016, 40, 77). This definitely goes for questions regarding the rise, heydays, presence and future of literary trials—legal procedures that try to find out whether texts regarded as literary are violating specific rules or other values protected by the law. A recent example for that branch of research is the research project A01 "Law and Literature in Disagreement on Censorship" of the Sonderforschungsbereich CRC 1385 "Law and Literature" in Münster: it aims at describing how in literary trials legal and literary studies act in what is basically a conflict over which interpretation prevails. However, a problem for this kind of research is the general dearth of evidence for reconstructing what judges or other parts of the judicial elites think of literature. Of the 19.000 cases that the European Court of Human Rights had dealt with until 2014, only 10 touched upon works of literature, as Eleni Polypoloumenou (2016) has demonstrated. Or to put it in more general terms: only a very small part of all trials are literary trials; only a small part of all judicial verdicts are published; an even smaller part is substantially documented concerning the arguments of all parties involved; and within literary trials the attorneys and judges are generally very reluctant to be too explicit about their ideas of what literature is, and to what degree it should get special protection in society compared to other types of human utterances. How can scholars deal with this problem? In this article I will reflect on the possibilities and limitations of possible roads towards more evidence for answering two types of questions; one aiming at poetics, the other at institutional relations (Grüttemeier 2016, 8–17). What kind of conceptions of literature are at stake on the judicial side in literary

R. Grüttemeier (✉)
Niederlandistik, Carl von Ossietzky Universität Oldenburg, Oldenburg, Germany
e-mail: ralf.gruettemeier@uni-oldenburg.de

K. Stierstorfer (ed.), *Law and Literature in Europe and Beyond*, Literatur und Recht 15, https://doi.org/10.1007/978-3-662-69851-8_6

trials? And what kind of ideas prevail on the societal status of literature and its degree of autonomy?

Bundesverfassungsgericht: Bundesarchiv Koblenz

One type of evidence that might offer more insight into the hidden ways how legal decisions come about and what ideas prevail in dominant juridical circles, are judicial archives at the highest level of jurisdiction. In a recent article, Dieter Grimm (2019) has demonstrated the fascinating possibilities and problems of an approach using this evidence with an analysis of the archive material around the 'Elfes-judgement' of the 'Bundesverfassungsgericht' from 1957—a benchmark especially for jurisprudence on the free development of one's personality (Art. 2 para. 1 GG). Concerning questions about the institutional and poetic contexts of literary trials, in Germany the leading cases would be the 'Bundesverfassungsgericht' decisions in 1971 on Klaus Mann's novel *Mephisto* and the 2007 decision on Maxim Biller's novel *Esra*. Both decisions not only set benchmarks for future prosecutions. They were also relatively explicit and elaborate at length what the highest judges in Germany think about works of literature. But how exactly did the judges' ideas about what literature is, about how to distinguish between texts that fall under the normative notion of "art" in Art. 5 para. 3 GG, and about the degree of autonomy of literature with regard to other constitutional values, find their way into their decision? Since judges are no specialists in art, one would expect that they will have made use of literary expertise, delivered by scholars or academics regarded as competent for the questions to be decided on, as judges do in in other cases with other disciplines ('Sachverständige') regularly. For judges it also seems functional to take notice of what is the state of art in literary studies and where there is consensus among literary experts in order to save the judiciary from becoming a laughing stock for literary insiders. So, to what extent was there a dialogue with literary experts, which arguments were successful and which unsuccessful in convincing the majority behind the legal decision?

The published decision from 1971 indicates that there indeed seems to have been a dialogue of some kind between judicial and literary experts. Its most explicit traces can be found where the court states that all previous courts have rightfully ("mit Recht") regarded *Mephisto* to be a work of art, in consensus with all parties involved in the trial "and, as far as one can see, including the judgement of all experts involved" ("und soweit ersichtlich mit dem Urteil aller kompetenten Sachverständigen"; BVerfG 1971, 2007). Furthermore, the *Mephisto* case seems to echo to a number of philosophical and theoretical texts, such as, among others, Hans-Georg Gadamers *Wahrheit und Methode* from 1960. The extensive use in the decision of the *Abbild-Urbild* terminology in combination with parallel reflections on the special position of the *roman-á-clef* point into this direction—without Gadamer or anyone in his tradition being explicitly mentioned in the published verdict. The same goes for the 2007 decision where the final rejection of the claim of the real-life-mother of real-life-Esra was based on an argument in which literary scholars will recognize a narratological distinction we owe to Mieke Bal (1985) and others. Without using the names of narratologists or their technical vocabulary, the court does differentiate between who tells and who sees, between narration and focalization. In its decision, the court held that the incriminated negative information and the negative judgments on Lale – the mother of Esra in the novel – are never uttered from the point of view of the narrator, but of that of other characters in the novel (Grüttemeier 2016, 150–154).

Yet, the indications for literary expertise in the published decisions of the 'Bundesverfassungsgericht' are rather vague, and therefore the foundation for specific claims is small. When the judges write "aller kompetenten Sachverständigen," who exactly was consulted? Furthermore: are "Abbild" and "Urbild" not very common notions that could point also to other experts than Gadamer? In order to get a sharper and more reliable picture, one would need more evidence and more context. This is where the judicial archives might come in: here, the 'Bundesarchiv' in Koblenz. Unfortunately, the files of the 'Bundesverfassungsgericht' in the 'Bundesarchiv' are closed until sixty years after a decision. Therefore, concerning the two leading cases on literature, for quite some years to come, we will have to work only with the decision and the dissenting opinions published on the usual judicial platforms: that is until 2031 respectively 2067.

International comparative research, however, may be helpful, at least in parts: while it will not give answers to the specific questions concerning the German decisions, it may give some plausible contextual information about practices on the highest judicial level, especially when the legal systems are comparable and closely related to each other. So while waiting for a timeslot in Koblenz in 2031, one could turn to the Netherlands where there are many judicial structures rather similar to the German ones; where there is a long tradition of literary cases since the beginning of the twentieth century; and where there are other archive-rules. In how far could this testcase confirm some of the structural expectations articulated above?

Hoge Raad: *Nationaal Archief Den Haag*

The highest court of the Netherlands is the 'Hoge Raad', which is, from a German perspective, comparable to the 'Bundesgerichtshof'. In the Netherlands, there is no court that guards over the Dutch constitution (Voermans 2023, 667–677; van der Velden 2015) and there is also no explicit legal protection of art in the Netherlands, neither in the constitution nor in any other law (cf. Grüttemeier 2016, 8–12; Beekman 2016). Yet, how close both jurisdictions are related is indicated by the fact that in the published jurisdiction of the 'Hoge Raad' on the 'Danslessen'-case from 2001, the jurisdiction of the 'Bundesverfassungsgericht' on *Mephisto* from 1971 did play a substantial role (Beekman and Grüttemeier 2005, 176, 177). From its founding in 1838, six cases related to literature – understood in a broad sense – have been dealt with by the 'Hoge Raad':

- A 1920 obscenity case against a bookseller for selling the Dutch translation of the novel *L'Enfer* by the French socialist writer Henri Barbusse; acquittal confirmed.
- Between 1963 and 1965 three decisions on an obscenity case against the Dutch novel *Liesbeth en de wereld van Bob en Daphne* by Han B. Aalberse; after two formal acquittals in 1963 and 1964 finally in 1965 conviction confirmed (which was symbolic: €13).
- A 1968 blasphemy case against the famous Dutch writer Gerard Reve, based on parts of his novel-in-letters *Nader tot* U (Nearer to Thee); acquittal confirmed.
- In 1971 and 1972 two obscenity decisions on Rudolf Kraawinkel's theatre performance *Erotisch panorama* (Erotic panorama); acquittal by an appeal court.
- A 2001 discrimination/defamation case against the novel *Danslessen* (Dancing lessons) by the Dutch writer Pieter Waterdrinker; acquitted by the *Hoge Raad.*
- A 2018 discrimination case against the Dutch rapper Ismo; conviction confirmed (€1500).

Of all these cases we do have as sources three types of published documents, among others in *Nederlandse Jurisprudentie*: the motivation for revision (at least in summary), the conclusion by the Attorney General (advocaat-generaal), and the decision of the court. The documentation of the decisions of the 'Hoge Raad' is in principle transferred to the National Archives at The Hague, where, at this moment, all files of the 'Hoge Raad' until 1979 are located. Of the four cases before 1979 named above, only the documents of the Barbusse-trial are accessible without restrictions—the access to the other three is officially denied to the public until 2055. It was lifted on my request in the summer of 2022, for which I would like to thank the 'algemene rijksarchivaris' and their staff.

To cut a long story short: the number and sort of unpublished documentation in the archives concerning these trials is very limited. The procedure that the 'Hoge Raad' follows in literary cases is obviously judicial business as usual. After having read and/or heard the party asking for revision (sometimes in a session that is in principle open for the public) and after having read the conclusion by the Attorney General, one of the judges—appointed from the group that will make the decision—writes a first draft of the decision to which the other judges can react, before the final decision is taken and made available to the public. In the four trials under scrutiny here, there are no traces whatsoever of judges having read literary theory, let alone traces of a direct or indirect dialogue, written or oral, between the judges and literary scholars. What the archives however do offer—apart from technical judicial correspondence—are basically additions to the three types of published documents mentioned above.

Concerning documents around the prosecution, one can find in the case of Barbusse the full version of the motivation for revision ('memorie van cassatie'): four pages written and signed by the prosecutor van den Brandeler, arguing against the acquittal of the seller of the incriminated novel by Barbusse (HR (2.09.28) 446). In the published version of the decision, van den Brandelers arguments only had been summarized. Second, the archive contains five pleas by the defense of the artists: three by Arie Mout in the three sessions on *Liesbeth en de wereld van Bob and Daphne* between 1963 and 1965 (HR (2.09.65) 1018, 1031, 1042); two by his nephew and partner Peter Mout on *Erotisch Panorama*, dating from 1971 and 1972 (HR (2.09.65) 1251, 1275). But the pleas by the advocates of the writers did not survive in all cases: apparently, the defense of Ernst Polak in the session of

March 15 1920 is lost. Reve, by the way, explicitly did not want to be defended at the 'Hoge Raad', since, as he wrote, he already had said everything on his behalf in the court of appeal and did not want to add anything. In his preparation for the appeal at the time, he had dismissed his lawyer (i.e., Hans Richard Eyl) of the lower court and had chosen to defend himself. Reve explained all this in a one-page-letter from November 22, 1967 to the president of the 'Hoge Raad'—a letter that is not part of the many published letter-books by Reve, as far as I can see (HR (2.09.65) 1112). This letter also includes Reve's polite advice what the 'Hoge Raad' should do with the prosecutor's request for revision—which in its effect did not differ much from what the 'Hoge Raad' decided in the end.

Finally, concerning the third type of evidence, there are concept-versions of the final decisions of all four cases (Barbusse, Aalberse, Reve, *Erotisch Panorama*) in the archives. This documentation ranges from fragments (for example two pages in the case of Aalberse, 1963) up to the whole decision as a concept, as for example in the case of Barbusse. Mostly, the concept-versions only contain minor linguistic corrections in the margins or between the lines.

However, there is one exception where we have written comments from different judges on the first draft: in the Aalberse case from 1965, where in the end the 'Hoge Raad' confirmed the conviction (HR (2.09.65) 1042). In the published decision of that case, careful readers might already have discovered a fog of disagreement within the 'Hoge Raad', especially one concerning the 'exceptio artis'. In Dutch jurisdiction, the emergence of the 'exceptio artis' dates from 1920 when the 'Hoge Raad' ruled (concerning the translation of a Barbusse-novel into Dutch, see above) that incriminated parts of a text can be judged differently when they are part of a work of art. The 1965 decision stated in that regard that the incriminated novel at the time—*Liesbeth en de wereld van Bob and Daphne*—was very poor literature. But the decision explicitly avoided saying what would have been the consequences, if it had not been. Starting out from the motivation of the verdict by the Appeal Court which had ruled that the book "cannot be regarded as a work of art", the 'Hoge Raad' added that the defense had contradicted this point with statements of "several literary experts whose names were explicitly mentioned". Then the 'Hoge Raad' continued, in arguing against the defense:

> that nevertheless, whatever one may think about the idea—that is obviously at the core of this argument—that a work of art as such cannot be offensive to public decency, according to the judgment of the *Hoge Raad* no such literary value can be attributed to the incriminated book that this argument needs further reflection in evaluating the contested decision of the Appeal Court […]. (Hoge Raad 1965, 947, 948; [my translation])

Especially the formulation "whatever one may think" ("wat er zij van de stelling") shows that the Supreme Court avoids making explicitly clear how to balance a work of literature against the fact that parts of it might violate the obscenity-law with its explicit description of sexual acts, especially those of young adolescents. An informed reader also might have raised an eyebrow when reading that this point of view ("that a work of art as such cannot be offensive to public decency";

"dat een kunstwerk als zodanig niet aanstotelijk voor de eerbaarheid kan zijn") was attributed to the defense. This was not what the defense had argued. Mr. A. Mout, speaking on behalf of his client, had defended a functional idea of the 'exceptio artis', not a principled one (as in the phrasing of the court: "cannot be"; "niet […] kan zijn"). Instead, Mout's argument was in line with what had been jurisprudentially established, for example in his defense in the literary trial against W.F. Hermans' novel *Ik heb altijd gelijk* (I am always right) from 1952 (acquittal by first circuit and by the appeal court; the trial did not make it to the Hoge Raad; Beekman and Grüttemeier 2005, 100–103). With regard to *Liesbeth en de wereld van Bob and Daphne*, Mout argued:

> The book is: erotic realism, it shows the truth […]; it shows that the sexuality of the children is, among other things, a consequence of the dramatic lack of adequate housing. It is a sincere effort to educate and to warn. The Appeal Court denies that the book has literary value. May I hold against this the judgments of the chairman of the international PEN-club—an organization that hosts writers from the whole world—Dr. van Vriesland, of Adriaan van der Veen, literary editor of the newspaper *NRC* and Dr. Jef Last?

In literature (and, Mout tries to make clear, this novel *is* literature, three experts say), judges have to look at the function of the incriminated passages within the whole work of art. From this point of view the many explicit sex scenes between kids were functional within the book as a warning to do something about sex education and the social circumstances of children, according to Mout. Yet, the idea that the proposition 'x is art' should be identical to stopping all prosecution against x, is nowhere to be found in the plea of Mout—nor in any other of the literary trials where he defended literary texts (Grüttemeier et al. 2022).

The archives confirm now that an internal discussion, indeed, lay behind the evasive formulation in the decision ("whatever one may think about the idea") and the speculative—to say the least—interpretation of the defense by the 'Hoge Raad'. In that debate, the first draft of the decision by Judge Kazemier held the position that the Appeal Court itself had implicitly argued that a significant literary value might take away the offensiveness towards public decency. Concerning this draft, judge Feber reacted with two pages, handwritten. According to him, to attribute this position to the Appeal Court was probably stretching the words of the court too far; furthermore, for Feber, the fact that something was a work of art—be it literature or painting—might, in fact, *not* take its offensiveness away, but in some cases, for example in painting, even *increase* the offensiveness of an utterance. Therefore, the 'Hoge Raad' had better not attribute ideas to the Appeal Court the latter may not have had. Instead the 'Hoge Raad' could consider giving—if giving anything at all—its own decision on "the exceptio artis", Feber remarked.

At stake here are different ideas on the degree of autonomy attributed to literature and art. The first position—when something is a work of art, its incriminated parts might not constitute a legal offense when interpreted within the artwork as a whole—offers art and literature a route towards a higher degree of autonomy. This greater freedom can be achieved when a functional interpretation of the incriminated passage within the whole of the work of literature seems plausible enough to the judges. The foundation for this approach to literature in law was laid, as mentioned above, in the Netherlands in 1920 when the 'Hoge Raad' held that the nature ("aard") of a work of art demands that it must be analyzed, evaluated and judged as a whole ("in zijn geheel", Hoge Raad 1920, 449). All recent decisions by the 'Hoge Raad' over the last sixty years or so, too, are based on this principle: the Reve decision in 1968, the *Erotisch panorama* decision in 1971, the Waterdrinker decision in 2001 and the Ismo decision in 2018. Looking at the 1965 decision in its specific chronological setting, it is remarkable that it was the first one in which the 'Hoge Raad' might have had to apply their 1920 *exceptio artis* guideline to the judicial interpretation of a specific text. In 1920 the establishing of the rule as such had already cleared the path to a decision, since the charges of the prosecution had contradicted this principle ("in zijn geheel"): the prosecution had—only—objected to specific passages of Barbusse's *De hel*. Therefore, establishing the guideline was sufficient for the 'Hoge Raad' to confirm the acquittal of the bookseller of the translation at the time. This 1920-decision, however, left open how exactly judges should deal with incriminated passages interpreted within the whole of a literary work of art. When judge Kazemier suggested now that in case something is a work of art, its incriminated passages may not be considered a legal offense, the 'Hoge Raad' would lay the foundation for what later would become the dominant line in the Netherlands to deal judicially with literature. As Jaap de Hullu has summarized, the rationale of this line basically is to keep away from literature and art judicially whenever possible (de Hullu 2002, 564): a rather high degree of autonomy of literature within the judiciary.

The second position, however, that can be reconstructed from the archives—that art can in some cases increase the offensiveness of incriminated passages—turns into an expression of a more traditional position against this backdrop; a position less willing to give art a structurally high degree of protection within the jurisdiction. That art might also be taken to intensify criminal offenses, opposes what later became the general tendency of 'Hoge Raad' jurisprudence of the twentieth century: to stay away from literature whenever possible. In the end, such a position on art did not make it into the 1965 decision, nor into any of the following. In retrospect, the comments by Feber can be characterized as a minority view that did not have time on its side. But in 1965, in the first 'Hoge Raad' trial possibly to apply the 1920 guideline, such a view was obviously within the 'Hoge Raad' still strong enough to keep the judges from taking a consensual stand on the precise relation between the literariness of the whole and the offensiveness of its parts: "whatever one may think". One should add: strong enough at least in a case when obviously all judges regarded the incriminated text as poor literature, and neither the defense nor the accused did change that evaluation. Looked at from this perspective, the concept versions of the decision in combination with the final, published version, indicate that at the beginning of the 1960s the degree of autonomization of modern literature within the Dutch judiciary was still relatively precarious, compared to the dominant tendencies from the end of the 1960s onwards.

Going through all the evidence one can find the National Archive concerning the 'Hoge Raad', the conclusion must be that the archives do not offer much new material for research that tries to dig deeper into the impact of poetics and literary theory on the judiciary. What is more, it may be striking from a literary perspective how absent literary expertise seems to be in legal decision making on the highest level—even if one adds that the surviving documents might give a selective image of the procedure. As has become obvious, except for the formal minimum there is no clear standard of what has to be documented in every trial: this seems to depend in large part on the choices of those who make the drafts or interventions, and what the defense wants to add to the files. What is said in the oral debates and the meetings is lost forever, since there are no minutes. Still, concluding from what is in the files, it seems very unlikely that one might have found references to specific literary experts in these oral exchanges of arguments.

Contextual Evidence: Legal Specialists as Mediators

Still, there might be other ways to tackle the dearth of evidence in the sense stated above—as the following tentative remarks may indicate. As a stepping stone, one can use interesting claims that have been made by the former judge of the Bundesverfassungsgericht, Dieter Grimm, in an article on the difficulties that constitutional law has with art (Grimm 2007). His reflections depart from the idea that the question what art is, can in differentiated societies be answered only within the art system. Therefore, the judiciary should turn to experts from that system when to deal with works of art or literature. But there is a problem. According to Grimm, the professional behavior of scholars of literature (or art) differs from that of other academic disciplines. This is why the suggested judicial move will not find what it looks for, i.e. a reliable answer to the question 'what is art':

> In contrast with the legal system or the system of sciences, the system of art seems to lack criteria with which this question can be decided within the system in order to reach a sufficient degree of disciplinary binding agreement. […] Where other systems can offer experts, art offers a void. (Grimm 2007, 502; *my translation*)

Probably most literary experts would contradict Grimm at this point—at least from within the perspective of their own view on literature and how to deal with it, and from within their own theoretical foundations. But that is not the point here. The question pursued by the present article is not whether Grimm is right, but: what are the ideas of relevant parts of the judicial elite on literature and literary expertise? That impression, then, seems to be that of a disciplinary "lack" of criteria to reach "a sufficient degree of binding agreement" ("Verbindlichkeitsgrad"), so that judges might rely on it in the courtroom. This goes at least for the development of the disciplinary state of the last fifty years, since—as we have seen above—in 1971 the Bundesverfassungsgericht did recur to literary experts ("all competent experts"). But after that, no explicit references to literary experts can be found in the majority decisions of the 'Bundesverfassungsgericht', which is explained by Grimm with the "void" ("Leerstelle") above ("Das Verfassungsgericht kam *daher* später auf den Sachverstand nicht mehr zurück."; Grimm 2007, 504; *my italics, RG*). Apparently, there are indications that the dominant impression within relevant parts of the judicial elite is that scholars in literature and art cannot offer expertise in a way that judges might use it in their decisions: in dealing with art, "the judiciary cannot rely on the help of the theory of art, due to the exceptionally far developed autonomization of art" ("der besonders weit fortgeschrittenen Autonomisierung der Kunst", Grimm 2007, 509). In other words, contextualizing the same diagnosis from the perspective of literary scholarship: the dominant parameters of knowledge production in the field of literary studies over the last half a century or so seem to have circled around the pole of variation, pluralism, difference, diversity, or innovation, as opposed to the pole circling around the accumulation of disciplinary knowledge, intersubjectivity or systematicity. This interpretation of Grimm's view is, by the way, a diagnosis that one can arrive at, too, when analyzing literary debates as the one on the role of intention in interpretation from a historical perspective (Grüttemeier 2022, 199–203). In how far Grimm's diagnosis is right seems to be therefore without any doubt a very relevant question not only for the legal system but for literary scholarship, too—but that would be another book, and definitely beyond the scope of the present article.

Returning to the questions pursued here, Grimm's view on the relation between the judiciary and art/literary scholars corroborates the impression taken from the archives that literary/art expertise hardly plays a role in legal decision making, and even decreasingly so. At the same time, judges—at least those who engage in an interdisciplinary dialogue as Dieter Grimm, writing here in a *Festschrift* for the renowned art historian Horst Bredekamp—obviously do offer in their writings outside the courtroom relevant evidence for research into how legal elites do look at the societal status of literature and its degree of autonomy within the law and society in general.

I would hold the same for the second type of question raised above, concerning theories of literature: at least some contours of what may be called the 'poetics' of Grimm can be reconstructed from the very same article—poetics taken here as normative ideas on the nature, function and properties of art. In spite of Grimm's (2007, 503) presumption about the "impossibility to define art generally," there are several sentences in which he makes general statements on art. Taking the well-known typology of M.H. Abrams (1971) as a tool for classification, one could hold tentatively that Grimm seems closest to the objective or autonomous pole of the four types of poetics Abrams distinguishes, and less so concerning the mimetic, pragmatic/didactic or expressive pole. Art "as a symbolic form" is for Grimm (2007, 507) not aiming at "new truths" ("neue Gewißheiten"), but is always polyvalent ("mehrdeutig"). Because of this polyvalence and because of the "usually higher complexity" of artworks, the "meaning of a work of art" can neither be found nor missed by the recipient ("[…]weder zutreffend erfaßt oder verfehlt werden kann"), due to the "openness for interpretation" that is essential for the work of art ("der dem Kunstwerk eigenen Deutungsoffenheit"; Grimm 2007,

507). Politically engaged art, for Grimm, then, is 'reductive' because it turns away deliberately from what the essence of art is: "Works of art can contain views of its author or factual statements. In these cases, the artist himself reduces the degree of complexity of his works and does not aim for the openness of interpretation" (Grimm 2007, 507). Of course, these tentative efforts on the basis of a single text cannot claim to be a solid reconstruction Grimm's poetics and his view on the degree of autonomy of the literary field, let alone a reconstruction of the poetics of the Bundesverfassungsgericht at a certain time. But they should suffice to illustrate that a systematic reconstruction of all published sources (be it scholarly works, essays, speeches, notes etc.) by legal experts within the jurisdiction—judges, lawyers and prosecutors—may deliver substantial new evidence for answering more reliably the two types of questions raised above.

A last example may point in the same direction: this goes especially for lawyers defending literature in trials. Those lawyers are legal professionals, who enjoyed a strongly regulated and strongly institutionalized training. At the same time, when they take over the defense of a work of literature, they show at least a certain affinity with literature. To fulfill their task adequately, they must have judicial expertise *and* a feeling for the game concerning literature. Whatever they say about literature, it should not contradict legitimate positionings around the incriminated text in the literary field, while at the same time it should offer possibilities for docking at the conceptions of literature of the judges and prosecutors in their trial. When these lawyers do their job in literary trials professionally, one may expect that they build up symbolic capital concerning the judicial treatment of literature and art which might give their ideas on literature a certain impact within the legal system (as do judges on the highest level that at the same time show openness for and affinity with art, one might add). In that sense, these lawyers can be regarded as mediators between law and literature whose published writings promise insights into their individual concepts of literature *and* into that of the judiciary, too. Recently, the case of the Dutch lawyer and at the same time critic, essayist and novelist Arie Mout was used as a testcase that confirmed these expectations (Grüttemeier et al. 2022).

Systematic research into these groups of persons, in the long run preferably in international comparative perspective, should allow to test what we already think we know about the structural homology—in the sense Pierre Bourdieu uses this term—of the shared tastes within elites, especially between the literary and the legal field, but also with regard to other parts of what Bourdieu calls the field of power.[1] Whether the views attributed to Grimm are shared by larger parts of the legal elites and whether they can be corroborated (or contradicted) by the archive material of the Bundesverfassungsgericht from 2031 onwards, will be interesting

[1] Within the DFG-project GR 1875/9–1 Lotte van den Bosch looks systematically at all lawyers in Dutch literary trials of the twentieth century and Lina Blank at the conception of literature of Dutch politicians in the twentieth century, with regard to their poetics and ideas on the societal status of literature. See elsewhere in this volume.

to find out. But what is more: there seems to be sufficient evidence available to make plausible statements on the questions what conceptions of literature and what ideas on the societal status of literature and its degree of autonomy are at stake on the judicial side in literary trials.

References

Abrams, M.H. 1971. *The Mirror and the Lamp. Romantic Theory and the Critical Tradition*. Oxford: OUP.

Bal, Mieke. 1985. *Narratology. Introduction to the Theory of Narrative*. Toronto, Buffalo & London: University of Toronto Press.

Beekman, Klaus. 2016. De Sade as a Benchmark. Dutch Legal Actions Against Obscenity in Literature, Theatre and Film in the 1960s and 1970s, *Literary Trials.* Exceptio Artis *and Theories of Literature in Court*, ed. Ralf Grüttemeier, 89–106. New York: Bloomsbury.

Beekman, Klaus, and Ralf Grüttemeier. 2005. *De wet van de letter. Literatuur en rechtspraak*. Amsterdam: Athenaeum & Polak.

BVerfG, *Urteil des Bundesverfassungsgerichts*. 1971. *Neue Juristische Wochenschrift* (37), 1645–1655.

BVerfG, *Urteil des Bundesverfassungsgerichts*. 2007. 1 BvR 1783/05, 1–151. https://www.bundesverfassungsgericht.de/SharedDocs/Entscheidungen/DE/2007/06/rs20070613_1bvr178305.html. Accessed: 1 May 2023.

Grimm, Dieter. 2007. Über einige Schwierigkeiten des Verfassungsrechts mit der Kunst. In *Bild/Geschichte: Festschrift für Horst Bredekamp*, ed. Ph. Helas, M. Polte & C. Rückert, 499–509. Berlin: De Gruyter.

Grimm, Dieter. 2019. Das Elfes-Urteil. In *Verfassungsgerichtsbarkeit in der Bonner Republik. Aspekte einer Geschichte des Bundesverfassungsgerichts*, ed. F. Meinel, 155–185. Tübingen: Mohr Siebeck.

Grüttemeier, Ralf, ed. 2016. *Literary Trials.* Exceptio Artis *and Theories of Literature in Court*. New York: Bloomsbury.

Grüttemeier, Ralf. 2022. *Intention and Interpretation. A Short History*. Berlin: De Gruyter.

Grüttemeier, Ralf, Lotte van den Bosch and Lennart Bartsch. 2022. Achter de schermen van het recht. De advocaat Arie Mout als bemiddelaar tussen literatuur en recht. *Nederlandse Letterkunde* 27(2): 161–186.

Hiebaum, Christian, Susanne Knaller, and Doris Pichler, ed. 2016. *Recht und Literatur im Zwischenraum / Law and Literature In-Between. Aktuelle Inter- und transdisziplinäre Zugänge / Contemporary Inter- and Transdisciplinary Approaches*. Bielefeld: transcript.

Hoge Raad. 1920. Ter verspreiding in voorraad hebben van "De hel" van Barbusse. Voor de eerbaarheid aanstootelijk geschrift. 12.04.1920. *Nederlandse Jurisprudentie*: 446–449.

Hoge Raad. 1965. "Liesbeth en de wereld van Bob en Daphne" aanstotelijk voor de eerbaarheid. 23.03.1965. *Nederlandse Jurisprudentie*: 945–952.

Hullu, Jaap de. 2002. Noot onder arrest Hoge Raad van 09.10.2001 [*Danslessen*]. *Nederlandse Jurisprudentie*: 563–564.

Polymenopoulou, Eleni. 2016. Does One Swallow Make a Spring? Artistic and Literary Freedom at the European Court of Human Rights. *Human Rights Law Review* 16: 511–539.

Velden, Bastiaan D. van der. 2015. Die Niederlande, ein Land ohne Verfassungsgericht. *Pázmány Law Review* 3: 67–72.

Voermans, Wim. 2023. *Onze constitutie. De geschreven en ongeschreven regels van het Nederlandse staatsbestel*. Amsterdam: Prometheus.

Mediators as the Founding Fathers of Literary Autonomy in Law: The Case of Ernest Polak

Lotte van den Bosch

The texts in this volume offer multiple insights into the vital role that literature plays, or arts in general play, in Europe. Art can be seen as “a powerful means for maintaining constructive dialogue in [Europe’s] democratic and open societies” (Andel et al. 2020). This is how a European 2020 expert group formulated art’s role in a manifesto on the freedom of expression of arts and culture for the Council of Europe. The writers of this manifest stress the importance of legally acknowledging art’s autonomy on a European level. Concerns about threats to or attacks on this autonomy are, for instance, expressed by *Freemuse*, an (international) organization advocating for freedom of artistic expression and cultural diversity; *Artists at Risk*, an organization active at the intersection of human rights and the arts and *Index on Censorship*, an organization that campaigns for and defends free expression worldwide. All three organizations listed here mention the important role that the European Court of Human Rights (ECtHR) could and sometimes does play in delineating and thus guaranteeing art’s autonomy.

The abovementioned calls for strengthening the freedom of artistic expression re-invoke the question: how autonomous *is* art in Europe currently? To what extent is art regulated, and to what extent does it regulate itself? Is art’s autonomy (in the sense of Bourdieu) implemented in law and jurisprudence and if so, to which extent? When one looks for European legal answers to these and related questions, however, it stands out that notwithstanding the European emphasis on the role that European and national judges might play in protecting the freedom of artistic expression, judgments by both national courts and the European Court of Human Rights that explicitly mention or qualify the autonomy of art are scarce. Court cases discussing the autonomy of literature—the art form which is in focus

L. van den Bosch (✉)
Abteilung für Staats- und Verwaltungsrecht, Leiden University, Leiden, Netherlands
e-mail: l.m.van.den.bosch@law.leidenuniv.nl

K. Stierstorfer (ed.), *Law and Literature in Europe and Beyond*, Literatur und Recht 15, https://doi.org/10.1007/978-3-662-69851-8_7

here—are even scarcer (Polymenopoulou 2016). An illustration makes this more insightful. If one dives into the official online case law database of the European Court of Human Rights (HUDOC)[1] and searches for judgments by the European Court of Human Rights in which freedom of literary expression is explicitly mentioned, like in the *Handyside* case (ECtHR 7 December 1976), one finds only 66 judgments, whereas the database contains 22,267 decisions. That is a meagre 0.3%.[2] There is, thus, a discrepancy between the vital role of literary autonomy in European society and the limited number of cases in which the European Court has explicitly outlined guidelines for its delineation and protection. At first sight, this makes it relatively hard to embark on an in-depth study of the European concept of literary autonomy. What could be done about this? To answer that question, it is relevant to note that this is not the first time in legal history that a contradiction like the one sketched manifests itself. In other words, it is not the first time there is a reason to investigate literary autonomy and, simultaneously, a shortage of jurisprudence on this topic. The situation is comparable with the Dutch national context of a legal development in the early twentieth century when the so-called *exceptio artis* first emerged in Dutch jurisprudence.

The facts of the case in question had to do with a bookseller in The Hague, who was keeping copies of the Dutch translation of the novel *L'enfer* (1908) by the French writer and politician Henri Barbusse in his bookshop. *L'enfer*, and thus its Dutch translation, *De Hel* (1919) too, is (literally) told from a remarkable point of view since the focalizer in this novel is spying on his neighbours in a Paris boarding house through a hole in the wall, which enables him to witness multiple sex scenes that he describes in detail. At the beginning of the twentieth century, in a Dutch national context in which pillarization formed the core of society—with two of the four pillars being a catholic and a protestant one—this book was seen as offensive. The fact that the bookseller in question had stored quite a few copies of the provocative work in his shop led to the question of whether this entailed a breach of good morals. The Dutch Public Prosecutor saw cause for legal action based on article 240 of the Dutch Penal Code. In dealing with this plea, the Dutch Supreme Court (Hoge Raad) then introduced the *exceptio artis* in Dutch jurisprudence (12 April 1920): an exception for artworks such as novels, meaning that utterances that are usually condemned by a judge are not necessarily to be convicted when expressed within the boundaries of a literary work, because they need to be studied within the whole of the artwork. Because of this exception, the bookseller was discharged from prosecution.

This Barbusse case raised the question of what social and legal rules a novel must comply with and, thus, that of the autonomy of literature. Since the Dutch Supreme Court coined the *exceptio artis* in this case, my expectation regarding

---

[1] This database contains judgments from 1960 onwards.

[2] When taking the Global Database of Freedom of Expression as an example: if we search for political expressions, 252 cases can be found in the case law database, versus only 44 cases about artistic expression, of which only 4 cases are explicitly about the freedom of literary expression.

legally-enhanced perspectives on literature's autonomy was that the Barbusse trial before the Dutch Supreme Court fitted a more general and advanced societal-juridical tendency in which literature was gradually acknowledged as an independent field. However, no other Dutch Supreme Court cases could confirm this, for the court did not use the term *exceptio artis* again until 1965. To understand what implications this official legal acknowledgement of the *exceptio artis* thus had for literature's autonomy in the Netherlands at the beginning of the twentieth century, one needs to look for other sources. My PhD research at the University of Oldenburg—which forms part of the DFG project "“A country of mediocre literature”. Literary concepts of the juridical and political elites in the Netherlands in the twentieth century" (DFG GR 1875/9–1)—shows that one of the fruitful ways to learn more about the autonomy of literature is to examine mediators between law and literature. The term 'mediators' has been explored in literary research about translation processes—a field of research within which this terminology was used when examining writers who operated in different nations, translating texts from one language to another (Casanova 2004; Missinne 2000). Like in these translation-oriented studies, the 'mediator' term in this essay is used as a metaphorical category to describe a person who has, to a certain extent, affinity with two fields and a professional function in at least one of both—here referring to the literary and the legal field. The methodological approach used to analyze mediators in both the dissertation project and this essay will primarily be based on Van Rees and Dorleijn (1993) and Van Rees (1994). Their central idea is that for a more reliable assessment of concepts of literature, two complementary approaches are needed: the traditional reconstruction approach of poetics on the one hand (cf. Abrams 1971), framed by an institutional approach *sensu* Bourdieu on the other hand. Positioning oneself with the aid of views on literature is always part of an interaction between and within the institutions in the literary field and therefore always knows a strategic dimension. Thus, conceptions of literature can be analyzed more reliably, when this strategic and institutional dimension of the positionings is systematically taken into account (cf. van Rees and Dorleijn 1993, 9; van Rees 1994, 108). Conversely, a mediator's views regarding the institutional position of literature can be further complemented by a reconstruction of poetics, which is the approach presented in this essay.

The mediator that can be analyzed in context of the Barbusse trial, using this methodology, is the bookseller's lawyer, Ernest Polak. Polak not only openly defended literature (the translation of Barbusse's book) in front of a judge as a lawyer, but had also written a dissertation about two Dutch Penal Code articles in their relation to art and science, and took an active part in the literary life of his time. Because of their work on the interface between law and literature, it can be assumed that mediators like Ernest Polak are capable of connecting to literary and legal discourses. It is therefore plausible that Polak generates both insights into the recognition of autonomy within the literary field itself, and the recognition outside that field—more specifically: that of legal elites. Research into literary concepts as presented by mediators such as Polak can thus provide insight into the societal-juridical developments concerning literature's autonomy at the time.

Some research into literary trials has already provided us with some first indications regarding Ernest Polak's poetics and his thoughts about the institutional position of literature. It has been described that it is likely that the Tachtigers (Movement of Eighty) poetics that were prominent in the Netherlands around 1890 proved their influence on the legal field at the beginning of the twentieth century, and that Ernest Polak was one of the legal-literary experts who, in his utterances, suggested that (Grüttemeier 2009 and Van den Akker; Dorleijn 2000). In *De wet van de letter*, Klaus Beekman and Ralf Grüttemeier note that:

> In his 1912 dissertation on the morality paragraphs 240 and 451 [bis], the jurist Ernest Polak uses a formulation that makes his literary view refer directly to that of the Tachtigers. About the special status of art and science in law, Polak writes: "In general, the artist seeks to express and arouse the emotions of beauty in others; the scientist seeks to establish an objective truth." (Beekman and Grüttemeier 2005, 18)[3]

It is this emphasis on beauty, on the artist's expression of emotions related to that beauty and on the effects on the reader, viewer or listener that is strongly similar to the poetics of Tachtigers authorities like Willem Kloos, who is known for describing literature as "the most individual expression of the most individual emotion" (cf. Beekman and Grüttemeier 2005, 78; Bel 2015, 22).

What is more, the already conducted research into Polak's views on literature also provides us with some information about his views on the institutional position of literature, specifically. As the authors of *De wet van de letter* point out, it was not Polak's aim to take this *exceptio* further than the domain of jurisprudence, for embedding this concept in written law could, in his view, lead to complications (Polak 1912, 39). Polak thus needed another way to connect the *exceptio artis* to written law. This is where the concept of intention starts to play an important role in Polak's dissertation. He stresses the importance of the artist's intention when it comes to the question of whether the artist can be legally prosecuted for his or her literary work, and states that explicitly including the concept of intention in the law would be a possibility to jurisprudentially anchor the *exceptio artis*. For when intention was to be a legal criterion that would be decisive when answering the question of whether the artistic expression in a specific case should be condemned or protected, the question in court would then not be whether a work of art was, for example, an affront to human morality, but whether it had been made with that intention (92–96). All in all, based on studies into aspects of Polak's dissertation

[3] Original Dutch: "In zijn proefschrift over de zedelijkheidsparagrafen 240 en 451 WvSr uit 1912 gebruikt de jurist Ernest Polak een formulering die zijn literatuuropvatting rechtstreeks naar de Tachtigers laat verwijzen. Polak schrijft in verband met de bijzondere status van kunst en wetenschap in het recht: 'De kunstenaar zoekt in het algemeen schoonheidsemoties uit te drukken en op te wekken bij anderen, de beoefenaar der wetenschap zoekt naar het vaststellen ener objectieve waarheid.'" The authors refer to Ernest Polak, *De artt. 240 en 451 bis W.v.Sr. beschouwd in hunne verhouding tot kunst en wetenschap* (Amsterdam: Amsterdamsche Boek- en Steendrukkerij, 1912): 82.

on the one hand and some utterances formulated during his work as a lawyer—mainly in the Barbusse case—on the other, the current conclusion entails that both in his actions and his words, he followed the Tachtigers' dogmas. In the following, Polak's dissertation will be analysed as a whole—taking into account the less juridical aspects of it, as well –, accompanied by a systematic analysis of not yet examined archive material, in order to answer the question of to what extent the things we know about Polak's views on the institutional position of literature and about his poetics can be confirmed or nuanced. In the following, I will discuss some of the main findings.

In his 1912 dissertation, Ernest Polak discusses the articles 240 and 451 bis (articles on the protection of good morals) of the Dutch Penal Code in relation to art and science (Polak 1912). More specifically, he studies to what extent these articles endanger free expression in art and science. In order to do so, he first extensively elaborates on the history of the two articles, emphasising how minor formulation changes can have a profound impact on society, in which art and science play, according to Polak, an important role. Writing about what he considers to be the primary task of the legislator in the introduction of his dissertation, he concludes as follows:

> Educated in the doctrine that the criminal legislator should primarily act where certain 'interests' are manifest, he also knows how much he has to guard against the encroachment of another when protecting one of them; where morality ànd art and science are the interests of the nation, namely both cultural factors, he is wary of elevating the one to the legal interest at the expense of the other, as long as the legal conviction is not generally present in the nation that one interest may be sacrificed to the other (5, 6).[4]

What becomes clear, here, is that Polak sees the perspective of the legislator as one from which a balance must be struck between different interests: morality, art, and science. Apart from a more general reflection on the role of the legislator, this piece offers insight into Polak's ideas on the institutional status of literature, in the sense that it provides the reader with a first indication of Polak's views on the institutional position of art in general. Art is seen as something of the same importance as both science and morality, and apart from that also explicitly marked as a distinct "cultural factor," which seems to be more than enough to let the legislator consider it when weighing interests. On the one hand, this suggests that art should, in Polak's view, be seen as something as autonomous and important as morality or science, which he considers to be distinguishable interests of the nation as a whole. On the other hand, acknowledging the fact that the legislator

---

[4] Original Dutch: "Opgevoed in de leer, dat de strafwetgever eerst daar hebbe op te treden waar bepaalde 'belangen' aanwezig zijn, weet hij ook hoezeer hij bij een beschermen van het ééne te waken heeft tegen het aantasten van een ander; waar èn zedelijkheid èn kunst en wetenschap belangen zijn der natie, immers beide cultuurfactoren, wachte hij zich er voor het eene ten koste van het andere tot rechtsbelang te verheffen, zoolang niet in de natie algemeen de rechtsovertuiging aanwezig is, dat het eene belang aan het andere mag worden opgeofferd."

weighs the field of art as one of the interests that have to be taken into account, means acknowledging that art's autonomy is relative, for it always exists in relation to other factors.

Besides the fact that part of the equation between art and science in general is inherent to Polak's dissertation—which the title of his dissertation already indicates—a similar kind of reflection is more subtly repeated throughout both Polak's dissertation and personal correspondence. An example hereof, that helps to sharpen this first sketch of Polak's institutional ideas, is a short piece in the introduction of the dissertation:

> We have now set ourselves the task of examining which way to go in handling the Articles 240 and 451 bis, [...] so that these articles can continue to fulfil their moral purpose, without however implying state intervention for the citizens when they are working in the field of art or science or for general interest (11).[5]

Apart from the fact that he again stresses that legally approaching art as a cultural factor to be taken into consideration means doing justice to the "moral purpose" of the Penal Code articles, Polak here also writes about his aversion to *staatsbevoogding* (here translated as "state intervention") where it concerns art or science, again emphasising art's potential to operate without any interference of that kind, though here explicitly stressing the importance of its autonomy in relation to societal regulation. In doing so, Polak admits that it is difficult to define art and to draw the lines of its boundaries, which Polak reflects on in the context of pornography, the topic of the articles he discusses in his dissertation: "The more difficult it becomes, after all, for us to determine where pornography begins and art ends, or vice versa" (4).[6] Herewith, the relativity of art's autonomy is stressed once again.

A somewhat more pragmatic view on the nature and function of art in society can be derived from the section of his dissertation in which Polak meticulously discusses advantages and disadvantages of the *exceptio artis* or art exception which, as becomes clear from its text, was under discussion at the time Polak wrote his dissertation. Although Polak, as was explained in the paragraph on the current stage of research, could be considered to be one of the founding fathers of the *exceptio artis*, he pleads against the explicit introduction of such an exception into the written law, for that would have undesirable effects: it would be "dangerous [...] for art and science!" (39). When summarizing some of these possible

[5]Original Dutch: "Wij hebben ons thans tot taak gesteld na te gaan welke weg bij het hanteeren der [...] artt. 240 en 451 bis dient te worden ingeslagen, welke hanteering deze artikelen aan het gestelde doel op zedelijkheidsgebied geheel kan blijven doen beantwoorden, zonder echter een staatsbevoogding voor de burgers te beteekenen daar, waar deze op het gebied van kunst of wetenschap of in het algemeen belang arbeiden."

[6]Original Dutch: "Hoe langer hoe moeilijker immers valt het ons af te bakenen het terrein, waar de pornographie begint en de kunst ophoudt of omgekeerd."

negative consequences of a written *exceptio artis*, Polak gives more insight into his views on the institutional position of literature, mentioning that:

> We now do not see salvation for the manufacturers in the construction of the art exception [...]. We should bear in mind that most writers, producers of illustrations or works of art almost never *only* have the intention of serving art, science or the public interest, but also have a convincing *profit* motive. We italicise two words here: *only* and *profit*. For apparently, some consider it fair that, when the motive of profit plays a role, an appeal to the exception would no longer be effective (65).[7]

Firstly, it deserves attention that Polak here explicitly mentions literature instead of the category of "art" as a whole, by paying special attention to "writers." Secondly, the emphasis that Polak places on the role that profit plays in the everyday lives of artists is an important indication that the autonomy of literature as described in this excerpt is, again, not meant in an absolute, but in a more relative way. In short, whereas Polak appears to think that art or literature should autonomously follow its own rules and thus operate free from state intervention, he also acknowledges that a certain amount of dependency on earthly affairs such as being appreciated by an audience and having enough money to live from are of importance to actors within the literary field.

On the one hand, Polak thus shows a high degree of restraint in terms of intervention in art; on the other hand, he emphasizes the interconnectedness between art and economy or society. That this connection between artistic and economic aspects also emerges in Polak's work as a lawyer in literary trials becomes clear when he—again in his dissertation—describes the effect of these trials on society: "legal interference brings about precisely what was not intended: public attention and curiosity about a piece of writing or an object are stimulated all the more. Thus, Flaubert could also call the persecution of 'Madame Bovary' in 1857, and Eekhoud the persecution of 'Escal Vigor' in 1900, an advertisement for their works" (ibid., 8, 9).[8] Here, Polak once again meticulously reflects on trials surrounding literary works specifically, showing his knowledge of earlier literary trials and indicating the relative autonomy of literature in a society in which trials

---

[7] Original Dutch: "Wij nu zien in de constructie van de kunstexceptie, [...] zelfs geen heil voor de vervaardigers. [...]. Wij bedenken hier, dat bij de meeste schrijvers, vervaardigers van afbeeldingen of kunstvoorwerpen bijna nimmer *alleen* het oogmerk om kunst, wetenschap of algemeen belang te dienen voorzit, doch ook bij hen een groote mate van *winstbejag* aanwezig is. Wij cursiveeren hier twee woorden: alleen en winstbejag. Want blijkbaar wordt door enkelen billijk geacht, dat daar, waar ook het motief winstbejag een rol speelt, een beroep op de exceptie al niet meer zoude baten."

[8] Original Dutch: "Eerst na wel overwogen motieven tot vervolgingen in deze materie over te gaan, is hier te meer van belang, daar justitieele bemoeiingen juist datgene te weeg brengen, wat men er allerminst mee bedoelde: de publieke aandacht en nieuwsgierigheid wordt des te meer naar een geschrift of voorwerp geprikkeld. Zoo konden ook Flaubert de vervolging van 'Madame Bovary' in 1857, Eekhoud de vervolging van 'Escal Vigor' in 1900 een reclame voor hun werken noemen."

play an influential role. That (relative) autonomy might be a dynamical concept is suggested when Polak describes that everyday practices and art interfere more often: he writes about "this society, which has also increasingly incorporated art into the commodity system so that e.g. art buyers' contracts with painters are nothing unusual at the moment" (65, 66).[9] This statement is another indication of the relative autonomy of art and literature that forms part of Polak's ideas about literature, and thus of a certain approach to the institutional position of literature.

The same relative autonomy comes across somewhat further in Polak's dissertation, be it in explicit connection with the criterion of intention, which was already described in the section on the state of research concerning Polak's views on literature. That art's or literature's dominance is not absolute becomes especially clear from the following passage:

> And for the jurist, from whom it can hardly be demanded that he brings the definition of 'art' and 'science' to a correct solution, these problems are reduced to the question: does not the intention of the artist, the scientific worker, and everyone else who trades in art and science differ entirely from that of the pornographer and the dealer in pornographic articles? An affirmative answer to this question can easily be given, and now entirely separate from the question of profit (95, 96).[10]

In order to distinguish between pornography and art, we must, Polak argues here, look at the intention of the manufacturer of an artwork, not at the perception of the jurist. The picture Polak paints here is that of a literary field that is institutionally independent and consists of artworks explicitly intended to be qualified as such.

When it comes to the "question of profit", Polak spends some extra pages describing the process of art buyers that sign contracts with painters (67–84). He thus explicitly pays attention to the institutional dimension of literary practice, showing an interest in the distribution of artworks such as paintings. It is an institutional practice that Polak takes part in himself, too. Describing institutional processes, he refers to Henriette (Goverdine Anna) Roland Holst-van der Schalk, in a footnote, more specifically to her piece called "De Intellektueelen, het Kapitalisme en de Sociaal-Democratie" (1911). Roland Holst-van der Schalk was a Dutch poet who initially wrote this piece in the form of a speech that was held for the Amsterdam Student Association for Social Readings in which she

[9]Original Dutch: "Het moge wat vreemd klinken, dat in deze maatschappij dat motief zoo heel erg op de kaak gesteld wordt en te bedenken is toch zèker, dat het niet aangaat, dat deze maatschappij, die ook de kunst meer en meer in het waren-stelsel betrokken heeft, zoodat b.v. contracten van kunstkopers met schilders niets bijzonders zijn […]."

[10]Original Dutch: "En voor den jurist, van wien men toch moeilijk eischen kan, dat hij de definieering van 'kunst', van 'wetenschap' tot een juiste oplossing brengen zal, zijn deze problemen teruggebracht tot de vraag: ligt niet bij den artiest, bij den wetenschappelijken werker, bij allen ook, die in zaken van kunst en wetenschap handeldrijven, een geheel andere bedoeling voor, dan bij den pornograaph en bij den handelaar in pornographische artikelen? Een bevestigend antwoord op deze vraag kan gemakkelijk, en thans geheel afgescheiden van de kwestie van winstbejag, gegeven worden."

explicitly calls for socialism, which she believed to be the only way to the future (Verlee 2008).[11] Roland Holst-van der Schalk was mainly known for her activities in emancipation movements and her outspoken socialism (Bel 2015, 49). With this prominent literary and political person, Polak appears to have had a personal correspondence. From the archive of the Literary Museum in The Hague, it becomes clear that Polak exchanged postcards with her. On 23 March 1902, Roland Holst-van der Schalk praised Polak with a piece of writing, which she calls "An excellent piece!—I wished that I had the chance to publish an excerpt thereof in G.V." (Roland-Holst van der Schalk 1902).[12] "G.V." is probably an abbreviation of *Gereformeerd Volksblad* ("Reformed Newspaper"); a Christian newspaper published in Amsterdam from 1895 on, which still appeared at least as late as 1904. By mentioning that she thought of Polak's short text as worthy of publication in this newspaper, Roland Holst-van der Schalk explicitly expressed her approval of Polak's writing, of which we, unfortunately, do not know the exact nature. More specific insight into Polak's artistic activities follows from a letter to François Henri Jacques Mijnssen. That this well-known playwright was closely connected to the literary elite of the Netherlands at the time, becomes apparent from the fact that he was a loyal member of the Literary Association ("Vereeniging van Letterkundigen"), which was originally established as a trade union (and therefore partly socialist) organisation in 1905, ensuring basic rights and financial incomes of literary authors (Bel 2015, 86, 87). It was the same François—or: Frans—Mijnssen who wrote a piece of remembrance in the yearbook of the prominent Dutch Society of Literature (Maatschappij der Nederlandse Letterkunde) (Polak 1931–1932) and who published his first literary piece in *De Nieuwe Gids* (1894), more specifically a few poems that were strongly influenced by Willem Kloos (Mijnssen 1894, 297). The close connection with this popular Tachtiger is, for instance, also affirmed by the fact that he formed part of a committee to cherish Willem Kloos in 1934, which consisted of many influential names of the time: Menno ter Braak, Lodewijk van Deyssel, Hélène Swarth, Aeg. W. Timmerman, Victor E. van Vriesland, Maurits Wagenvoort and Henriëtte Mooy (Oerlemans 2013, 281–288). It was with this acknowledged and Tachtigers-influenced literary figure that Ernest Polak exchanged letters shortly after the moment that Mijnssen decided to stop writing critiques on acting around 1910. In this letter, it becomes clear that nobody less than Polak himself will be Mijnssen's successor: "Your decision is a disappointment to us, because your pieces were, back then, read with great pleasure. And now will probably be the time, that I will venture onto the very slippery ice of theatre criticism" (Polak 1910).[13]

[11] The text was later printed by the office of the SDAP (Sociaal-Democratische Arbeiderspartij; Social-Democratic Workers' Party); a Dutch socialist political party.

[12] Original Dutch: "Een uitstekend stukje!—ik wilde, dat ik kans zag er een uittreksel van in G.V. te krijgen."

[13] Original Dutch: "Je beslissing is ons een teleurstelling, want je stukjes werden indertijd met graagte gelezen. Het zal er nu wel van moeten komen, dat ik mij op het waarlijk gladde ijs der tooneelcritiek ga wagen."

Whether Polak was already asked or even appointed to be Mijnssen's successor or comes up with the idea in this very letter does not become entirely clear. Whosever the decision was, Polak shortly addresses his suitability for the job by stating "I have always had great interest in drama literature," immediately nuancing it with "[b]ut in my youth, I lacked the money and later the time to visit the theatre".[14] The reason Polak wants to take over Mijnssen's work as a theatre critic remains unclear at first, for Polak makes known that he is "not under the illusion that newspaper articles can influence any form of art in such a way that it will benefit from them."[15] Describing that theatre is highly dependent on its audience, Polak writes that "[o]ne cannot improve that with newspaper pieces. And one cannot bother the reader with sermons every day."[16] The primary reason Polak nevertheless commits himself to theatre criticism becomes apparent from the conclusion of his letter to Mijnssen:

> But a theatre performance is an event that a newspaper should not fail to mention. It should report on it, as on so many other important occasions. It is with this in mind that I begin this new work. If I can make an occasional remark about the level of our times every now and then—well, I won't refrain from doing so. But I'm not going into the theatre with the illusion of being able to do something. Certain fellows have sunk their strong teeth into that in vain.[17]

Newspaper criticism, for Polak, is not an institution that has the potential to influence art in practice, whereas the audience does belong to that category of influential organs.

As to the question of where Polak himself is positioned in this power play of institutional forces, his dissertation and personal correspondence and activities offer a few clues, as well. Firstly, Polak does not refrain from mentioning and even citing a whole range of well-known literary authors: he cites Tolstoj (in German) when he writes about the relationship between art and people's sexual lives (6, 7), and he mentions several literary trials in which literary authors played a role, such as Béranger, Flaubert, Baudelaire, Richepin and Guy de Maupassant (83). Apart from the fact that this indicates a very broad cultural interest, herewith, Polak exhibits his knowledge about the important international literature of the time,

---

[14] Original Dutch: "Ik heb altijd wel veel belangstelling voor tooneelliteratuur gehad. Maar in m'n jeugd ontbrak mij het geld en later de tijd om veel in den schouwburg te komen."

[15] Original Dutch: "Nu heb ook ik niet de illusie, dat men door stukjes in de krant eenigen vorm van kunst kan beïnvloeden, zoo dat zij er beter van wordt."

[16] Original Dutch: "Met kranten-stukjes maakt men dat niet beter. En men kan elken dag de lezer niet met preken lastig vallen."

[17] Original Dutch: "Maar een tooneel-voorstelling is een gebeurtenis die en [*sic*] dagblad niet onvermeld mag laten. Het er verslag van geven,—als van zooveele andere—belangrijke gevallen. Van dat standpunt uit begin ik dit nieuwe werk. Kan ik daarbij zoo nu en dan een opmerking lanceren over het niveau van deze tijd—wel, ik zal het niet laten. Maar met de illusie wat te kunnen doen ga ik de schouwburg niet in. Daarop hebben zekere kerels de sterke tanden vergeefs stukgebeten."

positioning himself as part of the literary elites who are aware of the prevailing trends. That Polak belonged to the literary elite not only on paper becomes, for instance, clear from the fact that his first wife, Isabella Tas, must have had connections with this elite, for she was painted by Salvador Dalí (Dalí 1945).[18] For Ernest Polak himself, this status becomes clear from a letter he wrote to Frederik Schmidt Degener (1881–1941), who was not only an art historian, poet and essayist, but also the chief director of the Boijmans Museum in Rotterdam (1908–1921), and that of the Rijksmuseum in Amsterdam (1921–1941). The letter referred to here is written in 1927, meaning that Polak's letter is addressed to the Rijksmuseum. What is more remarkable, is that it is written on yellow stationery with a reference to a prominent literary society on it: the phrase "Nieuwe of Litteraire Societeit" indicates that Polak uses a letterhead of Nieuwe of Littéraire Sociëteit De Witte (New or Literary Society De Witte) (Polak 1927). This society, founded in 1782, still is a private The Hague association, located next to two leading heritage sites: the Mauritshuis—the former residence of Count Johan Maurits van Nassau—and the Binnenhof, which houses the States-General of the Netherlands, the Ministry of General Affairs and the Dutch Prime Minister's office. By the time Ernest Polak was part of this society, only male members were accepted. Those members came from all corners of the established elite at the time and consisted mainly of politicians, judges, high officers, lawyers and doctors (Arnouts and De Vries [unkn.], 202–217). What Polak wrote from this male elite establishment is only a short letter: "The contemporary may well decide nothing […]. [B]ut perhaps You will allow me, nevertheless, to express to You my great thanks for the enjoyable and happy hours that the reading of Your "Remembrance of Leopold" brought me this evening" (Polak 1927).[19]

This letter is about the essay "Remembrance of Leopold" ("Herinnering aan Leopold") that appeared in *Groot Nederland* (1927).[20] The essay was published after the death of the famous poet J.H. Leopold, who was of great influence on Schmidt Degener, for he taught Schmidt Degener Latin and Greek when he was at the Erasmian Gymnasium in Rotterdam. Given the quotation above, Polak seems to have been an admirer of the poet.[21] Nevertheless, he remains cautious in his opinion of Schmidt Degener's essay on the topic. In stating that "[t]he contemporary may well decide nothing," Polak seems to suggest that judgments about

[18] It here needs to be remarked, however, that Isabella Tas was painted by Dalí after Polak had already died.

[19] Original Dutch: "De tijdgenoot beslist wel niets… maar misschien wilt U mij toch wel veroorlooven U mijn grooten dank te betuigen voor de genotvolle en gelukkige uren die de lectuur van Uw "Herinnering aan Leopold" mij hedenavond bracht."

[20] This was a literary monthly between 1903 and 1944.

[21] This is confirmed by Schmidt Degeners response: "Such personal recollections are a dangerous terrain because it is so difficult to avoid the autobiographical slant. But I am pleased to see that you are fascinated by the retrieval of old times." See Schmidt Degener, 1927: "Zulke persoonlyke herinneringen zyn een gevaarlyk terrain omdat het zoo moeilyk is den autobiographischen inslag te vermyden. Maar het deed my genoegen dat het ophalen van oude tyden U geboeid heeft."

literary value might not be his to make. However, as the next section points out, that standpoint also knows its relativity.

That Polak had more explicit ideas about what literature should entail than is revealed in the letter to Schmidt Degener becomes, for instance, clear when one takes a closer look at the cultural activities he undertook during his life. The first remarkable thing in that respect is that he had a very broad cultural interest, as some examples in the previous section on institutional aspects already pointed out. The academic and societal interest or "search urge" ("speurdrift") (Schulman [unkn.]) of Ernest Polak—born on August 24, 1885, as the youngest child in the Jewish family of Marcus Polak (who was a doctor) and Engeltje de Jongh, in Rotterdam—was already noticeable from an early age. An illustration thereof is offered in the memorative piece in the yearbook of the Royal Dutch Society for Numismatics ('Koninklijk Nederlandsch Genootschap voor Munt- en Penningkunde') by M. Schulman (1940):

> [T]he young Polak was soon attracted to medals and I remember very well how in 1900 I got to know the then fifteen-year-old, who then already showed that he was not only interested in owning a few coins and medals, but that he also wanted to know the history of every piece, and where, when and by whom it was minted and what its value was in relation to today's standard.[22]

This initial interest in coins and their societal context flourished in the years after, and Polak published several articles within the field of numismatics, such as "Een Franeker Noodmunt uit 1573–1577?" (Polak 1929), "Over de penningen van het Huistimmermansgild te Zierikzee en te Middelburg (1697 en 1671)" (Polak 1931), "Nederlandsche gildepenningen" (1932) and "Een onbekende brandspuitpenning van Zierikzee" (1910). But Polak's academic interest appears to have been much broader than numismatics. In 1906, he started studying medicins at the University of Amsterdam, but soon converted to studying law at the same university. On 26 March 1912, he defended his PhD thesis, *De artt. 240 en 451 bis W.v.Sr. beschouwd in hunne verhouding tot kunst en wetenschap*, which was already discussed in the previous section. Polak would stay in Amsterdam to 1922. After receiving his doctorate, he married Isabella Tas (1887–1973) and became a lawyer and a public prosecutor. This was the time during which he operated as a lawyer in literary trials against the French writer and politician Henri Barbusse. Meanwhile, Polak made his name as an illustrator, as well. Several caricatures were published in *De Amsterdammer* and *De Nieuwe* Amsterdammer, and in 1919, the collection entitled *Amsterdammers, 45 teekeningen van Ernst Polak (bijschriften van hier en ginder)* (*Amsterdam people, 45 drawings by Ernst Polak (captions from here and*

[22] Original Dutch: "In 1885 te Rotterdam geboren voelde de jonge Polak zich al spoedig tot de penningkunde aangetrokken en herinner ik mij nog zeer goed hoe ik in 1900 den toen vijftienjarige leerde kennen, die toen reeds blijken gaf dat het hem niet alleen om het bezit van enkele munten en penningen te doen was, maar van elk stuk de geschiede- nis, waar, wanneer en door wien geslagen en de waarde in verhouding tot den tegenwoordigen standaard wilde weten."

there)) was issued. Cornelis Veth (1880–1962), a well-known Dutch writer, illustrator, drama and visual arts critic and journalist who, like François Mijnssen, was a loyal member of the Literary Association (Bel 2015, 87), wrote the introduction. More than Mijnssen, Veth was a realist and an outspoken trade unionist and, just like the earlier-discussed Henriëtte Roland Holst-van der Schalk, strongly associated with socialism, as evidenced by the fact that he wrote for the Socialist Guide ("Socialistische Gids") (cf. Wagner 2020). Part of Veth's realism can be recognized in the enhanced pragmatic approach that Polak seems to have to literature and society, as it was already described in the previous section. Further, the fact that Polak had such close contact with two fervent socialists suggests that he had an affinity with socialist ideas, or at least came into regular contact with them. In 1922, Polak moved to The Hague, only to move to Rotterdam shortly afterwards to become a district judge.

Notwithstanding his legal professions, Polak continued to deal with literary matters, as can, for instance, be derived from the fact that he kept close contact with at least two members of the Literary Association: Henriëtte Roland Holst-van der Schalk and François Mijnssen. In a letter to the latter, the famous Amsterdam playwright, Polak explicitly reflects on the nature, function and role of both theatre criticism and theatre as an art form per se, he states: "Art, including theatre art, cannot flourish beyond the culture of the time in which it is produced. Especially not theatre art" (Polak ca. 1910).[23] The explanation he gives is simple: "[A]s far as performance is concerned, it is entirely dependent on the audience's taste and the performers have, on penalty of starvation, to meticulously satisfy the demands of that audience" (Polak ca. 1910). The approach Polak chooses here seems to be more pragmatic, for he focuses on the role of the audience and even explicitly on the practical need to act in accordance with its wishes, for there is a real chance of financial discredit if actors refuse to do so (cf. Abrams 1971; Van Rees and Dorleijn 1993). Art is thus not only portrayed as something 'of the few, for the few', as it was traditionally seen by the first Tachtigers like Willem Kloos (cf. Bel 2015, 22). On the other hand, the dependency of the audience appears not to be something Polak advocates. After having described this as a given fact, he continues: "And that, I don't need to tell you, is her [i.e. theatre's, LvdB] misfortune in this day and age in our country" (Polak ca. 1910).[24] If we measure this all against Abrams' theoretical yardstick of different poetics, we thus see that the expressive character of Polak's poetics here (by necessity) leans towards a more pragmatic approach of which the (effect on an) audience and therewith a wider range of people—not only the happy intellectual few—lies at its core. This forms an indication that Polak had, in the Tachtigers dogmas that can be deduced from his words and actions, more affinity with the Tachtigers Gorter and Verwey than with Kloos. The

[23] Original Dutch: "Kunst, ook die van het tooneel, kan niet uitbloeien boven de cultuur van den tijd waarin zij wordt voortgebracht. Vooral niet die van het tooneel" (original emphasis).

[24] Original Dutch: "En dat is, ik behoef het je niet te zeggen, in dezen tijd en in ons land haar ongeluk."

latter, namely, held a more traditional aesthetic conception of literature and its role in society, in which literature was made by a few and meant for a few, and was still all about the individual expression of individual emotions. Gorter and Verwey, however, found more room for societal aspects in their approach to art, and for example also recognized the need for literary initiatives such as the Literary Association, against which Kloos kept arguing (cf. Bel 2015, 22, 44 and 59).

Polak's own close involvement in such discussions and themes came to a very sudden end. On May 15, 1940, only a few days after the German invasion of the Netherlands and the bombing of Rotterdam (May 14), Polak ended his life, leaving his second wife, Renee Johanna Hirsch, behind. She would die three years later, in Sobibor (July 9, 1943). The death of Ernest Polak must have been a great loss, not only to the field of numismatics. As M. Schulman describes it where it concerns this field of research, in which Polak must have been active until the last years of his short life:

> For many years, Mr Polak was a loyal and much-loved presence at the meetings of our Society, and it was a great pleasure to listen to his pithy and witty remarks. With Mr Polak, our Society has lost a great connoisseur and zealous practitioner of numismatics, a collector, who with his knowledge and studies was happy to help others and who as a co-worker and as a member of the editorial board of our yearbook rendered himself very meritorious towards our Society. His passing has left an empty place in our ranks, which will be very difficult to fill. (Schulman 1940)[25]

This essay, in which documents about and by Ernest Polak that are not directly related to literary trials were examined, has led to a further nuancing of the picture that could be painted of his views on literature, both concerning its institutional position and concerning poetics. Institutionally speaking, Ernest Polak strongly emphasized the relative autonomy of literature and, by stressing the importance of subjective criteria such as intention, took a rather pragmatic approach to literature's position in society. The latter is also connected to his poetic views on literature; a reconstruction of Polak's network shows that he possibly had an affinity with both realism and socialism, and approached literary circles through the Literary Association. Polak's somewhat ambivalent—or at least twofold—attitude towards literature is not necessarily intrinsically related to those of the Tachtiger Kloos, but more in line with the later Tachtigers Gorter and Verwey, who incorporated more pragmatism into their approaches and were less elite-oriented, although they recognised the relevance of literature's autonomy.

---

[25] Original Dutch: "Jarenlang was Mr. POLAK een trouwe, gaarne geziene verschijning op de vergaderingen van ons Genootschap en was het een groot genoegen naar zijne pittige en geestige opmerkingen te luisteren. / In Mr. POLAK verliest ons Genootschap een grooten kenner en ijverigen beoefenaar van de munt- en penningkunde, een verzamelaar, die met zijn kennis en studies gaarne anderen behulpzaam was en die zich als medewerker en als lid der Redactie van ons Jaarboek tegen over ons Genootschap zeer verdienstelijk gemaakt heeft. / Zijn heengaan heeft een ledige plaats in onze rangen veroorzaakt, die heel moeielijk bezet zal kunnen worden."

After having discussed his utterances and activities, we can now better characterize Ernest Polak and the role he played in the literary and juridical context of the Netherlands at the beginning of the twentieth century. As a man with a broad cultural interest and taste who formed part of the established cultural elite, his beliefs show an idealist concept of literature, with elements of societal engagement.

What is more, Polak strongly emphasized the relative autonomy of art and literature and, by stressing the importance of subjective criteria such as intention, took a rather pragmatic approach to literature's position in society. This idea is supported by Polak's actions in the institutional practice of the literary field of his time, in which he positioned himself as a socially active and self-conscious actor with influence on literary matters, despite or precisely because of his legal background.

Polak was able to make a very effective and—in contrast to the very small number of court cases—analysable contribution to the establishment of the legal limits of literary autonomy through both his legal and literary knowledge and perspectives. As one of the founding fathers of the *exceptio artis* in theory (his dissertation) and partly in practice (as a lawyer in the case in which the Supreme Court acknowledged the existence of an *exceptio artis*), he contributed to a tangible boundary of literary autonomy that we, as researchers in the field of law and literature, can explore and reflect upon. That is what research into mediators brings: a clearer assessment and delineation of the literary concepts that circulate in society and thus a clearer characterisation of what autonomy of literature actually means in practice. In the same way, one could look at modern European mediators of our time and use them as indicators of the state of literary autonomy at the European level. We might then even be better equipped to protect that autonomy where necessary, when threats to freedom of literary expression mount, at a time like ours.

References

Abrams, M. H. 1971. The Mirror and the Lamp. Romantic theory and the critical tradition. Oxford: OUP.

Andel, Jaroslav, Giuliana de Francesco, Kata Krasznahorkai, Mary Ann Devlieg, Sara Whyatt, supp. by Levan Kharatishvili. 2020. Manifesto on the Freedom of Expression of Arts and Culture in the Digital Era for the Council of Europe in the framework of the 70th anniversary of the European Convention on Human Rights. https://rm.coe.int/manifesto-on-the-freedom-of-expression-of-arts-and-culture-in-the-digi/1680a056a2. Accessed: 15 August 2023.

Akker, Wiljan van den, and Gillis Dorleijn. 2000. Hoe lang duurt tachtig? Reproductie van normen en literatuurgeschiedschrijving. In *Literatuurwetenschap tussen betrokkenheid en distantie*, ed. Liesbeth Korthals Altes and Dick Schram. Assen: Van Gorcum.

Beekman, Klaus, and Ralf Grüttemeier. 2005. De wet van de letter. Literatuur en rechtspraak. Amsterdam: Athenaeum & Polak.

Bel, Jacqueline. 2015. *Bloed en rozen*. Amsterdam: Uitgeverij Bert Bakker.

Casanova, Pascale. 2004. The World Republic of Letters. Translated by Malcolm B. DeBevoise. Cambridge etc.: Harvard University Press.

Dalí, Salvador. 1945. Portrait of Isabella Tas (1887–1973), or Melancolia. Berlin: Neue Nationalgalerie.

Grüttemeier, Ralf. 2009. "Zo schrijft hij en zo doet hij". *Nederlandse Letterkunde* 14, no. 2: 155–179.

Mijnssen, Frans. 1984. Verzen, door Frans Mijnssen. *De Nieuwe* Gids 9: 297, 298.

Missinne, Lut. 2000. Der intime Fremde. Literarische Vermittler zwischen den Niederlanden und Belgien. Jahrbuch des Zentrum für Niederlande-Studien 11, no. 10: 213–231.

Oerlemans, Frans. *De Amsterdamse jaren van Willem Kloos: Deel II (1888–1900)*. Amsterdam: UvA-DARE, 2013

Polak, Ernest. ca. 1910. Letter to François Henri Jacques Mijnssen, M 00984 Mijnssen, Fr. 1916–1941, Archive Literatuurmuseum, The Hague.

Polak, Ernest. 1912. *De artt. 240 en 451 bis W.v.Sr. beschouwd in hunne verhouding tot kunst en wetenschap*. Amsterdam: Amsterdamsche Boek- en Steendrukkerij.

Polak, Ernest. 1927. Letter to Frederik Schmidt Degener, 18 November 1927, S 00388 Schmidt-Degener, Fr., Archive Literatuurmuseum, The Hague.

Polak, Ernest. ca. 1929. Een Franeker Noodmunt uit 1573–1577 *Jaarboek voor Munt- en Penningkunde*: 1–7.

Polak, Ernest. 1931. Over de Penningen van het Huistimmermansgild te Zierikzee en te Middelburg (1679 en 1671). *Jaarboek voor Munt- en Penningkunde* XVIII: [unkn.].

Polak, Ernest. 1910. Een onbekende brandspuitpenning van Zierikzee. *Jaarboek voor Munt- en Penningkunde* XX: 1–5.

Polymenopoulou, E. 2016. Does One Swallow Make a Spring? Artistic and Literary Freedom at the European Court of Human Rights. *Human Rights Law Review* 16: 511–539.

Rees, C. van & G. Dorleijn 1993. *De impact van literatuuropvattingen in het literaire veld. Aandachtsgebied literaire opvattingen van de Stichting Literatuurwetenschap*. The Hague: Stichting Literatuurwetenschap.

Rees, C. van 1994. How Conceptions of Literature Are Instrumental in Image Building, in: K. Beekman [ed.]: *Institution & Innovation. Avant-Garde Critical Studies 8*. Amsterdam etc. 1994: 103–129.

Roland Holst-van der Schalk, H. 1902. Letter to E. Polak 24 March 1902, S 00243 van der Schalk, H.G.A. (Henriëtte) Roland Holst, Archive Literatuurmuseum, The Hague.

Schmidt Degener, F. 1927. Letter to Ernest Polak, 23 November 1927, S 00388 Schmidt-Degener, Fr, Archive Literatuurmuseum, The Hague.

Schulman, M. 1940. Mr. Ernst Polak. *Jaarboek van het Koninklijk Nederlandsch Genootschap voor Munt- en Penningkunde:* [unkn.].

Verlee, A. 2008. Henriette Roland Holst: de intellectuelen, het kapitalisme en de sociaaldemocratie. *Marxists Internet Archive* 2008, https://www.marxists.org/nederlands/roland-holst/1911/1911intellectuelen.htm.

Wagner, J. 2020. *"Sachlichkeit ist tödlich für das Wesen der Kunst". Funktionen der Debatte um 'Nieuwe Zakelijkheid' im niederländischen Kunstfeld der Zwischenkriegszeit aus feldtheoretischer Perspektive*. Münster: WWU.

The Resonance of Literary-Related Court Cases in Dutch Parliamentary Debates. Key Moments and Strategic Referencing

Lina L. Blank

The boundaries of what is considered to be art and therefore can be judged as art are contested constantly. Contemporary controversies are not hard to find. The art exhibition *documenta* in Germany, for example, led to many societal debates in the year 2022. The fifteenth edition of the famous series of exhibitions of contemporary art took place from June 18 to September 25 and was curated by an Indonesian artists' collective *ruangrupa*. It was accompanied by controversy from day one, as works in the exhibition were claimed to contain anti-Semitic symbolism and imagery. More claims and accusations followed, as well as open letters, positioning papers and artistic reactions by members of the collective. The case was covered widely in newspapers and podcasts, on television and social media. The newspaper *Süddeutsche Zeitung* for example, titled quite unambiguously: "documenta: A debate on the freedom of art and antisemitism" ["*documenta: Debatte über Kunstfreiheit und Antisemitismus*"] in June 2022 (dpa 2022). Fights around artistic products are not only a contemporary issue, as the banning of Homer (ca 750–700 BC) or the *Odyssey* (ca 800–700 BC) and many cases since illustrate (Aarts and van der Pluijm 1989, 10, 11). Analogous to previous work in the study of literature under trial, it can be argued that it is worthwhile taking a closer look at the literary concepts that underly such contemporary debates as well as the institutional circumstances in which they are being discussed (Grüttemeier and Laros 2013; Hupe 2019).

What unites the conflicts in recent times is the idea that art should be judged differently from non-art. The literary field and the field of cultural production are granted a certain degree of autonomy. Precisely speaking (relative) institutional autonomy: "[…] the degree to which the functioning of a field is governed

L. L. Blank (✉)
Niederlandistik, Carl Von Ossietzky Universität Oldenburg, Oldenburg, Germany
e-mail: lina.blank@uni-oldenburg.de

K. Stierstorfer (ed.), *Law and Literature in Europe and Beyond*, Literatur und Recht 15, https://doi.org/10.1007/978-3-662-69851-8_8

by rules that are more or less independent from those that govern other fields" (Grüttemeier and Laros 2013, 205). Inevitably, what goes hand in hand with this claim, is the question of how art can be differentiated from non-art as the answers to this question define what falls under the legal autonomy granted to art (Grimm 2007, 500). The aim of this study is to identify the concepts of literature that are being used by politicians in these controversies, within the legislative organs.[1] What I mean by concepts are the "normative presuppositions on the nature and function of literature" (van Rees 1994, 104) as well as the institutional circumstances of these claims.

One of the four major factors influencing the (relative) institutional autonomy of literature is field-external political power. The other three factors mentioned by Dorleijn et al. (2007, xiv) are market pressure, religion and morality, and concurring media productions. The object of the following analysis are parliamentary debates and therefore forces which exert pressure on to the literary field and the field of cultural production in general. Politicians often share their ideas of literature and art and they are sometimes expected to position themselves when conflicts arise. Their utterances are impedimentary in nature, since they "[…] influence literary activity (the writing of literary texts, as well as the critical writing about them) by requiring the thematization of a specific message, ethics or worldview, or at least requiring that these should not be questioned" (Dorleijn et al. 2007, xiii v).

Coming back to my contemporary example from the beginning, we saw this phenomenon in the pressure on the German minister of culture, Claudia Roth, to position herself in the case of the *documenta* in the summer of 2022. The pressure was palpable in the way she reportedly reacted to the demands: "Maybe, I should have been louder" ["*Vielleicht hätte ich lauter sein müssen*"] (Baum and Schmitz 2022) and in the fact that the decision of German Chancellor Olaf Scholz, to not visit the exhibition, was a newsworthy item. The journal *Der Spiegel* titled: "Chancellor Scholz foregoes Documenta[2] visit" ["*Kanzler Scholz verzichtet auf Documenta-Besuch*"], while opening the article with the following sentence: "Olaf Scholz normally likes going to the Documenta" (Spiegel 2022).

The question that arises from these considerations is where politicians draw the line between art and non-art and on what conceptions they base their decision. When do they decide that the alleged offense is too severe even for those special rights granted to art? Primary sources, consisting of the protocols of parliamentary debates, offer potential insight into these issues. In order to attempt an answer to the relevant questions, first, an inventory of all parliamentary debates held on

[1] Around the contemporary debates of the *documenta* we can see a focus on the second question, whereby a new 'concept of art' is explicitly proclaimed by the defenders of the exhibition in the open letter *We are angry, we are sad, we are tired, we are united: Letter from lumbung community* (Azeez et al. 2022).

[2] While the name of the exhibition is intentionally not capitalized by the organization, it is unsystematically capitalized in media coverage.

literary trials in the Dutch parliament will be given, whereby their qualitative as well as quantitative systematization is crucial. The results of a systemic search for a mentioning of all literary related trials from 1900 until today in the parliamentary archives can thereby be divided into two categories: longer, coherent debates on the one hand and references, quotations and mentions on the other. My contribution offers explanations for this heterogeneity, whereby in the following theses are substantiated: 1. The cases that lead to longer debates are culmination points in the definition of the degree of *exceptio artis*. Thus, they are conducive to the (relative) legal autonomy of literature granted by the political field which occurred around the years 1920 and 1960. The culmination points thereby function as pillars to distinctive phases in the relationship between the literary and the political field 2. The cases used as short references are instrumentalized as cultural knowledge for other political questions without commenting on the legal autonomy of literature or the literary status of the work, a technique which has occurred more frequently since approximately the year 2000 and which seems to indicate heteronomous tendencies.

In the following, the resonance of literary-related court cases in parliament will be discussed and I will argue that it offers the potential to reconstruct the interrelatedness of the literary, political and legal fields in Bourdieu's sociological terms (Bourdieu 2004). To support this view, I will show how parliamentary debates are homologous to the legal autonomy of literature whereby the literary field can, in this analysis, be viewed from the perspective of the political field. Thus far, parliamentary debates have not been used as source material for literary studies of this sort, at least not in Dutch Studies. Due to the novelty of this approach, it is especially beneficial to focus on the research design in the following.

Expectations

In the Netherlands, at least two, out of approximately seventeen literature-related trials of the twentieth century, led to extensive parliamentary debates: the trial of the Dutch translation of the novel *L'Enfer* by the French writer Henri Barbusse (1919) on the one hand and the trial of the novel *Nader tot U* by Dutch writer Gerard Reve (1966) on the other. This intermingling of the political and literary fields, which was covered in contemporary newspapers, has been analyzed and commented on within literary studies. The case of Gerard Reve especially, also known as the *Donkey Trial*, received a vast amount of attention and eventually made literary history. The nickname, *Donkey Trial*, derives from the fact that a donkey, God and a character named Gerard are all three involved in the sexually explicit scene from the novel that came before the judge. The role of parliament is thereby clearly described as rather reactionary, in the sense of its popular usage of a political view that favors a return to a previous state of society. At the very least, it is considered a lethargic force, if we look at the most common literary histories (Brems 2006, 264; Hubregtse 1980, 83).

The aim of this project is to test the existing images of the political field in literary studies while using the primary sources, the protocols of the parliamentary debates, for the first time. In doing so, politicians will not be treated as a homogeneous group but the goal is to reconstruct different positions and nuances in existence. The aim was to gather the original sources of the debates held in parliament to reconstruct the positions of the politicians mentioned in passing precisely. Based on this knowledge, the goal was to find the complete source material of the debates on the two cases and to find comparable extensive, coherent debates on all the literature-related trials of the twentieth and twenty-first century, known to the informed reader.

Findings

One of the difficulties in this reconstruction is to locate the debates in the sheer unmanageable quantity of archived parliamentary documents. For the compilation of the corpus the online archive of the Dutch parliament was used, whereby the following cases were searched for:

- 1919: Henri Barbusse, "De Hel"
- 1921: Herman Heijermans, "Allerzielen"
- 1952: Willem Frederik Hermans, "Ik heb altijd gelijk"
- 1955: Johan van Keulen, "De liefde van Bob en Daphne"
- 1961: Josephine Mutzenbacher, "Die Liebesgeschichte …"
- 1964: John Cleland, "Fanny Hill"
- 1966: Gerard Reve, "Nader tot U"
- 1967: Lodewijk-Henri Wiener, "Seizoenarbeid"
- 1969: Judicus Verstegen, "de Koekoek in de klok"
- 1979: Gerrit Komrij, "De Nederlandse poëzie […]"
- 1985: Theo van Gogh, "Een messias zonder kruis"
- 1990: Chris van Heijden, "Daghani, Daghani"
- 1998: Pieter Waterdrinker, "Danslessen"
- 2000: Hans Dorrestijn, "Finale Kwijting"
- 2013: Adrianus Francisus Theodorus van der Heijden, "De Helleveeg"
- 2014: Emma Curvers, "Iedereen kan schilderen"
- 2018: Nicolien Mizee, "De Porseleinkast"

The archive goes back as far as 1814. A list of search-terms was determined, based on the names of the authors, the books under trial and keywords of the literary debates. Guidelines were set up for the determination of the relevance of every document.[3] The two major guidelines for the compilation of the corpus thereby were:

[3] This approach was double-checked blindly by a scientific assistant, special thanks to the effort and precision of Lennart Bartsch.

1. First of all, the author or book had to be mentioned in the debate. The search for novels with an ambiguous title like Pieter Waterdrinker's *Danslessen*, which literally means 'dance lessons', for example, returned many debates about government funding of dance or the importance to learn it. These were not included in the corpus.
2. The second guideline was that the book or the author had to be mentioned within the context of a literature-related trial or conflict or the discourses evolving around and before a trial. Quotations of Barbusse's *de Hel* within the context of demilitarization where therefore not incorporated in this specific corpus.

The findings of this approach were quite astonishing. The picture that emerged during the compilation of the corpus was very different from what was expected at the beginning of this project. It was anticipated that comparable extensive debates could be identified. In the following the most striking findings of this approach will be described and possible explanations, the working hypothesis, will be presented.

Quantity of the Debates

First of all, from a quantitative perspective we can see that literary trials are referenced more or less frequently in the Dutch parliamentary debates throughout the twentieth and twenty-first century, from as early as 1906 to the present day (Fig. 1).

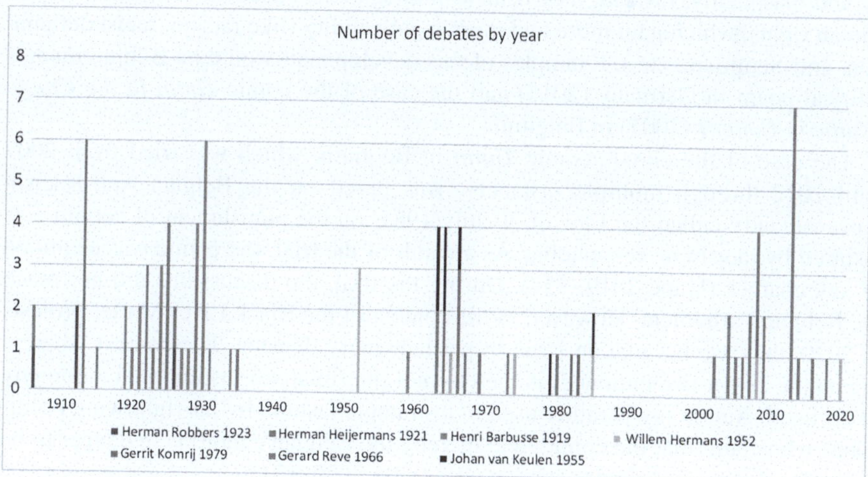

Fig. 1 Literary trials mentioned in Dutch parliamentary debates per year

But if we take a closer look we can see that only a fragment of the cases are referred to at all, seven out of seventeen, to be precise. More astonishing even than the sheer amount of trials is the common denominator of these findings: all of the trials referred to took place before the nineteen-seventies. No statements, debates or references on those trials which can be classified as literary trials over the past fifty years could be found in the archives of the parliamentary debates, with the methods that were applied to scrape the data.

So far, two factors can be hypothesized to explain these circumstances. First of all, the silence around the trials correlates with the charges that led to the trials. Broadly speaking, we can see that the charges of the Dutch cases shifted from what can be called collective or moral concerns (like obscenity and blasphemy etc.) in the early twentieth century to rather private accusations, in the sense of civil charges (like the violation of personality rights etc.) in the second half of the twentieth century. While contemporary literary trials lead to discussions in literary circles, they are not discussed in parliament. On trials in which mothers recognize themselves in (auto)biographical fictional novels, parliament is silent. One may wonder why this should be otherwise if public concern does not generate a debate on the topic.

This hypothesis seems plausible if we expand our view to the international arena. There are contemporary literary trials that find their way into parliamentary debates. We are currently seeing developments that point to the direction of a renewed emergence of more general reasons of concern leading to literary trials or playing a major role in the discussion of these trials. At least this seems to be a common denominator of the contemporary trials that are being discussed and mentioned by politicians in the Belgian and German parliaments. These cases are not based on the same moral standards as the classic literary trials on obscenity and blasphemy. Instead, they deal with allegations based on ethical and moral human rights, which gain more and more legal validity (like racism, racist defamation, anti-Semitism, etc.). Examples of this development would be Böhmermann's satirical poem in Germany (2016) and the case of the comic *Tintin in the Congo [Kuifje in Congo]* (2007) in Belgium.

The case of the classic comic *Tintin* in Belgium, which was tried from 2007 until 2012 through multiple instances, was based on the Belgian Anti-Racism Law, officially called the Law of 30 July 1981, on the punishment of certain acts inspired by racism or xenophobia. As a result of the trial, the comic was acquitted of any charges (Hupe 2019, 252). During the trial, the discussions did not reach the Belgian Parliament. However, in the context of the Black Lives Matter protests in 2020, the case became an issue in parliamentary debates. The context wherein the comic *Tintin* is mentioned, is thereby not the (relative) institutional autonomy of art itself. Autonomy is rather used in a strategic fashion by far-right wing politicians, who claim that the comic (and thereby the Belgian canon) is in danger to be forbidden due to civil rights activism (BE 18.06.2020, 13).

While the juridical case around Jan Böhmermann, the German comedian, was based on §103 StGB, which prohibits insulting organs and representatives of foreign states, in this case the president of Turkey, [*Beleidigung von Organen und*

Vertretern ausländischer Staaten], the societal debates on the case also touched upon the racist slurs that were part of the satirical poem. In the Böhmermann case, too, there was no conviction, as the charges were dropped eventually. Nevertheless, the daily newspaper *taz*, for example, ran the headline: "Judicial dispute with Böhmermann. Racism or performance?" [*Justizstreit mit Böhmermann: Rassismus oder Performance?*] (Rath 2016). The question if the usage of racist swearwords is acceptable within the context of a satirical poem thereby reached the German parliament. The case of Böhmermann was extensively discussed and the social democrat Michelle Müntefering (SPD) uttered her concern as follows: "If we look closely, we see that in many places on the internet these remarks are not satire, not art, but incitement, also from the right."[4]

The jurisdiction in these cases is widely read as a reinforcement and reaffirmation of the (relative) institutional autonomy of literature in relation to the legal field (Hupe 2019). The resonance of these cases within the German and Belgian political field paints a more heteronomous picture. In these discussions, a broader range of positions and topics satellite to the cases, as well as a strategic usage of the cases within other political discussions emerge. To be bold enough to proclaim a new shift, one would need more examples and an international, comparative perspective. The current events do support the hypothesis that more general charges correlate with a discussion of the topic in parliament. Nevertheless, there are some limitations to this explanation as it cannot explain the silence around all trials from the seventies to the early two thousands. The case of Theo van Gogh in the eighties, for example, was grounded on accusations of antisemitism and did not lead to parliamentary debates during the trial.[5]

The second hypothesis that emerges is that the cases of the first half of the twentieth century have functioned not only as societal culmination points in juridical practice but the parliamentary debates surrounding these cases have set important standards for dealing with such issues in the political arena. If a general discussion on the *exceptio artis* took place in parliament in the early twentieth century and this consensus was consecrated by the highest court of the Netherlands [*Hooge Raad*], the discussion did not have to be evoked in parliament again, at least not in the same way. More generally speaking, the findings might be taken to indicate key moments in the rise of *exceptio artis*, in which the debates of political elites function as a crystallization of field development. They show a major moment of consecration around 1920, the qualitative widening of institutional autonomy around 1960 and the emergence of more heteronomous tendencies in the form of strategic referencing from around the year 2000. This second hypothesis can be supported by a closer look at the content of these debates.

---

[4] "Wenn wir genau hinsehen, stellen wir fest: An vielen Stellen im Internet sind diese Bemerkungen eben auch keine Satire, keine Kunst sondern Hetze, auch von rechts" (DE 27.04.2016, 16335).

[5] For a detailed discussion of the literary trial surrounding van Gogh, see Beekman and Grüttemeier (2005, 99–114).

Qualitative Content Analysis

Also, from a qualitive perspective, the findings did not match the expectations at the start of this project. Instead of longer, coherent debates most of the findings can be classified as shorter references usually containing no more than one to three sentences. The references are mostly being made in a different context than the trial itself. What will be shown in this contribution are the outer poles of the spectrum of the findings.

Longer, Coherent Debates

Let us take a look at one side of the spectrum, where we can find longer, coherent debates. The legal treatment of literary trials has already been extensively studied in the Netherlands and has proven to be an extremely productive field of research.[6] It therefore seems promising to further investigate the court cases in which political authorities are known to have been involved. The *Donkey Trial*, for example, was broadly discussed in parliament, and it was even possible to reconstruct its antecedents. The run-up in 1963 and 1964, was influenced by the Calvinist member of parliament Algra (ARP), who repeatedly refered to the author Reve in general budgetary debates and thus sparked a discussion about the qualities of contemporary writers.

This run-up was followed by a written question handed in by the Calvinist MP van Dis (SGP). In reaction to the publication of the author's text *Brief aan mijn Bank* in the literary magazine *Dialoog*, the MP asked the acting Minister of Justice Samkalden (PvdA) as well as the Minister for Culture, Recreation and Social Affairs [*Cultuur, Recreatie en Maatschappelijk Werk*] Vrolijk (PvdA), to initiate juridical prosecution on the basis of §147, the blasphemy paragraph, in February of the year 1966. On these grounds, a prosecution was initiated. In May of the same year, a lengthy discussion on the prosecution fired up in Parliament, with the participation of several deputies [Beerekamp (CHU), Algra (ARP) and Vrolijk, (PvdA)]. This brief summary seems to confirm the reactionary impression some scholars already have of the political field in relation to the literary field.[7]

However, the positions, in the sense of literary concepts, within these debates held from 1963 until 1966, which were possible to be reconstructed, show a high degree of diversity among the participants and give us the possibility to nuance the knowledge we have on the case. The utterances of politicians explicitly and

[6] See also in the contributions of Ralf Grüttemeier and Lotte van den Bosch in this volume.

[7] In *Geschiedenis van de Nederlandse literatuur* political protagonists are described as rushed: "The Dutch government rushed [haastte zich] to adapt legislation and its application to changing views as quickly as possible [after the Donkey Trial], in an attempt to control the developments" (Brems 2006, 264) and Hubregtse describes the actions of politicians in the case as an "embarrassing performance" (Hubregtse 1980, 83).

implicitly define the concepts of literature that are being used by the politicians and their presuppositions on the nature and functioning of literature. Positions that match the stereotype of the reactionary or lethargic reacting politician can be found in these debates, like the one of the MP Algra or van Dis, who strongly oppose the novel written by Reve. They believe in a 'higher' and 'perfect' unity as the goal of art, and in a clear idealism in the sense of the Platonian Trinity of, the Good, the True and the Beautiful: "Truth and beauty in a work of art that has achieved a higher unity, reaches beyond reality and points to perfection: In such a work of art, as it were, a hand beckons from eternity."[8]

These positions are strongly contradicted and opposed by other MPs, who themselves are part of Christian and conservative parties, as we can see in the statement of the Catholic MP Janssen (KVP): "What the congressman [Algra] particularly objects to, however, is the strong emphasis on animality by modern writers. I think the deputy lumps all modern literature too much together here." (EKR, 2313)[9] This is only one example for a much stronger opposition to these idealist and conservative claims, than the canonization of the process would anticipate. As we can see, several MP's handle contemporary concepts of literature: "Perhaps, one may ask, provoking, shocking, is one of the most essential tasks of art; it shakes us up from our complacency, our self-satisfaction; it kicks over what we have considered, possibly wrongly, as sacred cows." (EKR, 767)[10] And above all, most politicians in the debates, agree on the special status that should be granted to literature. Even the governing ministers, who had initiated the prosecution of the novel due to the written questions handed in by a deputy, do not position themselves as in favor of a conviction in court but in favor thereof that the delicate question should be answered by a juridical entity. They repeatedly stress the importance of the separation of power: "The issue is therefore *sub judice* and I will refrain at this time from passing judgment on passages such as those which have aroused Mr. Beerekamps annoyance."[11] In summary, it can be said that critics

---

[8] "Dit is nu precies mijn opvatting en daarom heb ik mij juist in eerste instantie verzet tegen pogingen, die men telkens weer aantreft en die ik als verouderd beschouw, om wat men dan noemt het artistiek element, te scheiden van het kunstwerk als geheel. Waarheid en schoonheid in een kunstwerk, gekomen tot een hogere eenheid, een uitgrijpen boven de werkelijkheid, een heenwijzen naar de volmaaktheid: dan wenkt in zulk een kunstwerk als het ware een hand uit de eeuwigheid" (EKR 12.05.1964, 833).

[9] "Wat de geachte afgevaardigde [Algra] echter vooral tegenstaat, is de sterke nadruk, die bij de moderne schrijvers op het animale wordt gelegd. Ik geloof toch wel, dat de geachte afgevaardigde hier alle moderne literatuur te zeer over één kam scheert" (EKR 21.05.1963, 2313).

[10] "Misschien, zo kan men zich afvragen, is het provoceren, het schokken, wel een van de meest essentiële taken van de kunst; zij schokt ons dan op uit onze gezapigheid, uit onze zelfgenoegzaamheid; zij schopt omver, wat wij, mogelijk ten onrechte, als heilige huisjes hebben beschouwd" (EKR 11.05.1966, 767).

[11] "De kwestie is dus sub judice en ik zal mij thans van een oordeel over passages als die, welke de ergernis van de heer Beerekamp hebben opgewekt, onthouden" (EKR 11.05.1966, 766).

of the contemporary writer are in the clear minority in parliament whereby modern concepts of literature are being used frequently by politicians and the consensus on (relative) literary autonomy is strong.

Shorter, Strategic References

The longer debates that were found paint a rather clear picture on behalf of the autonomy of literature with regard to the political field from the beginning of the twentieth century until the 1970s. The other side of the spectrum of the findings, the short references paint a different picture. While longer debates took place more or less simultaneously to the trials, shorter references are used far beyond the actual events. And this from a temporal point of view as well as from a thematic point of view. The totality of the results of this category would exceed the scope of this article, but a few examples should be able to illustrate the impression described.

Let us take a closer look at a comment made by the MP Zijlstra from the VVD, which is a conservative, liberal political party. The comment was made in September 2007. The MP uses a reference to the *Donkey Trial* to compare it with a contemporary controversial case, that of Theo van Gogh which will be contextualized here very briefly. Theo van Gogh was a Dutch director and publicist who was murdered in 2004, by an Islamic fundamentalist, after the screening of a short film called *Submission* on national television which he directed (it was screened once on the 29th of August 2004 on VPRO, cf. van Gogh 2004)[12]. In the movie, we see four women wearing a niqab, telling the audience their supposedly biographical stories of oppression, sexual assault and domestic violence. The murder of van Gogh forms the tragic climax of controversies surrounding his work for several decades. Apart from regularly angering people of Islamic beliefs by using racist swearwords, he was sued for charges of antisemitism in a caricature, a pamphlet and a novel in the nineteen eighties and nineties. But neither was he convicted, nor did the charges lead to debates in the Dutch parliament at the time. After his death, though, he is regularly being mentioned in parliament. This was the case in a discussion on “the dynamic of Islamic activism” held in parliament in 2007, where Zijlstra says:

> Do you remember when Gerard van het Reve’s book *Nader tot U* came out in 1966? In it he described God as a donkey, and with that he had sex. The left loved it. When it came to faith and apostasy, anything was possible, because believers had to get rid of their faith.

[12] The Screenplay was written by Ayaan Hirsi Ali, who herself was a former MP (for the VVD, thus the same party as the MP Zijlstra).

> But where is the left forty years later? Where is the left when it comes to faith and apostasy? We must not offend people, it is said. But why the difference? Why was Gerard van het Reve a hero and why wasn't Theo van Gogh? (TKR, 93–5278)[13]

What we can see in the quotation is that the trial around Reve is used as a point of reference, Zijlstra utters that especially leftwing politicians supposedly were in favor of Reve's book. He further states: "When it came to faith and apostasy, anything was allowed, because the believers had to get rid of their faith". These utterances make a literary scholar shake her head vehemently, as the author Reve had based his defense in court mainly on the fact that he understood himself as deeply religious and his art as a form of expression of his faith (Grüttemeier and Leuker 2006, 300). It cannot be denied that the cases of van Gogh and Reve offer themselves for a comparison but such a systematic comparison of the two cases is not what is happening here. The politician uses the general knowledge on the case and its verdict for a comparison, whereby the case functions as a symbol of an absolute autonomy of art which seems to be canonized around the trial in the sense of an absolute freedom of expression. He asks: Why was Reve a hero and van Gogh wasn't? Or to put it into other words, he implies, why was Reve allowed to insult Christians, but van Gogh was not allowed to insult Muslims through his art. Even though, juridically speaking, both authors have been treated more or less comparable when it came to their literary work, both have been trialed and both authors have been acquitted in the end[14].

A comparable logic can also be found in the utterances by the MP Van der Ham (D66) in the year 2008, whereby this time it is not Theo van Gogh but Gregorius Nekshot, a controversial cartoonist and the controversial movie *Fitna* by the populist right-wing politician Geert Wilders who are being compared to Reve. Both Nekshot and Wilders have hashly critiqued Islamic beliefs.

> The prosecutor's office has found it necessary to arrest him [Gregorius Nekshot] on the basis of eight of his drawings. I was very shocked by this news. Can the Minister of Justice confirm that the cartoonist Gregorius Nekschot—that is his pseudonym—was taken from his apartment by 10 police officers and that his computer and other personal belongings were taken? [...] In the debate about *Fitna*, for example, Muslims have said: come on, freedom of expression is good. They are not as easily offended as the minister makes us believe in his statements. [...] In the past, offenses of opinion were also prosecuted. At least there were indictments of, for example, W.F. Hermans and Gerard Reve;

---

[13] "Weet u nog dat in 1966 het boek *Nader tot U* uitkwam van Gerard van het Reve? Daarin beschreef hij God als een ezel, en daarmee had hij nog seks ook. Links vond het prachtig. Als het over geloof en geloofsafval ging, kon alles, want de gelovigen moesten toch vooral van het geloof af. Maar waar is links veertig jaar later? Waar is links als het gaat over geloof en geloofsafval? Wij mogen mensen niet krenken, wordt er gezegd. Maar waarom dit verschil? Waarom was Gerard van het Reve een held en waarom was Theo van Gogh dat niet?" (TKR 06.09.2007, 93–5278)

[14] See footnote 5.

> Theodor Holman has added yesterday, that this had happened to him as well. They were simply summoned and asked to come to the police station· (TKR, 85–6010)[15]

In comparison to Reve, contemporary cases would be treated disproportionally harsh, so far the argument of van der Ham and Zijlstra. The prosecution of a literature or art related case is principally seen as a limitation to the freedom of expression and the freedom of art. Whereby autonomy is not seen as relative but as absolute.

Strategic referencing is not a new phenomenon. It can also be seen in the equation of the acquittal of a trial with absolute freedom of art as we can see in an utterance of the MP De Jong (PvdA). When he talks about the writer Hermans, he classifies his acquittal as proof that art is truly free in the Netherlands, in a debate that took place as early as 1952:

> The writer Hermans has been exonerated. I don't want to say, I did expect this. That would be too cheap. I did rejoice it. Of course, not because it may appear by this verdict, that the Secretary of State [Cals] is wrong, but because this verdict proves, that art in the Netherlands is truly free. (EKWH, 739)[16]

The writer had been indicted in 1952 on the basis of articles 111 and 137c of the Dutch Penal Code, the insulting of an ethnic group, in his case those of Catholic beliefs. This indictment had led to confiscations of the May issue of the magazine *Podium* in which fragments of his novel *Ik heb altijd gelijk* were pre-published. Art, in this case literature, De Jong implies, would only be truly free if literary trials ended in acquittals. Every court case which is literature related would thus represent a threat to the freedom of art. These are only a few examples of cases being used as short references, which are instrumentalized as cultural knowledge for other political questions without commenting directly on the legal (relative) autonomy of literature. All references will be studied systematically in the scope of this DFG project to test this impression.

---

[15] "Het Openbaar Ministerie heeft gemeend, hem [Gregorius Nekshot] voor acht van zijn tekeningen op te moeten pakken. Dat bericht heeft mij zeer geschokt. Kan de minister van Justitie bevestigen dat de cartoonist Gregorius Nekschot—dat is zijn pseudoniem—door tien politieagenten van huis is gehaald en dat zijn computer en andere persoonlijke zaken zijn meegenomen? [...] In het debat rond Fitna hebben moslims bijvoorbeeld gezegd: kom maar op, vrijheid van meningsuiting is prima. Zij zijn niet zo snel gekwetst als de minister in zijn uitingen doet voorkomen. [...] Ook in het verleden zijn opiniedelicten vervolgd. Althans, er zijn aanklachten geweest tegen bijvoorbeeld W.F. Hermans en Gerard Reve; Theodor Holman voegde mij gisteren toe dat ook hem dat is overkomen. Zij zijn gewoon gedagvaard en uitgenodigd op het bureau" (TKR 20.05.2008, 85–6010).

[16] "De schrijver Hermans is vrijgesproken. Ik wil niet zeggen, dat ik dit wel had verwacht. Dat zou te goedkoop zijn. Ik heb mij er wel over verheugd. Natuurlijk niet, omdat het door deze uitspraak kan lijken, dat de Staatssecretaris [Cals] ongelijk heeft, maar wel omdat deze uitspraak bewijst, dat de kunst in Nederlands waarlijk vrij is" (EKWH 22.04.1952, 739).

Preliminary Conclusion

The cases that lead to those longer debates are culmination points not only in the definition of the degree of *exceptio artis* granted in court, but also in the way politicians talk about literature related court cases. They shape a consensus on the special status of literature. An important moment of consecration can be reconstructed in the 1920s on the basis of the parliamentary debates on court cases: The first explicit recognition of a special legal status for literature, by the Dutch parliament. This can be considered a groundbreaking step in the process of gaining autonomy of the Dutch literary field in the face of the political field. Hereby it is particularly noteworthy that traces of the acceptance of a (relative) autonomy of the literary field can already be recognized in parliament several years before the landmark-case of the Supreme Court. At the beginning of the twentieth century, the political elites (in parts) appear to have been considerably more progressive than literary historiography has so far given them credit for. The consensus that has been reached exists among law, politics and literature. In Bourdieu's terms, they seem to be structured in homology, whereby the societal consensus within legal and political elites is made explicit: The acceptance of the literary field as a domain that follows its own rules.

This institutional autonomy is further extended in the debates of the nineteen sixties, to the extent that contemporary cases do not lead to further discussion. Furthermore, the extensive debates in the nineteen sixties reveal an orientation of politicians towards the literary subfield of restricted production in their literary conceptions and an increased interest in institutions that mediate between the political and the literary field, such as the *Fonds voor de Letteren* to avoid an interference of politicians in the literary field when subsidizing art. These two phases of autonomy do not seem to be followed by a third phase at the end of the twentieth century and the beginning of the twenty-first century. On the contrary, the increasing tendency to reference the landmark cases of the past as strategic references while demanding absolute freedom of expression, as well as the growing criticism of the mediating institutions, can be seen as clear heteronomous tendencies in the relationship between the political and the literary fields. These hypotheses urge further research in this area. In particular, computer-aided methods could be beneficial in investigating the phenomenon of strategic references.

References

Azeez, Abdul Halik, Abiye Okujagu, Agus Nuramal, Ahmed El-Faour, Ahmed El-Jumaa, Alice Yard, et al. 2022. *We are angry, we are sad, we are tired, we are united: Letter from Lumbung Community.* https://www.e-flux.com/notes/489580/we-are-angry-we-are-sad-we-are-tired-we-are-united-letter-from-lumbung-community. Accessed: 22 May 2023.

Aarts, C.J., and van der Pluijm, Mizzi. 1989. *Verboden boeken. Verboden door pausen en dictators puriteinen en boekenhaters*. Amsterdam: De Bijenkorf.

Baum, David, and Schmitz, Stefan. 2022. Claudia Roths Bekenntnis nach dem Documenta-Skandal: "Vielleicht hätte ich lauter sein müssen". In *Der Stern* https://www.stern.de/politik/deutschland/claudia-roths-bekenntnis---vielleicht-haette-ich-lauter-sein-muessen--32613966.html. Accessed: 22 May 2023.

BE 18.06.2020. Vlaams Parlement, debat, 'Commissie voor Wonen en Ontroerend Erfgoed', vlaamsparlement.be, 18 juni 2020 zie: https://vlaamsparlement.be/parlementaire-documenten/vragen-en-interpellaties/139717311. Accessed: 22 May 2023.

Beekmann, Klaus, and Grüttemeier, Ralf. 2005. *De wet van de letter.* Literatuur en rechtspraak. Amsterdam: Singel Uitgevers.

Bourdieu, Pierre. 2004. *Der Staatsadel*. Konstanz: UVK.

Brems, Hugo. 2006. *Altijd weer vogels die nesten beginnen: geschiedenis van de Nederlandse literatuur, 1945–2005.* Amsterdam: Uitgeverij Bert Bakker.

DE 27.04.2016. Deutscher Bundestag. 'Plenarprotokoll der 166. Sitzung'. 16303–16349. Bundestag.de. https://dip21.bundestag.de/dip21/btp/18/18166.pdf, Accessed: 26 May 2023.

Dorleijn, Gillis, Grüttemeier, Ralf, and Korthals Altes, Liesbeth. 2007. *The Autonomy of Literature at the Fins de Siècles*. Leuven etc.: Vantilt.

dpa. 2022. Documenta: Debatte über Kunstfreiheit und Antisemitismus. In *Süddeutsche Zeitung Online*. https://www.sueddeutsche.de/kultur/ausstellungen-kassel-documenta-debatte-ueber-kunstfreiheit-und-antisemitismus-dpa.urn-newsml-dpa-com-20090101-220617-99-705073. Accessed: 22 May 2023.

EKR 21.05.1963. Eerste Kamer, 39ste Vergadering: *Behandeling van het wetsontwerp tot vaststelling van hoofdstuk VIII (Onderwijs, Kunsten en Wetenschappen) der rijksbegroting voor het dienstjaar 1963 (6900).* 2293–2316. https://repository.overheid.nl/frbr/sgd/19621963/0000256563/1/pdf/SGD_19621963_0000736.pdf. Accessed: 22 May 2023.

EKR 12.05.1964. Eerste Kamer, 32ste Vergadering: *Behandeling van het wetsontwerp Vaststelling van hoofdstuk VIII (Department van Onderwijs, Kunsten en Wetenschappen) der rijksbegroting voor het dienstjaar 1964 (7400).* 805–847. https://repository.overheid.nl/frbr/sgd/19631964/0000252029/1/pdf/SGD_19631964_0000033.pdf. Accessed: 22 May 2023.

EKR 10.05.1966. Eerste Kamer, 34ste Vergadering: *Vaststelling van hoofdstuk XVI (Cultuur, Recreatie en Maatschap-nelijk Werk) der rijksbegroting voor het dienstjaar 1966 (8300).* 717–758. https://repository.overheid.nl/frbr/sgd/19651966/0000244668/1/pdf/SGD_19651966_0000035.pdf. Accessed: 22 May 2023.

EKWH 22.04.1952. Eerste Kamer, 37ste Vergadering: *Ingekomen stukken.* 713–746. https://repository.overheid.nl/frbr/sgd/19511952/0000288499/1/pdf/SGD_19511952_0000039.pdf. Accessed: 22 May 2023.

Van Gogh, Theo. 2004. Submission. YouTube. ed. Aguaresso. https://www.youtube.com/watch?v=iq8--myC9nM. Accessed: 22 May 2023.

Grimm, Dieter. 2007. Über einige Schwierigkeiten des Verfassungsrechts mit der Kunst. In *Bild/Geschichte: Festschrift für Horst Bredekamp*, ed. Philine Helas, Maren Polte Claudia Rückert, and Bettina Uppenkamp, 499–509. Berlin: De Gruyter.

Grüttemeier, Ralf, and Laros, Ted. 2013. Literature in Law: Exceptio Artis and the Emergence of Literary Field. *Law and Humanities* 7(2), 204–217.

Grüttemeier, Ralf, and Leuker, Maria-Theresia, ed. 2006. *Niederländische Literaturgeschichte*. Stuttgart: J.B. Metzler.

Hubregtse, Sjaak. 1980. *Over Op Weg Naar Het Einde en Nader Tot U van Gerard Reve*. Wetenschappelike Uitgeverij.

Hupe, Katharina. 2019. *Belgische Literatur vor Gericht: Über die Autonomie literarischer Texte in Gerichtsverfahren*. Oldenburg: BIS-Verlag.

Van Rees, Kees. 1994. How Conceptions of Literature Are Instrumental in Image Building. *Institution & Innovation*. Avant-Garde Critical Studies 8, ed. Klaus Beekman, 103–130. Amsterdam and Atlanta, GA: Rodopi.

Rath, Christian. 2016. Justizstreit mit Böhmermann. Rassismus oder Performance? In *taz. 02.11.2016*. https://taz.de/Justizstreit-mit-Boehmermann/!5351078. Accessed: 26 May 2023.

Spiegel. 2022. Kanzler Scholz verzichtet auf Documenta-Besuch. In *Der Spiegel*. 23.06.2022 https://www.spiegel.de/kultur/olaf-scholz-verzichtet-auf-documenta-besuch-a-8fc6d240-f048-4a24-b1ff-e2c0da7b8fd5. Accessed: 22 May 2023.

TKR 06.09.2007. Tweede Kamer, debat: *het kabinetstandpunt ten aanzien van het rapport "Dynamiek in islamistisch activisme" van de Wetenschappelijke Raad voor het Regeringsbeleid (WRR) (30800-VI, nr. 115).* 1–60. https://zoek.officielebekendmakingen.nl/h-tk-20062007-5260-5319.pdf. Accessed: 22 May 2023.

TKR 20.05.2008. Tweede Kamer, spoeddebat: *over het vastzetten van een cartoonist.* 1–28. https://zoek.officielebekendmakingen.nl/h-tk-20072008-6010-6037.pdf. Accessed: 22 May 2023.

Narrating Europe—A Literary Analysis of Legal Critique Between Ex-Yugoslavia and Vienna Using the Example of Juli Zeh's Debut Novel Adler und Engel

Alina Wolski

Introduction

When Juli Zeh published her debut novel *Adler und Engel* in 2001, the EU was far from existing in its current form. The image of Europe was shaped by Central Europe, the Yugoslav wars and their consequences were still present in the media. The idea that countries like Croatia would soon become members of the EU was far off. It is particularly rewarding, therefore, to engage with Juli Zeh's first work. In it, the qualified international lawyer packs the fatal story of the rising international lawyer Max, who is responsible for NATO's eastern expansion in a large law firm—sometimes in Vienna, sometimes in Leipzig. International legal documents on Yugoslavia also end up on his desk over the years. Throughout the novel, it becomes clear: Although Max wanted to do something good as a lawyer, his work led to the exact opposite due to criminal entanglements at the highest level. Here and elsewhere, general criticism of international law by the qualified international lawyer Zeh can be identified. At the same time, Max's life is caught between international law, which lets him "see the world from above", and his own existence, which is often influenced by national law, especially the penal code. At the center are Europe and the EU.

This contribution aims to address the question of how Juli Zeh, especially in *Adler und Engel*, narrates Europe. In this regard, the various prevailing European concepts in the novel should be worked out first and foremost and placed in a common context. To this end, theories will be used, which will be discussed in more detail at the appropriate place. Particularly within the framework of the law and

A. Wolski (✉)
Germanistisches Institut, Sektion für Allgemeine und Vergleichende Literaturwissenschaft, Ruhr-Universität Bochum, Bochum, Germany
e-mail: Alina.Wolski@ruhr-uni-bochum.de

K. Stierstorfer (ed.), *Law and Literature in Europe and Beyond*, Literatur und Recht 15, https://doi.org/10.1007/978-3-662-69851-8_9

literature movement, the elaboration of the understanding of Europe in the novel represents a defining element, on which further literature-legal analyses can be based. Juli Zeh, as a fully qualified lawyer, bestselling author and with most of her works representative of the German literature and law movement of the 21st plays a significant role in bridging the worlds of law and literature. The twentieth century is of particular interest in this regard for it allows us to exemplify central tendencies for the movement in Germany. For this reason, this contribution will conclude with a comparison to the author's later works—especially to *Unterleuten* and *Über Menschen*. Thus, this elaboration represents a step towards closing a research gap.

To find out how Juli Zeh weaves her narrative of Europe, the following four questions will be addressed in this contribution, building on each other: What spatial image of Europe is conveyed in *Adler und Engel*? To what extent is law used as a literary motif to create this image? What role do states then depicted as "peripheral" play in the narrative "delimitation" of this novel construction of Europe? Finally, a comparison to today is to be ventured by taking a look at Juli Zeh's newer works such as *Unterleuten* or *Über Menschen* and trying to apply the "center-periphery model" to this development. The focus of this work is on taking the literary-legal passages, especially differentiations between international law and national law, as a help.

The Spatial Image of Europe in the Novel

The first time Europe is mentioned in the novel is quite early, namely on the fifth printed page: "Do you see the majority of Europe devastated, I ask, the survivors deceived, violated and memoryless? No, she says. But I do, I reply" (Zeh 2009, 5). This passage is a foreshadowing and anticipates what will happen in the novel, or rather what has already happened historically, because the novel plays a lot with flashbacks and memories of Max's past—and in the end his youth is closely intertwined with his profession and Europe. This just quoted statement speaks for a defeatist, pessimistic image of the state of Europe. But what exactly is Europe spatially? There are different ideas and models about this: political, economic, geographical, cultural (Osterhammel 2004, 157–182), this is generally known and does not need to be elaborated on here. But how is Europe spatially understood within the framework of the novel?

In the novel, various entities appear first: the city, the state, Europe, the world. The city where Max lives—Leipzig, or previously Vienna. The state, whose national anthem Max hums to himself when he cannot think of another song (Zeh 2009, 21); otherwise, the state as a living space is less important than as an actor on the international law level. For Max's superior, "the countries of the earth in all their complexity are nothing more than closed personalities with their own individuality and a transparent character. They had a birth hour and a death day, a biography, they were exposed to imprints and traumas, had memories, hopes and wishes, they were poor or rich, strong or weak, had friends and enemies". (306). Then comes the world, which seems to be beyond saving anyway. And then Europe. The relationship to Europe is a bit more complicated than to the three entities mentioned before. This also has to do with the understanding of Europe:

First, European law appears in the novel, which Max applies in his law firm alongside international law and which is regularly cited in *Adler und Engel* (32). Max increasingly devalues this European law. He quits his job in the law firm with the justification that he has given up "doing something about the trickling at all walls and bridge piers" (34), which, in addition to the explicit understanding as a statement referring to European aid law, can certainly also be understood on a metaphorical level. Max himself sees both European and especially the International law is not only seen as law in the classical sense, but rather as a religion (147), in which one must believe and see oneself as an international and European law scholar and therefore not as a "real lawyer". European law, according to the legal definition, is the law that refers to Europe (cf. Streinz 2019, 1, 2). Thus, the first definition of Europe is found here in the fictional brackets of the novel—Europe is everything where European law applies. Juli Zeh uses a *positive legal-political* understanding of Europe.

This is supplemented by everything that lands on Max's desk—documents on the Yugoslav wars and the Balkans in general, occasionally also on EU enlargement to the east, i.e. countries like Estonia, Latvia, Lithuania, Cyprus, Malta, Poland, Slovakia, Slovenia, Czech Republic and Hungary. This is explicitly not Europe—not yet. Max emphasizes this explicitly and thus demarcates the spaces. So Europe is everything that is geographically Europe, except what is not yet part of the EU. This understanding could be described as *negative legal-political*.

And finally, Europe in the novel can also be understood in a certain personal-geographical way as everything where Max has already been and what is so close that it can be reached by car—Max's main mode of transportation both in his youth and during the course of the novel. Here we have a somewhat shifted image of Europe: Leipzig, Vienna, Italy, ex-Yugoslavia. But the perception changes over time: in 2000, when the novel is set, Europe seems to be particularly strong at the border crossings. Max says when entering Vienna: "This is Schengen and I like it" (Zeh 2009, 225). So this image of Europe has a lot to do with looking back, which in *Adler und Engel* is closely intertwined with the stay in Vienna: "This is Vienna, the city grabs you by the shoulders and turns you around so that you always look back, into the past" (Zeh 2009, 262). Vienna in the novel also represents a border. In a way, a border to the Balkans, to the East, a border of the known. The EU's external border is regularly alluded to, which is associated with the foreign (Zeh 2009, 333). So Europe is also personally-geographically shaped, oriented towards categories of the foreign and the familiar, and changes through political change, which is time-dependent.

In summary, it is noticeable: Although none of the countries of ex-Yugoslavia is a member of the EU in 2000, it plays a role in the context of the classification of this spatial-literary Europe, also apart from the geographical understanding—as the foreign, which is not quite so foreign. In a way, as the border or the end behind the EU, which cannot be separated from the EU at the same time.

Law as a Literary Motif for the Delimitation of Europe in the Novel

The answer to the question of how law as a literary motif works to delimit Europe in *Adler und Engel* is already largely contained in the previous explanations. Therefore, the following explanations should bring this to the point in summary and add some aspects. Law is central to both the *positive* and the *negative legal-political* understanding of Europe in the novel. It serves once as a spatial demarcation tool and another time as a delimitation tool. In the course of the novel, international legal hurdles such as visas, border controls, trade agreements are discussed and support the image of the familiar and the foreign in the sense of the premise: Where the legal effort is great to enter the ground, to make contact, another, foreign space begins, which cannot be Europe because Europe is everything that is connected, that has no border. Finally, the distinction between international law—which is predominantly what it is about—and national law. Juli Zeh describes the international legal events in Yugoslavia—both historically and the processing and work in Max's international law firm. At the same time, long passages appear in which Max clashes with German criminal law. In his resignation and hopelessness, the adult lawyer Max does what he learned as a student—write an expert opinion, which is printed in the novel. He checks his own criminal liability according to the StGB, thus delving into the depths of national law, which he left after the second state examination to devote himself to international law. As a result, national law seems foreign to Max. Yet it is so close to him, as he dealt with it very intensively in his exam preparation. Instead, at the time of the novel's events, he is concerned with what he considers to be the "big", important questions. His superior says at one point: "We are preventing the third world war here. You do not really believe that humanity would have survived the last fifty years without international law, without the United Nations, without disarmament agreements and nuclear treaties, do you?" (Zeh 2009, 474). International law is becoming increasingly important in the eyes of these novel characters, it serves the survival of each individual—it takes the position that is attributed to national law—the securing of peaceful coexistence. This is a phenomenon that will be discussed in more detail in the last chapter—the shift of center and periphery. However, we can already note here that international law and national law are used in the novel to delineate spaces. Max's handling of international law leads to the fact that a comprehensive, globalized image of Europe in the novel is even conceivable. Europe is always thought of as an overarching area in *Adler und Engel*, national borders seem anachronistic. Thus, the understanding that the novel characters have of international law is the basis for every spatial image of Europe in the novel.

The Role of States Portrayed as "Peripheral" in the Narrative "Delimitation" of the Novel's Construction of Europe

According to Niklas Luhmann, the German sociologist and social theorist, there is no periphery without a center (Magerski 2018, 71). This seems logical. After all, one could not even establish the first two of the three categories of understanding Europe if this principle had not applied. The foreign is a relational category that would not exist without the own—and vice versa—both condition each other. Something can only be perceived as foreign if it is compared to a point of comparison that is defined as one's own. An important element of the perception of the own is the feeling of belonging to a certain group (Scior 2009, 13). While the own is understood as normality, everything that lies outside this normality is perceived as foreign.

As already mentioned in the second chapter, ex-Yugoslavia represents this periphery in the novel's events. At the same time, the city of Vienna serves as a kind of *melting point*, where cultures meet—thus as a border region. Here it is decided what belongs to the own, i.e., what is still Europe, and what is already foreign. In addition to their function as an object of demarcation from the own, the states portrayed as peripheral have other tasks in the novel: they legally take on the role of the "weak" over whom the "own" judges. What exactly does this mean? Max and his superior, Rufus, symbolize with the international law firm in which Max works, the Central European, Western values—so from their perspective the "own". If I may remind you of the quote according to which states are personified as humans, the two of them only consider all states as objects with personality, or, if you like, as subjects with limited insight, who need international law to somehow get along with each other. The novel characters assume that the goal is to adapt to the "own" European to approximate values, whatever these are supposed to be. However, in the course of the novel, there is a content break when it turns out that people from Central European countries are entangled in the national problems of ex-Yugoslavia, even on an international law level, due to criminal machinations. Here, this construct of chasing after certain values collapses. The same applies to the role of international law. Until then, the novel had stated that international law was there to secure peace and the existence of states. But suddenly it turns into the opposite when it is revealed that major actors of international law are supposed to be responsible for maintaining the humanitarian situation, for human trafficking, drug smuggling, and also miserable conditions in prisons. Here we find literary criticism of international law. And at the same time, this concretizes the function of the periphery in the novel—it is initially an object of demarcation, as already explained, and later an instrument to assert one's own interests. This also happens both supported by legal motifs and legal themes.

The Application of the "Center-Periphery Model" to the Development in Juli Zeh's Novels

First, there are different models for center and periphery. These were initially developed in geography, then used in sociology, and now further developed within the framework of literary space theories (Pisarz-Ramirez and Wöll 2019, 3). Here, no specific model will be discussed in detail, but instead a characteristic that is inherent to the "center-periphery models"—namely, that two centers are more similar than the periphery that directly adjoins the center. The same should also apply to two peripheral areas. To what extent can this knowledge now be applied to *Unterleuten* or *Über Menschen*? And especially—how is this related to *Adler und Engel*?

Unterleuten was Juli Zeh's major breakthrough novel, which spent over a year on the Spiegel bestseller list. Published in 2016, it is, like the 2021 published *Über Menschen*, a social novel that takes place in a village in Brandenburg. While in the Wende novel *Unterleuten* the East–West problem is in the foreground alongside the peculiar village life, in *Über Menschen* it is the handling of the Corona pandemic.

When the protagonist in the novel *Über Menschen* leaves Berlin and drives to her newly acquired house in the country, she describes the experience as follows: "With every kilometer driven, she felt lighter. She was not only leaving Robert behind, but also the big city, the tightness, the constant fire of information and emotions. It felt as if she was leaving the known world, in a spaceship on the way to new galaxies" (Zeh 2021, 33) and later: "In Bracken [the village she moves to] Corona seems not to take place at all. The air tastes clean, each day has a different aroma" (Zeh 2021, 37). Zeh describes the contrast between village and city in a similar way in *Unterleuten*. The microcosm village presents itself in both novels as something completely foreign to the characters who leave the city life to start anew in the country. For them, it is a step into a foreign world, which is larger than if they were to start a new life in another European city. This treatment of the theme *village vs. city* is peculiar to both of Juli Zeh's most recently published novels. The periphery is moved to the center of the action. But in essence, this is not a foreign topic. Already in her debut novel *Adler und Engel* she deals, as previously pointed out, with the periphery and uses this as a central element for her story and the conveyance of criticism.

A commonality that stands out is that both in her 2001 novel and also in the latest work from 2021, Europe heavily depends on the definition of peripheries and centers. If in 2001 it is still the periphery as a border, in 2021 the centers are located in the midst of peripheries and are more scattered. It seems in *Über Menschen*, as if Europe in the novel context is understood as all centers on the European continent, thus in a geographical sense. At the same time, Europe can already end at the city limits of Berlin, where the literary periphery begins and life appears more foreign than 1000 km away in Paris.

References

Magerski, Christine. 2018. *Imperiale Welten / Imperiale Ordnung: Das Zentrum-Peripherie-Problem oder: Von der Kunst der Balance*. Weilerswist: Velbrück Wissenschaft.

Osterhammel, Jürgen. Europamodelle und imperiale Kontexte. *Journal of Modern European History* 2.2 (2004): 157–182.

Pisarz-Ramirez, Gabriele; Wöll, Steffen Adrian. 2019. Zum Begriff der Peripherie/des peripheren Raums. In *Periphere Räume in der Amerikanistik*, 3–9. Berlin, Boston: De Gruyter Oldenburg.

Scior, Volker. 2009. *Das Eigene und das Fremde: Identität und Fremdheit in den Chroniken Adams von Bremen, Helmolds von Bosau und Arnolds von Lübeck*, (Orbis mediaevalis, Bd. 4) Berlin: Akademie Verlag.

Streinz, Rudolf. 2019. *Europarecht*. Heidelberg: C. F. Müller.

Zeh, Juli. 2009. *Adler und Engel*. München: btb Verlag.

Zeh, Juli. 2021. *Über Menschen*. München: Luchterhand Literaturverlag.

Old Law and Legal Culture in the Literature of Polish Romanticism

Piotr Pilarczyk

Introduction

Although Polish Romanticism is part of the broad Romanticism movement, this concept is understood slightly differently in individual national cultures and placed differently on the map of intellectual traditions. First and foremost, its chronological boundaries vary greatly according to different national cultures: while, for example, German Romanticism covers the period from the 1790s to the 1820s, Romanticism did not appear in Poland until the 1820s, when it was already the Biedermeier period in German culture. Different time frames also meant different political or social situations. And yet there are still a number of national Romanticisms with many distinct characteristics: there are differences between English, French and, for example, Russian Romanticism where writers struggled with the traditional enslavement of the individual and their subordination to the invincible empire (Zielińska 1998, 13, 14).

In Polish culture Romantic postulates fell on the ground of particular Polish culture at a very unusual moment in history. Romanticism was born at a time when Poles were living divided by national borders. Most Poles lived under Russian occupation, where persecution affected many spheres of everyday life. These intensified after an unsuccessful attempt to regain independence (the November Uprising of 1830–1831).

The purpose of this article is to show the peculiarities of Polish Romanticism in the context of legal issues appearing there. Actually, the above-mentioned socio-political situation made it favourable to write about the old law. It is not my aim

P. Pilarczyk (✉)
Faculty of Law and Administration, Adam Mickiewicz University, Poznań, Poland
e-mail: piotr.pilarczyk@amu.edu.pl

K. Stierstorfer (ed.), *Law and Literature in Europe and Beyond*, Literatur und Recht 15, https://doi.org/10.1007/978-3-662-69851-8_10

to explore the field of comparative literature but some juxtapositions with the literatures of other nations will be necessary here, especially German Romantic literature in order to give the readers an impression of Polish specifics in contrast to Mickiewicz, Rzewuski or Kraszewski.

History and Romantic Works

One of the characteristic features of many Romantic works is that they draw—especially in the later period—on very ancient traditions, even on the Middle Ages. It can be easily seen, for example, in German or English literature. This is the case with Novalis, as well as with Schiller's *William Tell* or *The Maid of Orleans*, or the poem *The Glove*. The English take similar aim: there are Byron's poems or Walter Scott's novels recreating medieval events; we have the fake *Poems of Ossian*; there is Shakespeare discovered as a model with his *Hamlet* or *Macbeth* at the forefront. Many authors of works set in the distant past raise legal issues, such as Kleist in *Michael Kohlhaas* or E.T.A. Hoffman in *Das Fräulein von Scudery*.

Of course, Polish Romantics also reached far into the past, especially in the early years, but it will be in vain to search for legal topics in these works. Theodore Ziolkowski pointed out various connections to law of those who raised legal issues, the combination of legal practice and writing, and, in the case of Germany, he even wrote that a lawyer-writer is the dominant model of the German Romantic author (Ziolkowski 1990, 69). Among Polish artists, lawyers were quite exceptional, and only in the later stage of Romanticism (e.g. Józef Dzierzkowski). However, this lack of lawyers cannot be seen as an explanation for the absence of legal topics.

When looking at Polish Romanticism, it is above all the specific socio-political background that draws attention. German Romanticism developed against the backdrop of Germany's political disintegration, its humiliatingly lost wars with Napoleon, its opposition to the revolutionary ideas coming from France (Citkowska-Kimla 2010, 55, 56, 60). Hence the understandable references to the past. It would seem that Poles were in a similar situation—deprived of their own state, divided by borders. But this is not the case—the lack of an independent Polish state meant that Polish Romantics, instead of looking back to past eras, referred to realities of the recent times—the Commonwealth did not disappear until 1795 as a result of the partitions. When the generation that lived in it passed away, it was the Romantics who came to the fore—those who knew it only from stories and began to create its image themselves.

Rehabilitation of the Past in Polish Romanticism

This reference to the past can be seen from the very birth of Romanticism. Considered one of the two cornerstones of Polish Romanticism, Antoni Malczewski's verse novel *Maria* takes us back to the seventeenth century and the time of the flourishing of the old Polish noble culture known as Sarmatism. Interestingly, it was precisely that Sarmatism that was deprecated in the Enlightenment as the source of various problems and led to the partitions and the eventual collapse of the state. But Romanticism was born in opposition to the strong Enlightenment Classicism which brought foreign patterns and criticised domestic traditions. Of course, one cannot accuse Enlightenment authors of the downfall of the Polish state, but this downfall made their ideals susceptible to criticism, because despite reforms, despite adopting foreign patterns, Poland collapsed.

Here, the gradual rehabilitation of what was recent and what was actually vanishing right before their eyes begins: the Sarmatian culture was dying after the collapse of the state. The new generation of Poles living in the nineteenth century, separated by borders in the states that had seized Polish lands (Russia, Prussia, Austria) did not and could not cultivate what belonged to the canon of attitudes of Sarmatism. This was because the Polish nobles could not be politicians because they had ceased to be citizens and had become subjects; could not be knights (soldiers) because there was no country to defend; could not be farmers (agriculturists) as they had been before, because the social reforms were overturning the basis of the former existence of the independent nobleman—the peasants were slowly being freed from dependence, and the growth of cities and industrial civilisation was taking place; could not be lawyers either because after the partitions the original Polish law, institutions and the whole legal culture disappeared, replaced by solutions introduced by the partitioning states. And it is precisely that last element, namely, the reconstruction of Old Polish legal reality in the works of Polish Romantics that I want to talk about. Some scholars even speak of 'Romantic Sarmatism' (neo-Sarmatism) as a separate literary current which developed in Polish literature in the period between the two national uprisings, i.e. between 1831 and 1863, the inter-insurrectionary era (Waśko 2001, 8).

The old reality showed its potential best through comparison. Hence the most frequent reference to the times when Sarmatian realities coexisted with novelties coming mainly from France at the time. This made it possible to juxtapose characters, behaviour and customs by showing the Commonwealth in the last years of its existence, which fell during the reign of the last king, Stanisław August Poniatowski (1764–1795). It was a period of clash between the old Polish culture and the new, foreign one coming from abroad.

But it begins in an unusual way—with Adam Mickiewicz's *Pan Tadeusz*. This work, nowadays described as a national epic, perhaps the most important piece of Polish literature, describes events from the years 1811 and 1812. Exiled Mickiewicz published the work in 1834 in Paris, thus beyond the reach of the censors. The depiction of the "land of childhood" allows the reader to see what was ancient, old Polish, what was just passing away. This also covered the law and legal culture. Moreover, there are obvious traces of eighteenth-century realities in the work (Michalski 1978, 203–242).

From a legal point of view, *Pan Tadeusz* is a phenomenon because the whole story revolves around a lawsuit over the ruins of a castle. The lawsuit takes place after the downfall of Poland, in Russian reality, but the old laws, institutions and customs are still in place. The entire legal conflict is an example of old Polish litigiousness—litigating as if for entertainment. The meeting of the chamberlain's court, to decide to whom the object of the dispute belongs, is a great social event, an occasion for parties and feasts held within the walls of the object of the dispute (Breyer 1955, 27–29). In fact, the long-running lawsuit, going through successive phases and instances, does not interrupt the social relations between the parties. Moreover, there are evocative pre-partition realities, elements of the old legal culture, for example when the old Apparitor recalls years of his youth when he used to serve summons and sometimes had to flee from the defendant's anger. There are also references to various famous lawsuits of the eighteenth century. And finally, there is a foray (the subtitle of the work is: "The last foray in Lithuania")—a characteristic element of the old, pre-partition realities: when the public authority was too weak to enforce judgements and the customary legal institution of self-help was necessary (Breyer 1955, 127, 128).

Pan Tadeusz has a special significance because it is a work which, although not immediately but over time, increasingly conquered the hearts of the reading public, becoming a canonical piece of Polish literature, as well as an essential element in the education of young people. And its presentation of Old Polish culture in a sympathetic, benevolent way was an important step towards its rehabilitation.

Soon, however, a work comes out that shows the realities of the second half of the eighteenth century and openly takes the side of native traditions in the clash with contemporary culture flowing from the West. This is Henryk Rzewuski's *Pamiątki Soplicy* ("The Memoirs of Soplica") from 1839. In fact, before Rzewuski finally published his work, he had been recounting stories in his social circle for years, and Mickiewicz must have heard some of them and simply borrowed them from Rzewuski (Szleszyński 2007, 49).

The outstanding readership success of *The Memoirs of Soplica* marked the beginning of a new epic literary genre—*gawęda szlachecka. Gawęda* is a short narrative piece, a kind of tale recounted by a narrator about the old (pre-partition) time, people and events. The narrator, a nobleman storyteller, thus creates his own portrait, showing the mentality, views and attitudes characteristic of a typical representative of the old *szlachta. Gawęda* became extremely popular, and its collections as well as individual short pieces were created. Individual authors tried their hand at this form, which, of course, soon led to imitation, conventionalisation, and the emergence of less and less valuable tales (Waśko 2001, 205). However, a large-scale return to the pre-partition past can be seen not only in *gawęda* but also in other genres such as the historical novel or the '*kontusz* comedy' (where *kontusz* is a traditional male robe worn by the Polish nobility), of which Aleksander Fredro is the most prominent representative. Nevertheless, whether it is a *gawęda*, a novel or a comedy, many legal topics can be found in all of them, which is undoubtedly Rzewuski's contribution.

This is because for Rzewuski old law and lawyers, as well as old Polish courts, were part of the Sarmatian universe. Everything was original; the legal system which was a result of centuries of evolution, and in courts "it was probably wrong but [the judge] would have not signed a crooked decree" (Rzewuski

2004, 234)—which was contrasted with what was these days. There was an order stemming from respect for the law, or, finally, there was a model of legal education, or in fact, lack of it. This, of course, was nothing unusual; in Europe, only in Germany legal education took place at universities. In old Poland, as elsewhere, lawyers were educated through practice. Yet in the nineteenth century this was already an anachronism, but Rzewuski, as a conservative, very consistently argued that this was the right model.

> These laws are so homogeneous with the nation whose customs and habits they have revealed that, if one is not a Pole he cannot understand them, and if he is one, so to speak, then learns them without studying them, as if they were his native language, to the extent that every Pole who strongly retains his national features is a lawyer. (Rzewuski 2003, 47)

So, the law was part of national identity, something that did not need to be studied because it was simply absorbed. And

> [today] without all that, even if one spends ten years in Vilnius under [a supervision of] a professor, and learns all laws by heart, he will not become a lawyer. For to be a lawyer one has to be a citizen. Therefore in our state almost every citizen was a lawyer […]. (Rzewuski 2004, 212)

So, characters in many of Rzewuski's works are lawyers ("The memoirs of Soplica", "November", "The Zaporozhian") and if one of them is not a lawyer it is because he was more inclined to the sabre than to court. Lawyering was a service: it was taught through practice so that it could serve fellow citizens. Whereas—Rzewuski argued—today's university-educated lawyers only think about money.

Law was an inherent part of culture, an element of national identity, a product of its many centuries of development. Here, the influence of the German historical school of F.K. Savigny can be seen (Waśko 2001, 195). The law, which was a product of the nation, had only positive aspects—if only because it was obeyed. Therefore, there was virtually no need for authorities or police, so it was real freedom. According to Rzewuski, the departure from these values meant the downfall of the nation and Polishness. The Constitution of 3 May 1791 embodied the ideals of the French Enlightenment. Soon after the adoption of the constitution, Poland disappears. After the partitions, there was nothing to return to, because the law adopted new forms and regulations, for example through the imposition of modern French legislation (the Napoleonic Code). The departure from their own original law was one of the elements that led to the fall of Poland. The Polish, as Rzewuski argued, must pass away because they departed from their values, just as the Greeks or Romans once did. All that is left of Poles is a dead legacy, and it is not so much about the old law, but about the entirety, about that Sarmatism that no longer exists (Węgrzyn 2010, XXIV).

Rzewuski conveyed his views by describing various legal adventures or misadventures of his characters living in the last years of the Commonwealth. But he also depicted institutions: the Crown Tribunal, the highest appeal court in the Crown of the Polish Kingdom was simply magnificent in the pages of *The Memoirs of Soplica*.

> And in the hallways, there were hajduks, valets, harquebusiers and laufers; and in the square, there were carriages, carts, and horses such that even the Pope would not be disgraced to ride them; and gold dripped everywhere. At the tribunal, a nobleman learned about the greatness of his nation. When we, the courtiers of the Prince Voivode of Vilnus Voivodeship, were returning to our lodgings after the session, passing by the shop where the Germans and the French traded in foreign goods and grew rich on our coins, we looked at them with pity [...] What use would you have of your wits without our money! You neither have nor will have what we have. Wherever our lord appears, he cannot get rid of the French, Italians and Germans; and none of us goes to your lords, even though you boast that everything is better in your country than in the Polish Crown. (Rzewuski 2004, 117, 118)

It can be said that Rzewuski glorified the Sarmatian past, with its law and legal institutions as its inherent constituents. What may come as a surprise is a positive picture of *sejmiks* (that is local assemblies, bodies of the *szlachta* self-government) as an area of petty politics, but also as a place where old virtues were revealed. Despite fierce conflicts, disputes at the *sejmiks* ended amicably. Yet their role, as full of various pathologies, was attempted to be curbed even in the times of Stanisław August. Historians have also generally pointed out, and continue to point out, numerous flaws of these institutions. However, Rzewuski was at odds with this. The institutions portrayed were so magnificent and the attitudes often so naïve that it was sometimes even questioned whether it was written seriously or whether the author's intention was to ridicule rather than rehabilitate them. Today, however, the prevailing view is based on an analysis of the writer's outlook and his later works, indicating a deliberate intention to show an idealised past. What he wrote was simply related to his political views.

Therefore, it can be concluded that Rzewuski created a historical model, shaped the image of the ideal 'Sarmatian' embodied in the figure of a citizen-politician, a knight-defender of the homeland, a host-farmer and, finally, a lawyer. Of course, this was not completely new, because especially the first three figures were promoted in many literary pieces of the pre-partition era. Only this last element is questionable, because in Old Polish literature lawyers, judges or courts were presented in a negative light. And Rzewuski completely inverted this. The courts and lawyers, however, did not become the common motives taken up by other writers. And this is true regardless of whether the authors accepted or opposed Rzewuski's idealisation of the past. This was due to objective factors—it required the writers to have some knowledge of the old law, and not all of them could demonstrate it. For how could one know the law if it had never been taught anywhere, and which—when still alive—was learnt through practice? Rzewuski was an expert in the old law, so he explored the area freely. Many other authors merely feigned legal problems. These works were duplicative, imitative and epigonic. Besides, many authors of *minorum gentium* did not have such a coherent vision of the past as Rzewuski, so legal issues were not an important part of the old world for them. And for that reason, they were presented in a trivial, schematic, abbreviated and sometimes even ahistorical way, which only revealed the authors' lack of knowledge.

However, there were also authors who were able to cover the complexity of legal issues in a *gawęda.* Ignacy Chodźko was one of these. When Rzewuski described the Crown Tribunal, Chodźko, for contrast, depicted the second highest appeal court of the Commonwealth, namely the Lithuanian Tribunal. He showed both the bar and a convoluted lawsuit. When it comes to overtones, it is similar to that of Rzewuski. But of course, Chodźko did not slavishly follow the patterns of the older writer. We find here, for example, a picture of a sejmik, which in this case is by no means idealised: the victory of one side over the other occurs as a result of bribery.

Historical Novels

At the same time, a historical novel also emerges in Polish Romanticism. It paves its way to readers amidst numerous disputes among writers and critics trying to define its proper form. And although the influence of Walter Scott cannot be overlooked, this Polish historical novel of the Romantic era takes on its characteristic and specific features. In Polish literature, Józef Ignacy Kraszewski was the titan of historical fiction and its most prolific author. His legacy is so vast that it poses a problem for today's researchers. If we consider only his historical fiction, then, although the vast span of topics and chronology of Kraszewski's works (from the fairy-tale times to his contemporaries), his eighteenth-century themes simply stand out. Some have even argued that they need to be singled out, as his works about the era of the last Polish king were based on tradition and home stories which were still alive at that time.

Although Kraszewski sometimes presented problems similar to those of Rzewuski, he was able to show them differently. Kraszewski had distinct views and considered himself a historian, so he rejected Rzewuski's idealistic vision of the Sarmatian reality. This realism meant that he also did not want to ignore phenomena or events that could not be a source of pride. It can be said that in many respects, when it came to showing the decline of the Commonwealth, he engaged in a literary polemic with Rzewuski. Of course, not everything he wrote was contradictory, but Kraszewski showed both splendours and shadows—and the latter, after all, was omitted by Rzewuski. This was the case when he portrayed Prince Karol Radziwiłł, the archetype of the ideal Sarmatian in Rzewuski's works. This was also the case when it came to the functioning of the law. Kraszewski showed the Crown Tribunal in Lublin in his novel *Maleparta*, where he even mentioned at some point what historical resources he had used to paint his picture, and these were critical, Enlightenment sources. What we read in Kraszewski's is far from what we have in Rzewuski's. We even find the same motives, such as a poor widow embroiled in an unjust trial, but in Kraszewski's she does not live to see justice. There are characters of honest judges, or decent advocates, but yet evil, corruption, forgery and violence prevail. The Tribunal is not an idealised judicial institution but a hotbed of evil and corruption. The novel *Maleparta* is special because Kraszewski devoted as many as two of its volumes to advocates and the

Tribunal, but also in many other works he makes minor references to or creates characters of lawyers (Pilarczyk 2020, 62, 63). However, they are hardly positive. In *Hetman Sins* we have the disgusting figure of Advocate Kunasewicz, an unscrupulous man who made a fortune by suing his neighbours and stripping them of their property. Here too, one can see the ongoing polemics with Rzewuski, for example in the issue of education.

> The law was learnt, especially in practice, as a complex game, without disdaining the means that helped to circumvent the danger. […] A good lawyer knew when and at what time to put a case on the table, taking advantage of the absenteeism of some and the presence of others, of the after-dinner moods, or of the prolonged evening feasts;—a seasoned advocate knew how to grasp, frighten, prevent a reply, prepare a decree in advance, approach the foe, delude him, beguile him with hope, or with a word: strategically devise a campaign and lead it brilliantly. (Kraszewski 1879, 175)

It is difficult to see any admiration for the skills of the old Polish bar here. Practical legal education was not about learning how to serve others, but about how to exploit law, how to use tricks and ruses.

Finally, Zygmunt Kaczkowski and his historical novels which were very similar to *gawęda*. The Nieczuja cycle comprises novels from the youth of the narrator, a nobleman of the Sanok region (Jopek 1974, 71–75). The entire Sarmatian, local world appears there, and, thus, also various components of legal reality—from *sejmiks* to various types of disputes, conflicts or forays which today are one of the symbols of the weakness of Old Polish law. Kaczkowski is also far from a Rzewuski-style apotheosis of the past, although the main character represents Sarmatian views that are at odds with various—negatively depicted—new, foreign principles. Thus, we have a defence of various traditional legal and political principles of the pre-partition period, such as the Golden Liberty of the nobles or the 'Liberum Veto', that is the notorious, required unanimity when passing parliamentary resolutions. Needless to say, today it is difficult to find any rational arguments in support of such a position.

Conclusion

All of this is in contrast to the remarkable sparsity of contemporary law problems in Polish Romantic literature. There is nothing like Kleist's *The Broken Jug*, a work that shows the faults of the judiciary, nor anything like Victor Hugo's *The Last Day of a Condemned Man*, where the severity of criminal law is criticised. Gogol portrayed the paradoxes of Russian reality—the lawlessness in the provinces in *The Government Inspector*, or absurd contradictions in the law in *Dead Souls*. This is not the case in Polish Romanticism—topical legal issues are, of course, not completely absent, but they do not come to the fore. They are not independent, and have rather accompanying function, like in Juliusz Słowacki's *Kordian*, where the possibility of killing the tyrant tsar is, after all, more of a moral problem. Minor legal issues also appear in Fredro's comedies or in the context of social problems raised in the realist novels by Kraszewski, Korzeniowski or Dzierzkowski. Only authors of the following epoch, that is Positivism, would raise a number of legal problems, like the functioning of prisons, pathology of lower courts or the repressiveness of the judiciary towards Poles. But that was later, while Polish Romanticism showed the law of the recent past: the law, lawyers and judiciary institutions of the last years of the pre-partition Commonwealth. And since there was no single coherent vision of the old legal reality, we had conflict here, some presented it approvingly and uncritically, while others tried to be more realistic. Hence, the question of law in Polish Romantic literature remains very specific: there are no universal considerations, but there is a return to the recent past as an element of disputes and difficult national settlements.

References

Breyer, Stefan. 1955. *Spór Hereszków z Soplicami. Studium z dziedziny problematyki prawnej "Pana Tadeusza"*. Warszawa: Wydawnictwo Prawnicze.

Citkowska-Kimla, Anna. 2010. *Romantyzm polityczny w Niemczech. Reprezentanci, idee, model.* Kraków: Księgarnia Akademicka.

Jopek, Antoni. 1974. *Bard szlachty sanockiej. Opowiadania i powieści historyczne Zygmunta Kaczkowskiego*. Kraków: Wydawnictwo Literackie.

Kraszewski, Józef Ignacy. 1879. *Grzechy hetmańskie*. Warszawa: S. Lewental.

Michalski, Jerzy. 1978. Osiemnastowieczne realia Pana Tadeusza. In *Dzieło literackie jako źródło historyczne*, ed. Zofia Stefanowska and Janusz Sławiński, 203–242. Warszawa: Czytelnik.

Pilarczyk, Piotr M. 2020. Trybunał Koronny i jego palestra w powieści Maleparta J. I. Kraszewskiego. In *O historii adwokatury w Polsce i na świecie*, ed. Dorota Wiśniewska and Maciej Rakowski, 59–80. Łódź: Wydawnictwo Uniwersytetu Łódzkiego.

Rzewuski, Henryk. 2003. *Uwagi o dawnej Polsce przez starego Szlachcica Seweryna Soplicę Cześnika Parnawskiego napisane 1832*. Warszawa: Instytut Badań Literackich PAN.

Rzewuski, Henryk. 2004. *Pamiątki Soplicy*. Wrocław: Zakład Narodowy im. Ossolińskich.

Szleszyński, Bartłomiej. 2007. *Przymierzanie kontusza. Henryk Rzewuski i Henryk Sienkiewicz – najwybitniejsi twórcy XIX-wiecznego nurtu sarmackiego*. Warszawa: Instytut Badań Literackich PAN Wydawnictwo.

Waśko, Andrzej. 2001. *Romantyczny sarmatyzm. Tradycja szlachecka w literaturze polskiej lat 1831–1863*. Kraków: Arcana.

Węgrzyn, Iwona. 2010. Henryk Rzewuski. In *Wędrówki umysłowe. Mieszaniny obyczajowe*, Henryk Rzewuski, IX–XXXV. Kraków: Ośrodek Myśli Politycznej.

Zielińska, Marta. 1998. *Polacy, Rosjanie, romantyzm*. Warszawa: Instytut Badań Literackich PAN.

Ziolkowski, Theodore. 1990. *German Romanticism and Its Institutions*. Princeton: Princeton University Press.

“Law and (Which?) Literature”: Capture Theory, Law and the Poetry of Wole Soyinka

Owojecho Omoha

This is the voice of the people, the true people of the nation.
And they are telling you, Akintola, get out!
Get out and take with you your renegades who have lost all sense of shame.

(Soyinka 2001, 362)

Introduction

Whoever does not flow with interdisciplinary studies would ask, albeit blindly: where is poetry, and where is law in this vociferous epigraph with which this essay is anchored? “Renegades” echoes denials in law, and poetry is rooted in the unknown “voice of the people”. The unidentified voice sounds like the unheard voices of effigies holding the scale to balance equity and justice at our courts. “Akintola” personifies denials, even as “justice is the first condition of humanity” (Soyinka 1975, 96). Denials breach the “first condition” and we turn attention to the judicial dictum: “The man dies in all who keep silent in the face of tyranny” (Soyinka 1975, 13). This dictum is rooted in *The Rights of Man* (1791): “If the present generation, or any other, are disposed to be slaves it does not lessen the rights of the succeeding generation to be free. Wrongs cannot have a legal descent” (Paine 1996, 85). The epigraph with which I started, in this sense, is meant to capture attention on illegality of the “Premier’s Message,” and perhaps, to attract further attention on injustice: “we can break their haughty power, gain

O. Omoha (✉)
Department of English, University of Abuja, Abuja, Nigeria
e-mail: emman.owojecho@uniabuja.edu.ng

K. Stierstorfer (ed.), *Law and Literature in Europe and Beyond*, Literatur und Recht 15, https://doi.org/10.1007/978-3-662-69851-8_11

our freedom when we learn the union make us strong" (Chaplain 2005). The epigraph, therefore, is the stimulant for blending law and poetry in schemata.

Ralph Chaplain's poetics on dignity of labour "Solidarity Forever" above reverberates justice and succinctly captures Friedrich Nietzsche's morality lines translated by Brian Leiter (2002): "Slaves, unable to take physical action against the sources of their misery (their masters, their oppressors), are driven by their stewing hatred of their masters to do the only thing they can do, create new values" (203). The new values in the epigraph are the quest for justice translated in the metaphors of "the true people of the nation." Soyinka led "the true people" in November 1965 in a trial for seizing a radio station billed to announce false election results at gun point, but was acquitted on the technical ground of "casting doubt on the evidence of identification" (Dolin 2007, 167). Poetry intertwines, here, seamlessly with law. The unidentified voice of the persona, that of Soyinka, maybe, weighed on the scale of justice gave no clear identification—a valid and justice-laden poetic metaphor tilting to "the voice of the people" and not that of Soyinka. The judgment raises a theoretical question: if the poet owes the nation a duty to question law breakers, does the poet at the same time carry the burden of the nation? The answer to this question, in the poetry of Wole Soyinka (1996) is emphasized unambiguously: "Nigeria cannot be the duty and the burden of the writer and intellectual alone" (134). This proposition functions, theoretically, at two levels: first, the adherence to law and justice, and second, the use of poetry to guarantee equity and justice. Both levels advocate revolutionary voices, either in the field of law, or in the field of literature, in particular, the genre of poetry. It is, therefore, feasible, to bring both disciplines to a centrifugal theoretical system to operate collectively—attention capture, law and poetry.

Capture Theory, Law and Poetry

The German researcher Klaus Stierstorfer confidently explored interconnections of culture, law and literature, and persuasively navigated his postulations to new grounds. His "new directions" points to a series of theories or what D. Patai and W. Coral have coined *Theory's Empire* (2005) that could further blend law and poetry into what may, in the final analysis, turn to be law-poetics. Law-poetics has the potential to deliver Stierstorfer's reader from the emotional tension in the question: "Law and (which?) Literature." This somewhat threatening question posed by the German philosopher demands selecting from the post-theory bag, if any, a sure-key theory. In other words, without a back-up theory, no significant answer to Stierstorfer's harassing research question. I had a theory right there at the conference on law and literature in Europe and beyond at the University of Munster in October 2022 to answer Stierstorfer. The theory was the post-theory, capture theory. Capture theory preceded Klaus Stierstorfer's new directions in post-theories, in a way, and certainly predicts the Idoma traditional trope "oyi bibi noge hada api"[1]—the mystic child who circumcises his father. That is to say, capture theory mysteriously answered Stierstorfer's question on new directions in post-theories years before the question was posed and published in 2011.

Capture theory, in strict-adherence-contextualization, derives its meaning from cognitive humanities. The theory "describes a process by which an author attempts to recreate the capture of his or her attentional awareness on specific salient features of a text—i.e., tropes—on a really existing external reader" (Omoha 2019, 89). Interestingly, cognitive humanities post-theory emerged following the inability of two other German philosophers, Wolfgang Iser's *The Implied Reader* (1974) and Robert Hans Jauss' *Toward an Aesthetic of Reception* (1982). These two philosophers could not deal with text/reader relationships beyond text boundaries. "The actual reader's interpretation of the text is possible if there is a cognitive harmony between the author and the reader" in addition to the relationship between the text and the author (Omoha 2019, 90). Capture theory, in this way, explores the author's emotional reactions: his or her twitches in the face, drops of ineffectual tropes and the addition of conceits that hold the reader captive, and, of course, the passion and the craving of writing and rewriting until finally a cognitive agreement is reached with the self, and the text produced.

Capture theory, for sure, as a post-theory (capture theory deviates from existing approaches in attention and reception studies, even as it feeds from both) enjoys cognitive encounters from the humanities. Cognitive humanities is a blend of the sciences and the arts. It operates in psychological science, for instance, when a cognitive analysis of a poem reveals the intent to attract attention or capture the mood of the reader. Attention study is peculiar to the science of psychology, while poetry in its conceits is exclusively in the domain of arts. Again, the reader may, for instance, guided by cognitive intuitions, drop a text, take the conceitedness to shreds, and physically move to embrace an author for his/her cognitive harmonies. Moving from theory to practicum, the meeting out there, i.e., between the reader and the writer, is ostentatiously a cognitive extension made possible by capture theory in its post-theory garb. Contrary to current approaches in favour of immediacy of the text or the "telepresence" of the text/reader model, capture theory reawakens the primacy of oral traditions, brings to life, once again, ancient Egyptology and reinvents ideals of the *griot*, the ancestors, and the talking drums in African folklores. The reawakening places oral traditions first even as it acknowledges the immediacy of modern texts in pursuit of Stierstorfer's new directions.

Capture theory, in its intentions, attractions, and cravings attempts to break the "prison-house of language" and sets against injustices masquerading as inmates

[1]Ogo is of the pumpkin family. The traditional Idoma use it as eating or drinking plate. It grows extensively to join Ape, another specie, again, of pumpkins. When planted close in the farms, the two species grow into one another such that except for the fruits, in outlook, they are hardly distinguishable.

in poetry. The theoretical underpinnings are golden ways to new directions in law and poetry. It admits that "[g]ood fences make good neighbors" (Frost 1969, 33). The admittance notwithstanding, the fence breaks the natural bond existing between two neighbors. Law and poetry assume the status of good neighbors by virtue of interdependence. The symbiotic relationship reminds us of the doctrine of separation of powers in the English legal system. Going by the proposition on new directions in post-theories, law mends her centuries-old legally standing walls to accommodate literature, poetry in particular. Poetry, in return mends her tropes to break centuries of literary boundaries to interact with law. This interdependence is consistent with Robert Frost's ideologies in "Mending Wall." Mending being the state of adjusting to attract the opposite neighbor to a new governorship system. Adjusting, breaking, or mending the wall either side emphasizes interdependency rather than flaunt aesthetics. As Stierstorfer (2011) has demonstrated, "the study of literature is more concerned with literature's characteristics as an art form, i.e. characteristics it may share with the other arts" (45).

Other arts, in the context of post-theories, highlights the right to associate, i.e. poetry associates in one way, or the other, with law, and law in its cultural ties relates freely with poetry. The relationship attracts attention to the law of fundamental human rights and literature demonstrates that aesthetics in poetry is the freedom to associate with the other. The immersion validates the Idoma saying on interdependency in human relations: "ogo tagolape, apetagologo".[2] In other words, there can be no absolute independence of law or poetry—the two co-exist and reinforce each other in the manner "plants and animals, most remote in the scale of nature, are bound together by a web of complex relations" (Darwin 2009, 118). Charles Darwin's "complex relations" idea builds on mutual confidence and equality before the law of nature, and of men. On this note ends "Mending Wall" with the captivating lines: "Men work together; I told him from the heart,/Whether they work together or apart" (Frost 1969, 31). Frost insists on the interdependence of men, and the insistence takes hold on the relationships between law and literature.

Law and poetry, as Frost argues, are "Men." They work together in the inexplicable medium of metaphor. The metaphor in legalese: "interlocutory and perpetual injunctions" masquerade as place holder for the judge, "temple of justice" speedily loses it sanctuary standing to a house of hunger, and the most common slogan "My Lord" dramatically turns an obfuscating jargon, neither master nor monster in Niyi Osundare's poem that is law personified. In "My Lord, Tell me Where to Keep your Bribe," the poet turns the "Chief Justice" to a big and eternal fool: "Just one judgement sold to the highest bidder/Will catapult Judge and Lawyer to the Billionaire's Club" (2021, 67). This eloquence perforates the gown and the wigs—the law, the bench, and the bar turn to poetry in unprecedented metaphors:

[2] The mystery of a child circumcising the father expresses the unthinkable in human life—providing an answer to a question before the question is asked.

The Law, they say, is an ass
Sometimes fast, sometimes slow
But the Law in Nigeria is a vulture
Fat on the cash-and-carry carrion of murdered Conscience. (Osundare 2021, 65)

The cadence of intentional oratory unbelievably draws attention to street talcs of arrests, detentions and revelations, and to the media and court trials of judges and corrupt politicians in Nigeria. While the lines authenticate corruption as "A terrible plague in the land," they also combine the primacy of African oral traditions with the immediacy of modern law text. The orality awfully turns the actual reader's inner shame to a huge public embarrassment. In this paraphernalia on law and poetry, attention capture is intricately woven. The poetry draws extraordinary attention of the world to judges and lawyers. It has been argued that there is a drastic reduction in "mind-wandering during the performance of cognitively demanding tasks without altering the semantic content or complexity" (Lavie 2010, 146).

Attention, therefore, is on the judges, as well as the lawyers, who feel the earth would "open up and swallow" the bribery scandal to summarily end the game of shame. Weird cognitive feud between the judiciary and the world emanating from the extemporaneous poem is, to say the least, the trial and imprisonment of the corrupt in judiciary. "Where potholes swallow up the hugest jeep" is so captivating that it raises African oral traditions to points of primacy as the oldest form of art. The verbal interactions between law and poetry at court sittings give impressions that "[w]hile the order of a court will be imposed on the body or the property of the parties to the case, it will originally have been spoken as a sentence" (Dolin 2007, 2). That is, poetry persuasively interweaves judicial pronouncements at the courts to make verdicts captivating and tolerably acceptable to the hearer.

John Dryden's "Absalom and Achitophel" (1681) effectively employs oral traditions in Britain for intuitive, reflective, inventive, and captivating thought transfer on legality or otherwise of acrimonies between popery and puritans. The philanderer, King David, (here called Absalom) and Charles II's illegitimate son, James, Duke of Monmouth or Shaftesbury (here called Achitophel) are entangled in legal processes to determine who is entitled to the throne. Dryden's conflation of law and poetry, in this instance, shows where polygamy was outlawed and concubinary became a crime:

In pious times, e'r priest-craft did begin,
Before polygamy was made a sin;
When man, on many, multiply'd his kind,
E'r one to one was, cursedly confind:
When Nature prompted, and no law deny'd. (1972, 5)

An aura of licentiousness skews these lines, twitching and attracting attention to possibilities of advancing "[g]ood, gracious, just, observant of the law". The legal twitch unwittingly draws on mock poetry to intensify confusion on the legality or otherwise of the King's ascension to the throne. While the Jews clamoured to stop James, the legitimate heir, from ascending to the throne, Dryden, in his narrative poem, cohesively converts Roman Catholics to Jebusites to exaggerate the rebellion between popery and puritans. The poetic conversion reengages the audience on the nexus between law and poetry. The attention generated by the leadership crisis anchored on the Biblical narrative unambiguously projects law in poetry: "If a poem have a genius, it will force its own reception in the world. For there's sweetness in good verse, which tickles even while it hurts" (Dryden 1972, 3). The poem "tickles" because it is partly founded on oral traditions and the law of ascendency. It "hurts" because the law has been partly violated by popery thereby accommodating illegality of the process.

Reading and misreading in literature do occur, and even T.S. Eliot's reading of Shakespeare's *Hamlet* led to his uncompromising position, in spite of the "intractable" evidence of a master piece, that the play "is most certainly an artistic failure" (Eliot 1960, 98). When subjected to capture theory, *Hamlet* exhibits traits of law and drama. The play has "the effect of a mother's guilt upon her son" (Eliot 1960, 99) Eliot's judgment inexorably triggers attention on the pathological guilt of the supposed desperate Australian exhibitionist, Joseph Mandgele. Mandgele "[m]ade omelette of their [black] brains for white/Rights of passage" and experientially "made anesthetic/Optional—blue cornea graft, heart-liver swap,/Organic variants—eyes in earholes, leg to armpit" in the years of apartheid in South Africa (Soyinka 1989, 202). Soyinka's testament on the false scientific research in poetry has a tincture of guilt—that is, Joseph Mandgele claims to be a scientist while criminally subjecting humanity to suffering. Fyodor Dostoevsky's hero, Rodion Romanovitch Raskolnikov's awareness of the crime and lack of punishment in the society whimsically declares to Sonia: "I did not bow down to you; I bowed down to all the suffering of humanity" (Dostoevsky 1866, 99). Bowing down to kiss Sonia's feet, in the eye of Raskolnikov, is not a sign of love, but a symbol of denial of human rights as indicated in Joseph Mandgele's pathological guilt. The black man's denial of right to life without any consequence makes Soyinka's poem intricately tied to the law. The poem suggests, in the manner *Crime and Punishment* (1866) does, that humanity be made to legally bear the burden of their crimes—or be subjected to trials in the courts and punished, if found guilty. That sense of guilt resonates in Nathaniel Hawthorne's *The Scarlet Letter*. The Puritans, in downplaying natural accommodations to human inhibitions, inevitably draw our attention to the law of nature and the law of man in Hester Prynne's pregnancy and the morality question:

> The law we broke!—[…]
> God knows; and He is merciful! He hath proved his mercy, most of all, in my afflictions. By giving me this burning torture to bear upon my breast. By sending yonder dark and terrible old man to keep the torture always at red-heat! By bringing me hither, to die this death of triumphant ignominy before the people. Had either of these agonies been wanting, I had been lost for ever! (Hawthorne 1990, 256–7)

Hester Prynne's claim to natural justice clandestinely opposes the Puritans' right to punishment and the statute. Either way, literature comingles with law to etch out crime and punishment. The idea ultimately flattens our reasoning on law and literature to a question posed by Joseph Raz (2009) in *On Theory of Law and Practical Reasoning*: "Why Interpret?" (223). It is in pursuit of "practical reasoning," on the nexus between law and poetry on the one hand and the connection between attention capture, law and poetry on the other that this exploratory inquiry on the poetry of Wole Soyinka is conceived. The experimental inquiry, no doubt, gives vent to Klaus Stierstorfer's "new directions" in the understanding of Wole Soyinka's poetry.

Capture Theory, Law and the Poetry of Wole Soyinka

Soyinka, the Nigerian-born poet and winner of the 1986 Nobel Prize for literature, like any other social critic, writes poetry to gain attention of his reader: "The man dies in all who keep silent in the face of tyranny" (Soyinka 1975, 13). "Silent" negates the doctrine of equality before the law and Soyinka's avowed social maxim: "justice is the first condition of humanity" (96). Surreptitiously, this social and judicial commitment points to a new direction in Soyinka's poetry volumes: *Idanre*, (1967), *A Shuttle in the Crypt* (1972), *Ogun Abibima* (1976), *Mandela's Earth* (1989), and *Samarkand and Other Markets I Have Known* (2002).

Undeniably, these volumes are further explicable under any of "...the various kinds of insight which the far-flung and heterogeneous approaches literary theories have brought to the field" of law and literature (Stierstorfer 2011, 45). Soyinka's poetry inherently exhibits judicial activism: "My Tongue does not Marry Slogans" (Soyinka 1989, 241). The term "slogan" apparently expresses the monotonous publicity of events deemed to have taken place, or about to take place, while in actual fact, there is nothing on the ground to show for the events repeatedly publicized. The intention of the sloganeer is to deceive the hearer and at the same time gain popularity for the self and the body represented. The attitude is criminally motivated, and so, has some judicial stint—the sense that the sloganeer reaps where he/she does not sow—a dangerous cheat to the unsuspecting public. Speaking on "Trust, Confidence and Public Institutions," former High Court Justice, Kenneth Hayne, noted that "sloganeering" damages government and institutional trust: "If those within institutions of government seek to lead by resorting to slogans, others must do whatever can be done to provide reasoned and peaceful debate—based on truth—for all to see and judge" (Neilson 2020). This is what is meant by "We can never separate our judgments from the contexts in which they are made, those judments are nevertheless authoritative and even, in the only way that matters, objective" (Fish 1989).

Lack of trust suggests criminality, sort of, and Soyinka's poetry warning on sloganeering becomes legally relevant to restore public confidence in governments and institutions. Reasoning on poetry, law and attention capture borders on "what, if" to undermine politically dangerous institutional campaigns. And so, what if the poetry's abhorrence of slogans ends the impunity of falsehood, what if the poetry stealthily restores social justice, what if the question is asked, at what point does Soyinka's poetry intervene in law, and what if Soyinka's poetry mindfully takes sloganeering to shreds, do we confidently cry that Soyinka's poetry fails justice in spite of the posture for poetic justice? "My Tongue does not Marry Slogans," no wonder, unprecedentedly attracts attention of a greater majority of humanity—hence the theoretical basis of attention capture, law and poetry on which this essay stands. Daniel J. Simons asserts that "[a]ttention is thought to be captured if performance is slowed by this irrelevant singleton relative to performance on trials with no irrelevant singleton" (2000, 148). That is to say, while Soyinka's poetry mounts as "My Tongue" and positively attracts, the "irrelevant singleton" called "slogans" simultaneously acts negatively and discreetly as a distractive cue. A cue is a trope deployed by the writer to stimulate a reader to reactions. Conversely, and in the manner of attention capture, only a small percentage of sloganeers in the greater majority of humanity certainly is likely to take Soyinka's alert on sloganeering as a radically invalid cue, that is, Soyinka's poetry may only be distractive to a negligible number of sloganeers.

Let's take the poem, "My Tongue does not Marry Slogans" as an indicting piece on public office holders. David J. Seipp (2011) citing Tamar Frankel describes trust as an "expectation that others will act in one's own interest" and fiduciary duties as "duties enforced by law and imposed on persons in certain relationships requiring them to act entirely in the interest of another, a beneficiary, and not in their own interest" (1011). The sloganeer, in this sense, dishonestly acts only in the interest of the government or institution. By doing so, he/she derives some pecuniary advantage by virtue of the official position. In "My Tongue does not Marry Slogans," the "Multi-naira clinic" stands as evidence of performance in the slogan of "health for all," but emptiness at the shelves erodes public trust in the clinics. The "lawman" equally owes the public the fiduciary duty of dispensing justice to all. Failure in the fiduciary duty is often characterized by unwillingness to equitably serve justice at all times:

> Since justice is but one, it must
> Be seized not piecemeal but entire, or not at all,
> And pleas for the moment's justice shall not be. (Soyinka 1989, 245)

Soyinka's contention is that doubt should not becloud the sense of justice at one court and in another the very doubt be seen to be absent. The ambivalence twist is there in Western courts. It reflects in his conversation with Adekunle Fajuyi: "I do believe in the courage of that court, and of that judge." The possibility of justice, here, is hardly negotiable, but the twist, the overall verdict on Western courts that follows is unprecedented: "Subverted. No one believes in the courts any more" (Soyinka 1975, 157). The twist implies that justice is served "piecemeal" as indicated in Soyinka's opinion which echoes throughout "For Fajuyi". In this poem, what looks like a momentary appearance and disappearance of a match flare in the dark, or the reward-related visual stimuli of a working memory, Soyinka captures the attention of his audience with a visual image of Lieutenant Colonel Adekunle Fajuyi, the first Military Governor of Western Nigeria. "Honour late restored, early ventured to a trial/Of Death's devising. Flare too rare/Too brief" (60) with which the poem begins coincidently turns attention to the captivating appearance of a "march-flare in wind's breath" elsewhere in "Watermaid" (Okigbo 1962, 11). Juxtaposing this poetry with law, "march-flare" or the appearance of "garlands" is fantastically judicial—the fancy gladdens the hearts. Gladness is short-lived as it is subverted by "weeds" that comically injects injustice, anarchy and martial law into Soyinka's poetry. The poetic attraction has legal connective to the "Weeds" that doubly oblique the garlands to attract attention to the unjustifiable killing of Fajuyi by the 1966 coup plotters in Nigeria. Ultimately, "For Fajuyi" is an indictment of lawlessness, criminality and injustice in the reward-related memory poem designed to attract our attention to Fajuyi. Soyinka's memory load and by extension, Fajuyi's high reputation stimulate some sense of injustice in the gruesome murder. It has been argued that stimuli on working memory, and by further extension, this poem in memory of Fajuyi, has influence on "attentional capture, showing that greater memory load increases distraction by physically salient yet task-irrelevant stimuli" (Poppy Watson et al. 2019). That is to say, "garlands" or sense of justice is completely whittled down by the killers. Here, the swags become less attractive. Injustice masquerades as "Weeds" to our attention in the poetry of Soyinka.

Soyinka's poetry equally draws attention to law and justice in another memory threat-related appearance of a nibbling cockroach in prison. In "Conversation at Night with a Cockroach," lonely nights and mental agonies in detention create one of the most inhuman and unjustifiable conditions for political prisoners:

> During the first months of my detention, in 1969, I was in absolute isolation. I had no contact with the outside world and the only people I saw were my inquisitors. This absolute isolation, which accompanies the nightmare of interrogation, is an even greater torment and it has its purpose. They try with this barbarous isolation to open breaches in your thought, to shake your trust in the most simple human values which have supported your life until now, and thus to weaken your resistance to the continual waves of upsetting thoughts that they unleash against you during their interrogations and that constitute the perverse spiritual world of the dictator. (Mangakis 1975, 3)

George Mangakis, in this testament, legally draws attention to the barbarity of solitary imprisonment in a supposed world of justice and the rule of law. The "barbarous" incarceration and deprivation of persons provokes imaginations against the "riven hearts" (108) and their empiric "new-forged weapons" fashioned against law and justice. Soyinka's poetic indictment of the barbarity of solitary imprisonment unequivocally states, and the non-equivocation statement sounds legal, that if at a moment "On earth, our fears must teach us silence" (110), that moment tells us that law and justice, in one way or the other, have suffered violent denials. These denials encoded in "Conversation at Night with a Cockroach," are not too distant from the huge silence of the world on injustice. Theoretically speaking, and going by Stierstorfer's supposition on "Theory-After-Theory," in law and literature, breaking the huge silence on Soyinka's poetry and the relationships with law requires an all-engaging principle. The principle is our capacity to break the silence, or put in another way, the "ability to grab attention [and turn to law in the poetry], even if we try to ignore them" (Schmidt et al. 2015, 693). It is, indeed, herculean to ignore poetry's affinity to law in Soyinka's texts. The poetry seemingly has the fragrance of the liquid scent, perhaps the scent of interdisciplinarity suffused in attention. It is difficult to attempt to break justice and law free from the poetry by widening the "ledge of space" between the two. This is particularly so, when *A Shuttle in the Crypt* is subjected to a close scrutiny.

The poetry volume is more of a trial by ordeal. Assumedly equated to spiritual judgment or the trial of a restless human, the shuttle, nay, the prisoner facing trial "is a secretive seed, shrine, kernel, phallus, and well of creative mysteries. Self-identification with this essence of innate repletion was a natural weapon to employ against the dangers of an inhuman isolation" (Soyinka 1975, 95). This pre-trial prefatory address on what is yet to come in future proceedings has been tersely stimulated by poetry. The stimulation includes the obvious kinds of fantasies inviting ancestors and traditionally submitting to the dominance of fate. Tying to, and finally uniting the prefatory mind with spirits simply replicates a communal trial—the all-knowing Ogun and the worshipper bound together in fierce defense of truth and justice. Even "When Seasons Change," or fantasies switch to truth in the detention ordeal, the mind turns to look at no other for the ordeal, but the "dead recession of the silent host/Whispering judgements" of no meanings than the "[c]obweb hanging on the throne of death/In solitude" (114). In this judicial context, attention turns to *A Shuttle in the Crypt* as a poetry volume seeking liberties of all persons. Liberties resound as the volume breaks to prison notes, and the attention gripping inflammatory notes are "dedicated to all who participated in the two-year experiment on how to break down the human mind" (159). The ironies of the dedication and subtle lies in the prison bulletin: "He sleeps well, eats/Well. His doctors note/No damage/Our plastic surgeons tend his public image" (160) are sheer mockeries of those who worked to crack the mind in the two-year ordeal of incarceration.

Expectedly, the fake detention report genuinely turns attention to the law of denial. Denial law, so to say, is like "[d]oing justice to the past requires a political and theoretical attunement to the ways in which law, in purportedly attempting to address past political violence, inscribes itself into contemporary contexts of violence" (Ertür 2019, 5). In essence, Basak Ertur is saying that while detention law claims to be solving past political violence, it is often undermined by reversals of its mastery, that is, "the violence of the law, and especially its symbolic violence, becomes easily incorporated into *longue duree* of political violence, rather than mastering them, settling them, or providing closure" (2). Soyinka's "Wailing Wall" is suited to the context of denials and law. A replica of the Wailing Wall (Western Wall) in Jerusalem, the poem subtly incorporates "violence" in the denials the manner Israeli forces in a six-day war with Palestinians in 1967 captured, and summarily decimated the Wailing Wall and converted the site to Religious Affairs Ministry—the largest synagogue in the world. The Religious Affairs Ministry attracts attention as the largest worship center in the world. It also denounces past conspiracies of silence and the paradoxical live television trials of victims in Israel. Soyinka's "Wailing Wall," nonetheless, remains a symbol of denials in law and justice. While focusing on denials in law, the poem simultaneously attracts solidarity for the dispossessed: "evil feeds/Upon the wounds and tears of piety./O wall of prayers, preyed upon/By scavenger, undertaker" (1975, 134).

It, sort of, awakens memories of Adolf Eichmann accused of masterminding the Holocaust. While law was used for the arrest of Eichmann, his trial was "marked by public silence and some sort of statist denial regarding the Holocaust" (Lipstadt 1996, 214). Again, this denial brings attention to the Greek philosopher who had to chew pieces of paper he used to communicate to avoid wraths of the state: "This action was a valuable expression of solidarity and communicated to me an excellent picture of the great solidarity which exists among simple people. And it also saved me. Once again I acquire confidence that I was in the right, because I felt that I wasn't alone and so I wasn't mad" (Mangakis 1975, 3). Denial is evident in the detention law. The flack attracts attention "on the leaden conscience of the world" (Soyinka 1975, 11). Soyinka's "leaden conscience" to use Friedrich Nietzsche's master phrase, is a "malignant historical fever." The phrase recalls memories of injustice in the past, turns Soyinka's poetry to a new direction, in search of justice in text properties. The two, poetry as a text, and justice as an ideology embedded in the poetry ostensibly meet at a common ground—poetic justice. Nietzsche's "malignant historical fever" or the fret of television trials in the "Wailing Wail" at "Bet Ha'Am" (the Peoples' Hall) are obvious denials framed on the key figure of the Holocaust in Israel.

The key figure, Adolf Eichmann, accused of being responsible for implementing the "Final Solution to the Jewish Question" (Zertal 2000, 96) readily attracts attention and the attention ineluctably interweaves injustice and Soyinka's critical poetic commentary "on the leaden conscience of the world" (Soyinka 1975, 11). The allure of interweaving injustice and poetry draws greater attention to memories of the Holocaust. As Yehudah Elkana (1988) succinctly put it, "[w]hat has happened in Germany can happen everywhere, and to every people." Soyinka's poetry painfully affirms the injustice in "hope/Buried in soil of darkness" (1975, 135). Watching hope buried doubly and cynically draws on fairness in law. While victims of the Holocaust battle "In Praise of Forgetfulness" Soyinka's poetry emits sounds of a legal text. Stanley Fish describes a legal text as pronouncements "written in verse or take the form of narratives or parables" in court trials (138). Such poetics substantially build on law, and going by Klaus Stierstorfer's post-theory postulations, legal tales in poetry point to new directions in studies in law and literature.

Legal tales and parables abound in Soyinka's *Indanre* (1967), in particular, the October '66 series, and in further particulars, "Harvest of Hate" and "Massacre '66." These poems bluntly paint a picture of the German holocaust in Nigeria. While "Harvest of Hate", on the one hand, triggers the final question of the Igbos, the poem discreetly and in brotherhood asks for cessation of hostilities, and the enthronement of fairness and justice: "The heart is pocked with furnacing of teeth/ The air is heavy with rise of incense/For wings womb-moist from the sanctuary of nests/Fall, unfledged to the tribute of fire" (1967, 56). "Massacre, October '66" on the other hand, resolves the so-called final question with "A kind confusion to arithmetic of death" in "...a loud resolve of passion" (1967, 57). The tones of these poetic tales are indicative of failure of justice in Nigeria. Agreed that "much of human history has been a fight for survival against natural hazards and against real and imagined human enemies," (Rodney 1972, 10) the parabolic sad tales negate the receptive social principle of *salaam aleikun* for strangers, then and now, and insistently focus attention on Nigeria's unfortunate history of injustice against the Igbos in 1966. Additionally, when we attempt to justify the statement that "individuals and groups become defensive against the things that threaten their values, identity, security, and any privileges and advantages they may enjoy" our rationalization come close to equality before the law (Best 2006, 69).

Soyinka's negative feeling, in cases of massacre and injustice, is human. That is why "once the committed writer has analyzed the ills of the society, he is also morally bound to take concrete action, dictated by political circumstances, to remove those ills" (Jinadu 1980, 141). The poems "Harvest of Hate" and "Massacre '66" are part of the feelings for justice. Laura E. Little reveals, and the revelation is legally touching, that more than half of the fourteen contributors to the book *The Passions of Law* (1999) "are themselves path-breaking emotion scholars" (Little 2001, 980). The commentary shows that emotion in law is gaining ground and that the age-long argument that emotion is detachable from law is no longer sustainable, if not for anything else, the fact that Stierstorfer's argument on theory-after-theory subsists, and in addition, that this experimental essay on attention capture, law and the poetry of Wole Soyinka bridges the gaps.

If not for the emotion intensified in the rhythmic traumatic motion in "Tread. Drop. Dread Drop. Dead" that draws the audience's attention closer to "Procession" as a poem, the all-silent hanging processes in prisons impacts less, and again, if not for the disgusting line: "Let no man speak of justice, guilt" (Soyinka 1975, 142). Soyinka's admixture of justice and guilt emotionally alerts there is confusion in the minds, even as the forewarned is further alerted: "Take Justice/In your hands who can/Or dare. Insensate sword/Of Power/Outherods Herod and the law's outlawed" (165). The law, indeed, is mostly "outlawed" in Soyinka's *Samarkand and Other Markets I Have Known* (2002). In the poem "Calling Josef Brodsky for Ken Saro-Wiwa," justice in Ogoniland hangs in the balance: "Market forces write the law, rigs and derricks/Scorch the landscape, livelihood and lives" (2002, 27). The operations of the law, and how effective the law is predicated on market forces. This hints at *pro patria* and that the people whose land produces the oil are social parasites. In what follows, like the "comedy of law," a smile is comradelier enough to make a trial judge go bizarre: "The charges, questions multiply but you withdraw—/Your mind has moved to mould a likeness of/The prosecutor's head in horse manure./The judge records your furtive smile—another one year: A private gift from him above the Party line" (1972, 27). This bizarre attitude of a judge, again, draws unusual attention to the truism: "Let no man speak of justice, guilt". Weird as the axiom is, it underscores hypocrisies "Of Power" and the twitching phases of law in Ogoniland, and by extension, our world as a market place. It is like going to a market to buy some needs and leaving other buyers down the place. Soyinka's poetry takes this socio-psychological approach to argue the eclipse of justice as "A dream that never ends, a glimpse that still recedes,/That shimmering Golden Road to Samarkand" (2002, 57). Using this approach to negotiate justice is poetically strategic. It is strategic because "…

thinking and argument, rather than as process in the conventional way" elicits attention (Billing 1996, 150).

Soyinka's poetry does not contemplate armament to gain justice in Ogoniland. War, for sure, leads to wastes and shameful testimonies of surrender:

> My friend, blood shaking my heart
> The awful daring of a moment's surrender
> Which an age of prudence can never retract.
> By this, and this only, we have existed
> Which is not to be found in our obituaries
> Or in memories draped by the beneficent spider
> Or under seals broken by the lean solicitor
> In our empty arms. (Eliot 1960, 306, 403–10)

This argument that humans, in their quest for justice, erroneously opt for war; yet return with empty bags of justice is quite sensitive—"He who was living is now dead/We who were living are now dying/With a little patient" (Eliot 1960, 304), 327–30). The acceptance of the law, or at most, the resistance to the law signified by dying "with a little patient" alludes to "Insensate sword/Of Power" in Soyinka's poetry. Here and there, "law's outlawed" with a "[b]reaking speed/ Of the truth barrier by a swooping detention decree" (Soyinka 1975, 173). China's Mao Tse Tung ended in emptiness after he unconstitutionally seized power with insurgency, and Chiang Kai's "Two Bombs, One Satellite" military project remains a master stroke in lawlessness. Malawi's Hastings Banda's parliamentary manipulations of the law made Malawians die for their President to live. In Ghana, Kwame Nkrumah's detention protection decree maimed constitutionalism and justice.

Insisting on law of power and evolution, Soyinka's poetry contextually becomes legalist. In Israeli, and in the context of law and devolution of power, the poetry lawfully projects Golda Meir, the first Israeli woman to be head of government, from 1969–1974. The lawful projection shifts attention to Yasser Arafat's transition. Arafat fought from trenches to become President of Palestinian National Authority, from 1994–2004. Power in the context of lawful transition in poetry also focuses on revolutionary Fidel Castro. Castro became Prime Minister of Cuba, 1959–1976, and then President, 1976–2008. The attention-seeking poetry survey of democratic powers captivatedly ends in the context of the United States. The legal transition of Richard Nixon started, first, as a Representative and Senator from California, second as United States Vice President (1953–1961) and third as the thirty-seventh President of the United States, from 1969–1974. These legal standards in transitions are anchored on people, not on the threats of power and lawlessness highlighted in Soyinka's poetry.

In a phenobarbital circumstance, therefore, between complexity and over-familiarity, Soyinka's poetry, legally speaking, is neither very difficult as to be incomprehensible, nor very familiar as not to attract legal attention and expectations. Expectations are always there at instances when Soyinka flaunts legal idea in power and transitions or attempts to attract attention to law, most times, at first readings. Legal idea in Soyinka's poetry comes and goes like a flower pot that appears with a red rose on a table, and again, disappears. Expectations are that someone is behind the scene. Additionally the appearance and disappearance is logical. Of course, there is the "evidence that young infants have the cognitive capacities necessary to form certain specific expectations, although in the case of younger infants some of this evidence is disputed or in the need of replication" (Parrott and Gleitman 2008, 292). The logic of "replication" in appearance and disappearance is hinged on expectation—again, there is someone behind the scene. Logic as a poetic tool shares borderline with law.

So, when Soyinka poetically flaunts *Mandela's Earth* (1989) drawing attention of the world to apartheid law in "Your Logic Frightens Me, Mandela," he does not just depict the mind as a citadel of courage and knowledge, the legality of apartheid is quintessentially questioned. Questions arising from apartheid laws are logical in spite of the contradictions. How does a prisoner fight timelessness of illogical racial law from detention with patient: "Your patience grows inhuman, Mandela. Do you grow food? Do you make friends/Of mice and lizards? Measure the growth of grass/For time's unhurried pace?" (Soyinka 1989, 197). Law, timelessness and imprisonment frighten and attract unprecedented attention to any personality whose mind reads: "Go to jail. Go straight to jail." What follows the mind's reading like Sophocles' Antigone is apprehension and attention to empiric law: "What will be left of you, Mandela?" (1989, 199). The logic of apprehension, ostensibly on the illegality of the detention, sadly focuses attention on law, poetry and the banality of accepting to go to jail, and then, turn with patient to fight back. The logic builds on the legal principle of obedience to law, albeit forced on the prisoner by the apartheid regime. It is on this legal principle that Soyinka objects to the illogical comparison between a political detainee and a criminal in the poem "Like Rudolph Hess, the Man Said." Quoting Pik Botha as saying: "We keep him (Mandela) for the same reason the Allied Powers are holding Rudolf Hess" (Botha 1989, 200), the poem draws attention to Hess as a criminal in Britain and to Mandela as a political detainee held under apartheid laws in South Africa. Pik Botha's confusion in differentiating racial law from criminality is even more legally worrisome. Rudolf Hess, the Deputy to the Nazi Leader Adolf Hitler, in a solo flight landed in Scotland on May 10, 1941. Being aware of the criminal act, he falsely identified himself as Hauptmann Alfred Horn and claimed to have landed in Glasgow to negotiate peace talks with Britain. Hess was captured and charged for war crime. The confusion surrounding Hess's identity at the time of arrest is poetically replayed on the arrest and detention of Mandela under apartheid laws. The confusion, misreading, or misunderstandings generated by Botha significantly inflames the racial tensions generated by apartheid laws:

> I bet they flushed him out, raced him down
> From Auschwitz to Durban, and Robben Island.
> Mandela? Mandel…Mendel…Mengel…Mengele.
> It's he! Nazi superman in sneaky blackface! (Soyinka 1989, 200).

Incomprehensibilities of identities arising from racial laws created these monstrous shapes of lawlessness and identities in Soyinka's poetry. The poetry has redefined criminality and detention laws in Britain. The Austrian monk Gregor Johann Mendel whose legal genetic research gave birth to modern human genetics resurfaces in Soyinka's poetry. It is branded "caste research" to stress the illegality of apartheid laws that sought to "determine the genetic origin of the South African legend" and the insistence on the rule of law (Omoha 2012, 45). On point of apartheid law, Mandela is taken for Joseph Mengele, also known as "Angel of Death" in Nazi circles. Mengele's medical research in Auschwitz prisons aimed at determining genotypes of detainees illegally caused the death of thousands of Jews. The confusions surrounding identities of Hess, Mandela, Mendel and Mengele are the very confusions around apartheid laws in the poetry of Soyinka. In other words, "Like Rudolph Hess, the Man Said" is intricately woven around apartheid laws and criminal laws of Britain to elicit attention of Soyinka's audience. Rudolph Arnheim describes this kind of interdependent attention-centered language as "dynamic" and the structure and coherence of compositions of the language as "straightness and flexibility, expansion and contradiction, or openness and closeness" (1977, 253). These characteristics are typical of qualities in building constructions. Arnheim's theoretical bent on elasticity and ambiguity in building constructions suggest "openness" in our attempts at identifying law and poetry as distinct disciplines, and again, "closeness" in the dynamic moves at closing the gap between law and poetry. The attention generated in this process points to a new direction in interdisciplinary studies.

Conclusion

Capture theory's "openness" and "closeness" in bringing, law, poetry, and attention together acts as "the governing problem", that is to say, as a theoretical or a rotating legal engine. The rotating legal engine has emitted justice, freedom, logic, monopoly, race, apartheid, black and white, subversion, chess pieces, Auschwitz, and other law-related jargons in this essay. These jargons collectively have that patient-central-interdisciplinary stammering tonal quality—leg, leg, lega, legal sensibilities immersed in po, po, poe, poetry as imputations for debates. The imputations, by virtue of interdisciplinary attention consequentially impart on the close tonal qualities of the legal jargons in poetry. The impartation on the hitherto differing stammering tones coalesced to what looks like law-poetics—an apparent harmony. Law-poetics echoes *ogo tagolape apetagologo*. The union of the two distinct disciplines conflates theory-after-theory with the mythic wand *oyi bibi no ge hada api* hitherto applied to tickle this discourse. That is to say, again, this experimental essay mysteriously resolved the conflict "Law and (which?) Literature?" years before it was generated by the German philosopher Klaus Stierstorfer. This lay to rest the debate on literature and its affinity with law. No literature shares a common boundary better with law. It is poetry.

References

Arnheim, Rudolph. 1977. *The Dynamics of Architectural Form*. U of California P: Berkeley, CA.

Best, Shedrack Gaya, ed. 2006. Conflict Analysis. *Introduction to Peace and Conflict Studies in West Africa*. Ibadan: Spectrum Books Limited.

Billing, Michael. 1996. *A Rhetorical Approach to Social Psychology*. Cambridge: Cambridge UP.

Botha, Pik. 1989. In Wole Soyinka. *Selected Poems: Indare, A Shuttle in the Crypt and Mandela's Earth*. Methuen Publishing Limited.

Chaplain, Ralph. 2005. *Songs of the Workers To Fan the Flames of Discontent: The Litte Red Songbook*, Limited Centenary Concert Edition.

Darwin, Charles. 2009. *On the Origin of Species*, ed. William Bynum. London: Penguin Classics.

Dolin, Keiran. 2007. *A Critical Introduction to Law and Literature*. Cambridge: Cambridge UP.

Dostoevsky, Fyodor. 1866. *Crime and Punishment*. London: Vizetelly & Co.

Dryden, John. 1972. *The Works of John Dryden: Poems 1681–1684*, ed. H.T. Swedenberg, U of Califonia P.

T. S. Eliot, 1960. Hamlet and His Problems. *The Sacred Wood: Essays on Poetry and Criticism*. London: Methuen & Co.: 95–103.

Eliot, T. S. 1960. "The Waste Land." *Understanding Poetry* (eds.) Cleanth Brooks and Robert Penn Waren. Holt, Rinebart & Winston.

Elkana, Yehudah. 1988. In Praise of Forgetfulness. *Ha'aretz*, 2 March 1988.

Ertür, Başak. 2019. Law of Denial. *Law and Critique* 30(1): 1–20.

Fish, Stanley. 1989. *Doing What Comes Naturally: Change, Rhethoric, and the Practice of Theory in Literary & Legal Studies*. Duke University Press.

Frost, Robert. 1969. Mending Wall. *The Poetry of Robert Frost*, ed. Edward Connery Lathem. New York: Holt, Rinehart and Winston.

Hawthorne, Nathaniel. 1990. *The Scarlet Letter*. Oxford: Oxford UP, 1990.

Iser, Wolfgang. 1974. *The Implied Reader: Patterns of Communication in Prose Fiction from Bunyan to Beckett*. Baltimore: Johns Hopkins UP.

Jinadu, Adele. 1980. *Fanon: In Search of the African Revolution*. Enugu: Fourth Dimension Publishers.

Lavie, Nilli. 2010. Attention, Distraction and Cognitive Control Under Load. *Current Directions in Psychological Science* 19(4): 143–148.

Leiter, Brian. 2002. *Nietzsche on Morality*. New York: Routledge.

Lipstadt, Deborah. 1996. America and the Memory of the Holocaust, 1950–1965. *Modern Judaism* 16(3): 195–214.

Little, E. Laura. 2001. Negotiating the Tangle of Law and Emotion. *Cornell Law Review* 86(4): 974–1002.

Mangakis, George. 1975. Solidarity. *Index on Censorship* 4(4): 3–4.

Neilson, Naomi. 2020. Former High Court Justice Warns "Sloganeering" Damaged Government Trust. https://www.lawyersweekly.com.au/biglaw/29109-former-high-court-justice-warns-sloganeering-damaged-government-trust. Accessed: 29. August 2023.

Okigbo, Christopher. 1962. Heavensgate. *Labyrinths*. London: Heinemann.

Omoha, Owojecho. 2019. Capture Theory: Battling with Tropes in T.S. Eliot's Waste Land. *Arizona Quarterly: A Journal of American Literature, Culture & Theory* 75(3): 87–107.

Omoha, Owojecho. 2012. Genius and Creativity as Poetic Madness in the Poetry of Wole Soyinka, Christopher Okigbo and Jack Mapanje. PhD Thesis, University of Jos.

Osundare, Niyi. 2021. *Snapsongs: Homegroans and Foreignflares* Vol. 1. Ibadan: University Press PLC.

Parrott, W. Gerrod and Henry Gleitman. Infants' Expectations in Play: The Joy of Peek-a-boo. *Cognition and Emotion* 3.4 (2008): 291–311.

Paine, Thomas. 1996. *Rights of Man*. Chatham: Wordsworth Editions Limited.

Patai, Daphne, and Will H. Corral. 2005. *Theory's Empire: An Anthology of Dissent*. New York: Columbia UP.

Poppy, Watson et al. 2019. Capture and Control: Working Memory Modulates Attentional Capture by Reward-Related Stimuli. *Psychological Science* 1(12): 2.
Raz, Joseph. 2009. Why Interpret? In *Between Authority and Interpretation: On The Theory of Law and Practical Reason*. Oxford: Oxford UP.
Rodney, Walter. 1972. *How Europe Underdeveloped Africa*. London: Bogle L'Ouverture.
Schmidt, J. Lisette, Artem V. Belopolsky, and Jan Theeuwes. 2015. Attentional Capture by Signals of Threat. *Cognition and Emotion* 29(4): 687–694.
Seipp, J. David. 2011. Trust and Fiduciary Duty in the Early Common Law. *Boston University Law Review* 91: 1011–1037.
Simons, J. Daniel. 2000. Attentional Capture by Auto-cue and Allo-cue. *Trends in Cognitive Sciences* 4(4): 147–155.
Soyinka, Wole. 1967. *Selected Poems: Indanre, A Shuttle in the Crypt and Mandela's Earth*. London: Methuen & Co., Ltd.
Soyinka, Wole. 1975. *The Man Died*. 1975. Penguin Books.
Soyinka, Wole. 1989. *Selected Poems*. Methuen.
Soyinka, Wole. 1996. *The Open Sore of a Continent: A Personal Narrative of the Nigerian Crisis*. Oxford: Oxford UP.
Soyinka, Wole. 2001. *Ibadan: The Penkelemes Years: A Memoir 1946–65*. London: Methuen Publishing Limited.
Soyinka, Wole. 2002. *Samarkand and Other Markets I Have Known*, Methuen Publishing Ltd.
Stierstorfer, Klaus. 2011. Law and (which?) Literature: New Directions in Post-Theory? *Law and Humanities* 5(1): 41–51.
Zertal, Idith. 2000. From the People's Hall to the Wailing Wall: A Study in Memory, Fear and War. *Representations* 69: 96–126.

Narrative Comparatives of Social Media Comments During the Pandemic in Australia and Germany

Cassandra Sharp

Introduction

Emotions are an active component of identity and community. They help us to make sense of the world around us and help us to locate our identity as part of a collective. It is our emotions that inform our everyday decisions, structure our experiences, and importantly, help to inform how we perceive our individual and communal position in the world (Duncombe 2019, 414). We all know that emotions have the potential to be contagious. When a human being experiences an emotion, it is natural that another in proximity might respond in kind, even if the degree and experience is different, and it is the notion of emotional contagion with which this article engages. When a hashtag trends in response to an event or issue, emotions are the "vehicles through which tweets become widely shared" (Nelson 2016). This article highlights and showcases affective interactions within the context of both the Australian and German Governments' responses to the COVID-19 pandemic. It showcases an empirical analysis of social media narratives to demonstrate that emotions are an active component of legal consciousness.

Across my work in the law, literature, and humanities field, I have sought to demonstrate that stories, narratives, and conversation are a significant method for informing and constituting law, as well as provoking critique and challenge to our cultural justifications for legality and justice (Sharp 2022, 2015). Over the last decade, I have narrowed this focus to specifically reflect on the performance of social media in its provocative role of transforming and challenging understandings of law and the social construction of law (Sharp 2022). The focus has been to identify and recognize

C. Sharp (✉)
School of Law, University of Wollongong, Wollongong, Australia
e-mail: csharp@uow.edu.au

K. Stierstorfer (ed.), *Law and Literature in Europe and Beyond*, Literatur und Recht 15, https://doi.org/10.1007/978-3-662-69851-8_12

the dual layers inherent in social media analysis for law and humanities scholarship. The first layer highlights the way that social media storytelling (commenting, posting, or tweeting) gives rise to a collective narrative that questions the efficacy of law in our society. The second demonstrates that social media narratives can render visible the ways in which ideas and values about law are actively at work in our culture and consciousness. These connected layers at work are what I have called a 'hashtag jurisprudence', and as part of that I recognize that perceptions of law are open-ended, dynamic and co-constructed by both narratives and emotion (Sharp 2022).

In this article, I showcase a hashtag jurisprudence by analysing social media comments related to COVID-19 in both Australia and Germany. Social media activity surrounding this history-making crisis reflected substantial public apprehension and critique about the impact of government decision-making on everyday lives and the legitimacy and efficacy of law, as evidenced by these two tweet examples:

> A complete absence of control, containment & action from a Government lacking any meaningful policy and ability to respond to the national emergency. #COVID19Aus

> Moronic stupidity of #COVID restrictions: train crosses border from France (mask-wearing optional) to Germany (masks in trains obligatory). Passengers who had been sharing the same space for hours mask up. German police with guns make sure they do.[1]

The combined role of narrative and emotional storytelling in creating and maintaining legitimacy in law cannot be under-estimated. Each personal response to a crisis event that is tweeted contributes to the furtherance of legal consciousness, which in turn justifies (or challenges) the need for, and efficacy of, a cohesive democratic government. By viewing the hashtag as a jurisprudential device that weaves together meaning, expectations and narratives of law, the article will move through a contextualist account of how perceptions of law and democratic governing are shared and perpetuated through social media. This will be achieved first, by explaining the connection between narratives and the activity of social media, and second, by using hashtags deployed during COVID-19 as case study, to demonstrate that emotional narratives are deeply constitutive of the cultural formations of law.

Narratives and the Hashtags of Twitter

Narratives are essential to the human experience—to the ways we communicate, learn and reflectively make sense of the world.[2] In my work, I argue that narrative and stories are inseparably constitutive of the life experience, and are an indelible aspect of sense-making, both individually and collectively. Stories that

[1] All tweets quoted in this article are anonymized for the purposes discussed in Sect. 3. Each tweet has been allocated with a number on file with the author.

[2] Understanding that narrative is fundamental to human understanding and self-identity can be further explored in the seminal work of Jerome Bruner. See for example Bruner 2002 and Bruner 1987.

represent our lived experience do not pre-exist narrative. In fact, far from being purely representational, narrative plays an integral role in the movement between experience and meaning such that the relationship between story and narrative is therefore understood as dynamic, powerful, and formative of meaning (Ricoeur 1984). This is why Bruner argued that we "have no other way of describing 'lived time' save in the form of a narrative" (Bruner 1987, 12), and why Presser stated that narrative is therefore a "shaper of experience" (Presser 2010, 434). I argue that all human conversations are enacted narratives (MacIntyre 1984, 211, 212), which reconfigure "the relation between the past, present and future" (Graef et al. 2018, 432).[3] I have long believed that as individuals tell stories of their experiences, they actively engage in a sense-making activity; as they narrate, they give meaning to their experiences and make sense of what is happening in their lives. Naturally, this investment in storytelling extends to the framing and contextualisation of normative expectations of the legal system (Sharp 2011), and in the doing of this, individuals are complicit in the construction and the constitution of law itself. Moreover, Olson argues that "[l]aw is always embedded in cultural practices that at least in part have a narrative component" (Olson 2015, 57).

In the digital age of the twenty-first century, such storytelling in the shaping of experience has become much more widely available and visible in public discourse through social media platforms. As ubiquitous in the fabric of everyday life, social media provide an opportunity for individuals to listen, interpret, and tell their stories immediately, accessibly, and interactively. Such participatory media affords citizens the power to raise voices, challenge institutional authority (Robinson 2011, 149) and rethink their place in the everyday world. Social media are thus viewed as potential sites that extends Habermas' notion of the "public sphere" (Habermas 1991), where the informal telling of personal stories also occurs online for democratic deliberation and debate.[4] As individuals comment about an event or crisis on social media, they engage in conveying not only a re-crafting of what occurred, but they also convey the meaning they have created by and through that event. Interestingly, this context of contemporary digital advancements is what Delage, Goodrich and Wan have explicitly labelled as the "seachange in the mode of law's presence" (Delage et al. 2019, 1). They classify this as 'post-law'; that is, "law unbound, free of its former thresholds, relocated and in the process of reinvention" to be recognized as collective consciousness implanted within and contributing to the cultural fabric of life (Delage et al. 2019, 2, 23). The tweet (and retweet), the Facebook or Instagram comment, and even the 'like' button, are modes and methods that represent 'post-law'—a "remediation of legality by virtue of the move to the virtual and by dint of the novelty" of digital media and its malleable capacities (Delage et al. 2019, 16). Law, just

[3] This is especially so as they deploy stories to link meaning-making with the world around us (Graef et al. 2018, 432).

[4] Social media platforms provide 'online sociality' (van Dijck 2013, 4) which stimulates a participatory medium of expressing personal evaluation to many individuals (Polak 2018, 404).

like our social world, is deeply mediatized,[5] and social media provides access to informally articulated, and constituted, perceptions of law. It is important then to note that a collective understanding of law would not be possible were it not for the human ability to communicate experience through narratives (Bruner 2002, 14). As Jerome Bruner argued: "In time, the sharing of common stories creates an interpretive community, a matter of great moment not only for promoting cultural cohesion but for developing a body of law, *corpus juris*" (Bruner 2002, 25). Within such a context, this article emphasizes narrative engagement in shaping cultural and legal knowledge, and demonstrates that narratives emerge, transform, and proliferate from the activity of tweeting and deploying hashtags.

Twitter and the Hashtag (#)

Twitter is a micro-blogging social networking site (SNS) that enables users to broadcast personal opinions mixed with information based on current events and contemporary cultural realities.[6] Viewing social media, and in particular Twitter, as providing contextual links between that which is cultural, legal, emotional, and storied, value is placed on the meaning that is facilitated and produced by the use of the hashtag symbol (#), combined with a keyword.[7] Signifying an individual's desire to "take part in a wider communicative process" (Bruns and Moe 2014, 17), the choice to associate their evaluation, idea, or value (whether random or considered) with a keyword in their tweet involves a subconscious encoding and decoding of meaning for both dissemination and interpretation (Pond and Lewis 2019, 217). In other words, the allocation of a hashtag marks the intended significance of an utterance to performatively frame a context that might not otherwise be apparent, and in so doing, it becomes a tool for creating narratives by which individuals coalesce around an issue.[8] Individual tweets enjoined by a hashtag gain significance by their co-creation and multi-authorisation. Hashtags then play

[5] 'As a result, the ways in which we make sense of the world phenomenologically become necessarily entangled with the constraints, affordances and power- relations that are features of media as infrastructures for communication.' (Couldry and Hepp 2017, 30).

[6] Launched in 2006, Twitter is primarily utilized for public micro-blogging, although Twitter does have facilities for private communication via direct messages between users. Users are able to post messages constrained to 280 characters (tweets) across multiple devices, and allows them to follow any globally public account without the requirement for that account's user to follow them back. Once a tweet is posted by an individual and then received by their 'followers', it may be freely 'retweeted' so that each tweet has the potential to reach an unlimited number of followers.

[7] 'By including a hashtag in a tweet, a Twitter user is making an active decision, and this choice connects their post to other comments around a common topic, event, or theme'. (Highfield and Leaver 2015, 8).

[8] Hashtags are hybrids in the taxonomy of types of information: 'They are both text and metatext, information and tag, pragmatic and metapragmatic speech […] [yet they] point to themselves, to their own dual role in ongoing discourse.' (Rambukkana 2015, 161).

a significant role in facilitating the creation of, and participation in, collaborative narratives among disparate individuals by framing issues around dominant beliefs, emotions, and values (Benford 1993).

This is the context in which Bruns and Burgess have adapted the 'public sphere' for the internet age. They demonstrate that emergent communities form 'ad hoc' publics that connect and bond large numbers of users that would otherwise be unconnected if it were not for the central role of the hashtag (Bruns and Burgess 2011). In this article, I argue that the combination of a catalysing event, emotions, and the affordances of a hashtag (#), enables 'ad hoc' publics to coalesce around familiar narratives that are critical of, yet also deeply constitutive of, law. COVID-19 is one such catalysing event, and the uncertain and rapidly changing context of a global pandemic provoked both individual and collective vulnerabilities such that social media was a useful mechanism for weaving together communal legal consciousness in response. In the next section, a comparative account between Germany and Australia will demonstrate the emotional narratives that implicate (and imbricate) law on social media.

Comparative Narratives: Germany and Australia's Reaction to COVID-19

COVID-19 has been the most prevalent bio-medical threat of the twenty-first century, creating an international public health emergency with common global consequences such as catastrophic loss of life; devastating economic disruption; international travel bans; and significant imposition of governmental restrictions on movement and behaviour.[9] Our vernacular became infused with terms such as 'herd immunity', 'self-isolation', 'social distancing', and 'contact tracing' such that a new pandemic lexicon became part of our everyday experience. Crisis communication proliferated a stream of continuous information from a wide range of authoritative sources, with individuals, organisations and governments equally contributing to an unprecedented "flow of all types of voices, insights, comments, clips, and statements [...] often producing not only misinformation, but also contradictory and ambiguous messages" (Volkmer 2022, 4). This transnational crisis "assemblage" (Sassen 2006, 3) of insights was made possible through the unremitting interactivity of social media, which in the end helped to perpetuate and enable "an ongoing crisis mode" (Volkmer 2022, 4). Isolation poignantly fuels the need to seek out digital technology for the provision of information desperately needed during these times, and so interactions across social media were stimulated by a dependence on digital technology for information and connectivity. Facebook reported in 2020, that social media traffic unprecedently increased following the start of the pandemic (Schultz and Parikh 2020). On Twitter in 2020, the most

[9] It is the largest public health threat since the Spanish Flu in 1918 (Robert et al. 2020).

used hashtag was #covid19, and it was reported that across the first 12 months of the pandemic, #covid19 had been tweeted nearly 400 million times around the world (Price 2021).[10]

The analysis in this article is drawn from a study of two Twitter hashtags (#covid19 and #covid) across four months (March/April in 2020 and July/August in 2021) for both Germany and Australia. Adopting the Social Media Analytics Framework (Stieglitz et al. 2014), a topic-based approach was employed for retrieving and collecting the tweets. Delimited by the date ranges, specific keywords (e.g. 'government' 'law' or 'policy'), and the two key hashtags were searched using the advanced search function of Twitter's API.[11] Only the first 200 for each month in each country were saved, coded, and allocated a number for de-identification.[12] The analysis involved extensive coding to capture nuanced patterns of attitudes and expectations across the data. NVivo analysis (word frequency linguistic concordance) and manual critical discourse analyses of the data were undertaken to identify patterns in the meanings that underlie the public comments made during these months.

Interestingly, in many respects the response from each country to the pandemic was very similar—both from a governmental regulative perspective, and from a public reaction perspective. Even considering a number's perspective: despite Germany having over 3 times the population size of Australia, the proportion of COVID cases in each country's population has been approximately the same—at around 46%.[13] Being already endowed with a high degree of social cohesion, both countries also drew on their individual histories of constitutional and federalist understandings of citizenship to seek compliance with COVID response measures (Jasanoff and Hilgartner 2022, 295).

In Australia, the early focus appeared to be an attempt to suppress and stop the spread, with the goal of 'COVID-Zero' status fleetingly within grasp through

[10] Other frequently used hashtags that were related to diverse aspects of the pandemic included: #stayhomestaysafe, #flattenthecurve, #stopthespread and #covidiot (creative term for a person ignoring self-isolation rules or not using general common sense during the outbreak. It is sometimes used to publicly shame).

[11] The API or the 'application programming interface' is a set of protocols and definitions that build and organize the platform.

[12] This anonymizing is necessitated by the desire to adopt a distinctly ethical practice to the collection and analysis of publicly available social media data. For a lengthier discussion of this ethical framework and its application in my research see Sharp, 2022, 58, 59. Note that in relation to Germany, I was naturally limited by my capacity to only read those tweets that were posted in the English language.

[13] Since 3 January 2020, Australia has had 45,457 confirmed COVID cases per 100,000 and Germany has had 46,217 per 100,000. The death rate was much higher though in Germany (210 deaths per 100,000 as compared with Australia at 90 deaths per 100,000). Statistics gathered from *WHO Coronavirus (COVID-19) Dashboard* https://covid19.who.int/. Accessed: 13 September 2023.

wide-ranging and large-scale community lockdowns and restrictions.[14] A national cabinet was formed—comprised of both state and federal inter-department representatives—which sought to provide "uniform risk management and timelines as well as clarity and coherence in jurisdictional response," allowing for states to develop their own policy within their unique context (Beck and Hensher 2020, 76). Likewise Germany sought to stop the spread, but opted at first "for a relatively mild version of a shutdown: not an elimination but a mitigation strategy" aimed at reducing infections to with moderate controls (Wurster et al. 2022, 2). Reports indicated that there had been an "initial period of relatively consistent decision-making across all German 'Bundesländer'" (Wurster et al. 2022, 3).

Since that time however, and particularly across 2021 because of significant community transmission of the highly contagious Delta and Omicron variants, in both countries, the approach for fighting the virus became more regionally fragmented and incoherent (Wurster et al. 2022, 3). and there was much division and discord between the different levels of government. With lockdowns becoming tighter and harsher in both countries, debates loomed, and communities were divided over mandatory vaccination requirements, and around what were the normative legal and political expectations appropriate in the context of a global health crisis. Such discussion played out across social media and was concomitantly discordant and unifying.

The analysis that follows seeks to demonstrate a symbiotic connection between narratives, emotions, and legal meaning-making that proliferates through first, an attribution of blame that contributes to a decline in public trust of democratic governing and by extension law's legitimacy; and second through contagious emotions.

The Narrative of Blame in a Pandemic

Given that uncertainty and fear around an unknown future manifests itself in a widespread perception of powerlessness, it is in the very act of tweeting that individuals attempt to garner a heightened sense of control by holding others accountable (Choli and Kuss 2021, 8). The framing of responsibility during unexpected events becomes a crucial aspect of sense-making and a coping mechanism for individuals (Hewstone 1989). Indeed, it is said that the 'blame game' is one of mankind's oldest rituals, and that it is natural in times of a crisis to seek a scapegoat whom we can hold responsible (Campbell 2012). From the early days in the pandemic, the COVID-19 virus itself was framed on Twitter as a formidable threat to international security, for example: "#Germany is coming apart at the seams. Blame #COVID19." Blaming the virus was a direct natural response to the aversive emotion of fear experienced in the face of understanding what was happening

[14] For most of 2020 it appeared that Australia had 'largely avoided the high mortality rates associated with the exponential rise of cases of COVID-19 relative to many other first-world nations such as the US, UK, and Italy': (Trevor et al. 2020).

in the world. However, it was also highly stimulated by the familiar deployment of militarised language and a "war narrative" by global leaders and media commentators (Cusato 2022). As early as April 2020, the UN Secretary-General referred to the pandemic as the "fight of a generation" (Cusato 2022, 112) and worldwide crisis communication consistently invoked the language of 'fighting for lives', 'battling infection rates' and 'winning or losing the battle'. This simplified normative agenda portrayed humanity as sharing a vulnerability in relation to an 'invisible enemy'.[15] Moreover, the collective casting of 'victims' (affected populations and individuals) against a 'villain' (the virus),[16] became enthralling within a war narrative because it speaks of urgency, expediency, and necessity that each justifies the need for exceptional changes to policy:

> The rising #covid19 infections in #Germany and other European nations is a scary indicator that the #Pandemic is far from over, we can't let our guard down…it is imperative that we get everyone we know fully vaccinated (both shots), that's the only way to win this war.

> Australia is losing the war and we need leaders

The impact of a war narrative is to produce a streamlined prescriptive agenda. The urgency in fighting a "shadowy enemy" (Connolly 2020) in the battle for life and death, convinces individuals and populations that special control measures are necessitated, which then underpins far-reaching policy pronouncements related to mandatory behaviour control.[17] As Cusato has argued, the generalized war narrative "obfuscates the differentiated effects suffered by the most marginalised" and when deployed by governments or political institutions to promote an 'apolitical approach' to the crisis, it can significantly distract from systemic shortcomings that sustain inequity (Cusato 2022, 110). Yet, as this research demonstrates, engaging in the language of war does not necessarily achieve the desired results for institutional actors or governments.

Because the impact of a war metaphor imputes exceptional responsibility to the government, the failure to effectively lead a coordinated response is all the more stark, and has the potential to backfire on those using the war narrative to justify and legitimize exceptional policies. Despite the ubiquity of the war metaphor, and its long-time connection to "strong emotions and social values" (Steinert 2003, 268), research conducted during the last two years is increasingly pointing to a "limited effectiveness of a warfare framing of the pandemic situation" (Schnepf and Christmann 2022, 108) for trust and legitimacy in our sovereign institutions.

---

[15] Emmanuel Macron, the French President, used this term in relation to the 'war' against COVID: cited in Cusato 2022, 111.

[16] This heroes versus villains casting was a common response during previous health crises, including epidemics such as Ebola (Choli and Kuss 2021, 2). See also: Hagsstrom and Gustaffson 2021, 417.

[17] "The aim of this rhetoric was always the same: increase civil support for strict COVID-19 policies and encourage preventive behaviours." (Schnepf and Christmann 2022, 107)

This can be illustrated by the tweets below, where hashtags were used by many to share and amplify an attribution of responsibility, judgment and condemnation on governments for their (in)action in this space:

> The dispute between AstraZeneca and the #EU proves that no one takes it seriously. Naturally, we can blame #Merkel and #Germany for this development.
> It is very clear the current crisis in NSW and in Victoria is a direct result of the complete stuff up of the provision of vaccines due to the idiocy of the Morrison govt. #MorrisonFail and it is costing lives and Billions of $$$...INCOMPETENT #wheresmyvaccine
> The #COVID19 situation is out of control in Germany. Health System has collapsed, the number of gravely ill people has crashed the ICU capacities. While physicians still fight for every life, [German flag emoji] polititicans try to find the scapegoat of their messed up #Corona-strategy.

This amplification of a 'blame' narrative is the natural outworking of a cumulative frustration and anger regarding governmental responses during the pandemic, and it belies the expectation that governments are expected to provide a sense of calm, maintain public order, and provide meaning and context to how reality is to be understood and experienced. This is even more important during a crisis "when the everyday consensus on what it means to live together—that is normally maintained through routine interactions—is suspended or challenged" (Faucher and Boussaguet 2018, 170). The tendency to allocate blame is thus highly contextual, expressed in the moment and greatly dependent on the pre-existing political inclination of each individual and their community. As they tweet, individuals are not only constructing "their own 'normative orders'" that is representative of a desire for a particular kind of sovereignty, but also by curating, sharing and forwarding it "within their social media networks" (Volkmer 2022, 4), they are making visible the discursive conditions in which governmental actions (or inaction) are labelled as legitimate or otherwise. Within a hashtag jurisprudence, it is the telling and retelling of individual storied critique and fears that provide a frame of reference regarding how well the government is performing in defending and guaranteeing the public good. Social media narratives across both Germany and Australia consistently reflected a deep-seated rejection of the methods by which the pandemic was being handled by their respective governments. Take these tweets as further exemplars:

> Ridiculous actions everywhere. German people under massive pressure by corrupt and insane politicians. Fascism has completely returned!
> For the first time in the history of #Australia, the left and the right both hate the government in their own way! #australiahasfallen

In each of these tweets there is hyperbole that amplifies the frustration and anger around the efficacy of sovereign order—"Australia has fallen", "fascism has returned"—which represents extreme emotional judgment placed on the actions of the governments.

In Australia for example, it was argued that governmental responses were reactive, often inconsistent, and lacking in clear strategy, and this became continual fodder for public criticism. Mask wearing, social distancing, restricted movements: governments across Australia vacillated about appropriate measures to protect the Australian public, all the while attempting to anticipate the appetite for public compliance to the policies they were continually revising. Across the tweet corpus, evocative tweets repeatedly assigned negative descriptors for government (in)action, including: corrupt, neglect, crazy, reckless, negligent, lazy, appalling and arrogant. Moreover, the prospect of mandatory vaccination was a critical point of judgment for many in Australia—and the narrative about vaccination targets was closely tied to normative conceptions of what would be for the public good and national protection. This narrative came to represent the "prominent unresolved tension of the current (post)neoliberal order"—the dissonance between what would be for the public good and individual sovereignty (Benoit and Hay 2022, 392). One Australian noted in a tweet: "Mandatory vaccination has no place in a free society. Public health policy should never be coercive and should always be participatory #covid19aus", while another stated "a refusal to tighten restrictions puts the whole country at risk."

Of course, this narrative was not unique to Australia—it was also evident in Germany where blame was attributed to the government for 'harrowing numbers' of infections and 'a sluggish rollout of booster jabs'. Consider further this tweet where the language strongly attributes culpability for lack of effective action:

> The current covid10 response in Germany is tragically ABYSMAL. We've had 2 days in a row of 35k+ new infections (all time highs!), yet our government refuses to implement proper vaccine mandates because they fear backlash. A failure that will continue to cost people their lives.

Overwhelmingly across both countries, emotional accusatory comments were a challenge to the institutional structures vested with the authority to govern. In many tweets, individuals told stories of arrogant governments that vitiate responsibility in favour of other interests,[18] and they used expressions like abrogation, abandonment, failure, and hopelessness to collectively and emotionally critique the governments' capacity to fulfill their democratic responsibility of safeguarding the lives of their citizens in this pandemic. In this way the narrative of blame was operationalized unsurprisingly through articulations of frustration and anger in both countries.

> The German government is preparing more #covid measures for next winter… This is what happens when your leaders are serving BigPharma interests instead of working for their own people.

> There is palpable anger from my NSW Twitter people today… They have been let down by a government more interested in economics, during an outbreak of a global pandemic, than public health.

[18] For example, one tweet stated: "This isn't a position based on prioritising health, its one based on opening up the economy and getting profits flowing."

To 'let someone down' is to fail to support or help someone as they had hoped or expected, and so here we see desires for normative assurances being dashed or disappointed. Of course, such disappointment has the potential to fester and just like a virus that contagiously increased its reach into our communities, so too did an infectious mistrust in government dominate the narrative. In disseminating narratives of blame related to the pandemic, twitter hashtags were thus inextricably tied to the conferral (or withdrawal) of legitimacy. This was reflected in many tweets that conveyed a personal re-evaluation of the way government and its leaders should be perceived and believed.[19] In acknowledging the key objective of democratic government to be protection of its citizens, Australians often forewarned the consequences of failing to do so—a loss of legitimacy and a democratic ousting of power—as these tweets demonstrated.

> Australia needs a Federal election and a change of government to keep us safe

> the governor of NSW must sack @GladysB TODAY if she does not introduce additional restrictions.[20]

That law's legitimacy is intimately connected to an engendering of trust and confidence within the public[21] was also evident in Germany where according to a study conducted in May 2022, by infratest dimap, a German polling institute, one-fifth of Germans believed that politicians and the media have intentionally exaggerated the danger posed by the coronavirus in order to mislead the public (Karnitschnig 2020). More than forewarning, or simply paying lip-service, Germans orchestrated several nationwide demonstrations over the years of the pandemic in protest over institutional direction, and this was lauded on Twitter. For example:

> Germans hit the streets today against #covid tyranny #freedomconvoy

> People protested the governments Covid's regulations and globalist agenda in over 200 locations across Germany today. They only desire a return to their previous lives!

Online engagement about governmental responses to COVID functions as part of the narrative sense-making taking place within the "discursive environment" in which various policies may be designed and subsequently legitimized (Da Silva and Crilley 2017). Tweeting about an event enables a simultaneous documentation and transformation of experience that becomes revelatory about law's legitimacy, and so it is easy

---

[19] For example: "I have no faith at all in the NSW or the Fed Gov and I think that's depressing me." Atkeson and Maestas suggest that distressing and shocking events in society encourage this re-evaluation (Atkeson and Maestas 2012).

[20] GladysB refers to the then NSW Premier Gladys Berejiklian.

[21] Lockwood has argued that public comment has significant potential to temporarily destabilize or disrupt "the smooth functioning of capital and government" and to threaten the efficacy of our governing authorities (Lockwood 2013).

to appreciate how social media can facilitate the communication of an alternative 'normative order' to mobilize protests in defiance of national and international directives.

Confidence in law is fundamental to a functioning polity and society, and narratives of legality figure importantly in generating the legitimacy that undergirds that confidence. Thomas Keenan writes that the contemporary pervasive view is that to maintain authority and power through legitimation, governments and lawmakers must at some point be exposed to the force of public opinion (Keenan 2004, 435). Likewise, Darley and Gromet have argued that it would be perilous for law-makers to ignore social responses and public perspectives when developing normative arguments, lest they risk losing prescriptive force, or worse, legitimacy in the eyes of the people (Darley and Gromet 2010). For this reason, it is important to probe deeper into the cultural narratives through which institutions will legitimize their claims to govern (Olson 2015, 56). I argue that emotion is an important and inseparable connective force within these narratives, and that the performative and emotional act of appending a hashtag to a tweet serves as an ideological practice designed to assist in that connection. The last section of the article briefly illustrates the work of contagious emotions in the hashtag jurisprudence constructed in the pandemic.

Contagious Emotions: The Heart of the Matter

> I want to cry and scream in frustration and anger for NSW.

Emotion pervades our conceptions of justice, legal norms and institutions. To tweet is to blend "emotion with opinion, and drama with fact, reflecting deeply subjective accounts and interpretations of events" (Papacharissi and Oliveira 2012, 277) as they unfold. As has been demonstrated, connectedness through narratives facilitates the symbolic, cognitive, and emotional alignments on social media. As individuals comment on a particularly provocative event, they "produce and circulate affect as a binding technique" (Dean 2010, 95), which inscribes themselves into the story, and over time contributes to a collective narrativized emotional response.

The idea of emotions being contagious has been a concept long acknowledged by the social sciences as a central mechanism of individual and collective behaviour.[22] Over a century ago, Durkheim explained that emotions had significant transformative potential for creating collective "effervescence" (Durkheim, 1912). Exposure to others' expression of emotions via verbal or textual communication primes the activation of similar emotional experiences and appraisal (Moors et al 2013). In the context of social media research, digital emotion contagion thus refers to the process by which posted and shared individual emotions can spread and cultivate group emotions (Goldenberg and Gross 2020). We only need think of the #Black Lives Matter, #MeToo movements as explicit examples of provocative affective engagement (Penney 2015). By publicly sharing and displaying

[22] See Durkheim's theory of collective emotions (Durkheim 1912) or (Hatfield et al 1994).

these emotions, they become contagiously effervescent, which is "socially and politically powerful precisely because they are recognized as sites of emotional resonance," constituting the parameters of identity and circumscribing political potential (Duncombe 2019). In the context of this research into #covid19, it became apparent that expressions of anxiety, uncertainty, fear or distress, often became as transmissible as the very virus that was causing the torment.

> My heart seriously goes out to all the health workers and contract tracers working across NSW and Vic at the moment. Their days must be epic and incredibly stressful.

> Following #COVID19 with a sad heart reading about my dead colleagues in Germany

Building upon Butler who suggests an intimacy between materialization and intensification, Ahmed suggests that bodies and worlds materialize, take shape, and collide through the intensification of feeling (Ahmed 2014: 209). It is a bodily process of affecting and being affected by something, and that judgment arises by the intensity of affect in relation to that thing (Ahmed 2014, 209). To Ahmed, in moments of uncertainty or fear, "the world presses against the body" (Ahmed 2014, 2), and emotions embody the space where we become aware of its impact upon us. Associated with the 'mark' that is left on us by the press of one surface upon another (Ahmed 2014, 29), emotions can be sudden, significant, and without subtlety.

Many comments on Twitter to the ever-changing restrictions, case numbers, and border control under COVID, empirically illustrated that affect was registering as the trace of contact between the world and the body (Ahmed 2014, 6), and the contagiously affective experience of a pressing of emotion on bodies in response to COVID, was expressed through descriptions of suffering physical sensations. Across the analysis of this project, one recurring and contagious affective reference was the 'heart'—particularly as individuals discussed their fear and distress surrounding increased case numbers:

> Oh my heart. Another steep surge in Sydney. Its exponential now. I fear for my friends up there. #covid19aus

The concept of the heart is a common reference across cultures, and it is not only denotative of physical functionality in our bodies, but it has significant emblematic connotations that are connected to love.[23] Although often referred to as a physical sensation that could indeed be literally occurring ('my heart is thumping') the overwhelming affective description of this material impression was the metaphorical pain coming from the heart. For example, heartache and the hurting heart were common phrases used in this context.

---

[23] 'Heart metaphors abound in everyday life and language. To "take heart" is to have courage. To "speak from the heart" conveys sincerity. We say we "learned by heart" what we have understood thoroughly or committed to memory. To "take something to heart" reflects worry or sadness. If your "heart goes out to someone," you sympathize with his or her problems. Reconciliation or repentance requires a "change of heart"' (Jauhar 2018).

> Kids and parents have enough to deal with. Covid just brings heartache.

> Yikes. More than 100 exposure sites added in NSW. Not good. My heart hurts for the people up there.

> Honestly my heart aches for Germany. They have been hit so severely by #COVID19 with no relief in weeks. The effect on people will be deep rooted and last for generations.

The symbolism of a heart in distress, similar to these tweets here, can be found in many literary contexts. Whether it be the psalmist who cries out in the Judeo-Christian Bible: "My heart has turned to wax; it has melted within me" (Psalm 22:14), Antigonus from Shakespeare's *A Winter's Tale*, who exclaims: "Weep I cannot; But my heart bleeds," (3.3.55) or even Bonnie Tyler's timeless ballad *Total Eclipse of the Heart*, the heart is figuratively used to reference an impact to the very centre of one's soul. As such, it is easy to see why it is a concept that contagiously takes hold within the Twitter narrative.

Indeed, heartache is associated with extreme emotional and physical distress and is used in many tweets to represent the grief, isolation, loneliness and pain that the pandemic caused. Often, the intensity of this pressing in on the body was constituted by a symbolic weight on the heart, for example:

> What a tragic day for NSW. My heart aches and it just feels far to heavy. It's almost hard to believe we're in this situation. Love to all my fellow sydneysiders #covidnsw
> Honestly my heart aches for Germany. They have been hit so severely by #covid19 with no relief in weeks. The effect on our people will be deep rooted and last for generations

The idiom of a heavy heart that is *sinking* was also regularly expressed across social media, and reflected intense feelings of sorrow, dread or dismay. To sink, is to move downwards, (usually through water on the threat of darkness and death) and in response to the latest news related to the pandemic (particularly about 'surging' numbers or 'numbers jumping dramatically'), the body felt the weight of worry and distress pulling and moving it towards the dark place of fear: "My heart just sank to the floor when I saw today's figure. I just feel dead inside."

The articulated affective experience associated with the heart did not simply stop at heartache or heaviness. Interestingly, these expressions of anguish in the heart were contagiously amplified and transcribed into a larger collective narrative that hearts have a substantial propensity to be 'broken'. If your heart is breaking, it is usually because someone is suffering, and you are helpless to change the situation or do anything to help. The heart-breaking response was most often in relation to the separation of loved ones and isolation due to institutional policy-making. Take for example these tweets:

> The cost of this #covid19 pandemic is going to be felt for the generations to come. It truly breaks my heart

> People have been apart for two years now. Its heart-breaking. {broken heart emoji] #strandedAussies

My heart is breaking for the countless people who die from #COVID19 in Germany

The symbolism of a heart breaking in reaction to tragedy or crisis is a negative affective response whereby the body is shifting within its normal positioning. So, dovetailing with this imagery of a broken heart is the common exclamation across the case study that hearts were 'going out' to those affected—in Australia, one person tweeted "My heart really goes out to all in the country. This didn't have to happen." In Germany, another said: "I've just been told that its lock down again here in Germany as of today. My heart goes out to the business owners who've suffered so much lately."

This is such an interesting expression that collectively took hold within the narrative. The idea that a 'heart goes out' conveys that something more than rational argument and cognition was required to sufficiently empathize with those most acutely affected, and to communally respond to the tragedies around the pandemic, for example: "Germany have had so many deaths. RIP. my heart goes out to all families." It is a symbolic giving of one's body—a metaphorical transfer of affection to those who suffer. Bodies were responding to the crisis by creating affective resonances which in turn created "an experience of belonging, intimacy, affinity, togetherness and mutual understanding based on common experience and sentiments" (Miller 2015, 66). Miller explains that these resonances are reverberations resulting from interacting bodies which produce "an emotional connection based on appeals to sameness or common human experiences" (2015, 66).

Motivated by (and simultaneously motivating) a momentary experience of solidarity and community around anger at the government, "however evanescent those feelings may be" (Papacharissi 2016, 310), a contagious disruption pivoting the body towards something transformative was also evident in the tweet corpus—with the metaphor of a heart breaking for the suffering of others, was transformed into the contagious offering to 'send love'. In Australia this was articulated in in statements like: "I can just feel your pain and am sending you all the [heart emoji] I can muster #covidnsw #tears". While in Germany, an image of the DHL Post Tower in Bonn, and its office lights displaying the pattern of a heart was retweeted in an expression of gratitude to those on the frontline: "DHL Post Tower thanks all the corona crisis workers with an illuminated heart of lights. #solidarity."

Of course, what does the heart represent most, or at the least connote in the everyday sense, if not the concept of love. As an outworking of the heart, love becomes a prosocial norm that is served to reduce the negative impacts of fear, anxiety and distress, and expedite a return to peace, trust and calm. Through unifying messages that are "characterised by repetition [and] restating" (Papacharissi 2016, 278), Twitter narratives thus reflected the movement of the body away from fear and distress, towards the norm of love. Goodrich has argued that the affective bonds of love are expressed in the everyday drama of the juridical (Goodrich 2000), and are an urgent dimension of all law, traditions and practices which form the collective legal unconscious (Shaw and Shaw 2013, 47). With its immense importance for individuals or groups who face distress, sorrow and despair, the potential of love embraced and pursued, as a result of sustained exposure to others who express love is cumulatively significant. Take this idea of imploring others, through sentiments of love, to 'do the right thing' for example, which was common in the case study:

> Sending love to all the people doing the right thing—almost all of us #covid19aus

> Big love and shout out to New-Southers again tonight. This may turn into a longer haul than people expected but if everybody's doing the right thing, it will soon pass. Let's get through it. Xx #covidnsw

It could be argued that to love and be loved is one of the key purposes to life, and that it is facilitative of strength, which in turn spreads to hope. Here we see that the repetition of a simple utopian impulse of believing in the power of obedience to law, promotes an emotional pattern for love and hope to prevail within culture. These individual impassioned tweets become part of an empathetic imagination expressed by a collective where hope is made apparent in the desire to restabilize society, to restore order and balance, and to trust in a society where law benefits all.

Conclusion

It is argued that there is an intimate connection between how we conceive legal meaning and the practice of everyday living. This article has illuminated the way narratives of social media shifts other users towards a sense of communal expression of emotion. Indeed, it is not the content or text that often causes media to become viral, but instead it is the affects and emotions which that content produces. This, in turn, has enormous normative significance for law, which is "an expression and satisfaction of emotions" (Solomon 1999, 127). Indeed, Solomon argues that without an "empathetic perspective, there can be no adequate conception of justice or law," (Solomon 199, 127) and this analysis demonstrates that collective narratives that emerge on Twitter have the potential to define, rationalize and shape expectations of law, because they reflect, engage and circulate emotion. These expectations proceed from taken-for-granted assumptions that we live in a world where the goal of law is to protect citizens from harm. Any threat to security and safety provokes an interweaving of individual and collective emotions. As the analysis has demonstrated, emotions narrated through hashtags is one process through which individuals contribute to a collective shaping of social, political, and legal processes. As judgments of law are enacted through the articulated intensity of bodily responses to crisis, it becomes imperative to not under-estimate the powerful role of emotional narratives in creating and sustaining law's legitimacy.

References

Ahmed, Sara. 2014. *The Cultural Politics of Emotion.* 2nd ed. New York: Routledge.

Atkeson, Lonna Rae, and Cherie D. Maestas. 2012. *Catastrophic Politics: How Extraordinary Events Redefine Perceptions of Government.* New York: Cambridge University Press.

Beck, Matthew J., and David A. Hensher. 2020. Insights into the Impact of COVID-19 on Household Travel and Activities in Australia – The Early Days Under Restrictions. *Transport Policy* 96: 76–93.

Benford, Robert D. 1993. "You Could Be the Hundredth Monkey": Collective Action Frames and Vocabularies of Motive within the Nuclear Disarmament Movement. *The Sociological Quarterly* 34: 195–216.

Benoît, Cyril, and Colin Hay. 2022. The Antinomies of Sovereigntism, Statism and Liberalism in European Democratic Responses to the COVID-19 Crisis: A Comparison of Britain and France. *Comp Eur Polit* 20: 390–410.

Bruner, Jerome. 1987. Life as Narrative. *Social Research* 54: 11–32.

Bruner, Jerome. 2002. *Making Stories: Law, Literature, Life.* Cambridge, MA: Harvard University Press.

Bruns, Axel, and Jean Burgess. 2011. The Use of Twitter Hashtags in the Formation of ad hoc Publics, presented at the *6th European Consortium for Political Research General Conference*, August.

Bruns, Axel, and Hallvard Moe. 2014. Structural Layers of Communication on Twitter. In Twitter and Society, ed. Katrin Weller et al., 15–28. Peter Lang.

Campbell, Charlie. 2012. *Scapegoat: A History of Blaming Other People.* London and New York: The Overlook Press.

Choli, Marilena, and Daria Kuss. 2021. Perceptions of Blame on Social Media During the Coronavirus Pandemic. *Computers in Human Behavior* 124.

Couldry, Nick, and Andreas Hepp. 2017. *The Mediated Construction of Reality.* Cambridge: Polity Press.

Connolly, Catherine. 2020. War and the Coronavirus Pandemic. *Third World Approaches to International Law Review Reflections* 15: 1–7.

Cusato, Eliana. 2022. Beyond War Narratives. In *Crisis Narratives in International Law*, ed. Makane Moïse Mbengue and Jean d'Aspremont, 109–121. Leiden: Brill.

Darley, John M., and Dena M. Gromet. 2010. The Psychology of Punishment: Intuition and Reason, Retribution and Restoration. In *The Psychology of Justice and Legitimacy: The Ontario Symposium Volume 11*, ed. Bobocel, D Ramona et al., 229–250. New York: Psychology Press.

Da Silva, Raquel, and Rhys Crilley. 2017. "Talk about Terror in Our Back Gardens": An Analysis of Online Comments about British Foreign Fighters in Syria. *Critical Studies on Terrorism* 10: 162–186.

Dean, Jodi. 2010. *Blog Theory: Feedback and Capture in the Circuits of Drive.* Cambridge: Polity Press.

Delage, Christian, Peter Goodrich, and Marco Wan. 2019. Introduction: West of Everything. In *Law and New Media West of Everything,* ed. Christian Delage, Peter Goodrich and Marco Wan, 1–28. Edinburgh: Edinburgh University Press.

Duncombe, Constance. 2019. The Politics of Twitter: Emotions and the Power of Social Media. *International Political Sociology* 13: 409–429.

Durkheim, Émile. 1912. *The Elementary Forms of Religious Life*. The Free Press.

Faucher, Florence, and Laurie Boussaguet. 2018. The Politics of Symbols: Reflections on the French Government's Framing of the 2015 Terrorist Attacks. *Parliamentary Affairs* 71: 169–195.

Graef, Josefin Raquel da Silva, and Nicolas Lemay-Hebert. 2018. Narrative, Political Violence and Social Change. *Studies in Conflict & Terrorism* 43: 431–443.

Goldenberg, Amit, and James J Gross. 2020. Digital Emotion Contagion. *Trends in Cognitive Sciences* 24: 316–328.

Goodrich, Peter. 2000. Amatory jurisprudence and the Querelle des Lois. *Chicago-Kent Law Review* 76(2): 751–778.

Habermas, J. (1991). *The structural transformation of the public sphere: An inquiry into a category of bourgeoissociety*. MIT press.

Hagström, Linus, and Karl Gustafsson. 2021. The Limitations of Strategic Narratives: The Sino-American Struggle Over the Meaning of COVID-19. *Contemporary Security Policy*, 42(4): 415–449.

Hatfield, Elaine, John T. Cacioppo, and Richard L. Rapson. 1994. *Emotional Contagion*. Cambridge: Cambridge University Press.

Hewstone, Miles. 1989. *Causal Attribution: From Cognitive Processes to Collective Beliefs*. Basil Blackwell.

Highfield, Tim, and Tama Leaver. 2015. A Methodology for Mapping Instagram Hashtags. *First Monday* 20(1).

Jasanoff, Sheila, and Stephen Hilgartner. 2022. A Stress Test for Politics: A Comparative Perspective on Policy Responses to COVID-19. In *Routledge Handbook of Law and the Covid-19 Pandemic*, ed. Joelle Grogan and Alice Donald, 289–298. London: Routledge.

Jauhar, Sandeep. 2018. *Heart: A History*. India Viking.

Karnitschnig, Matthew. 2020. German Coronavirus Deniers Test Merkel Government. https://www.politicmag.net/politics-news/german-coronavirus-deniers-test-merkel-government-reports-4806-2020/. Accessed: 1. November 2023.

Keenan, Thomas. 2004. Mobilizing Shame. *South Atlantic Quarterly* 103: 435–449.

Lockwood, Alex. 2013. Affecting Environments: Mobilizing Emotions and Twitter in the UK Save Our Forests Campaign. In *Environmental Conflict and the Media*, ed. Libby Lester and Brett Hutchins, 49–60. Peter Lang.

MacIntyre, Alasdair. 1984. *After Virtue: A Study in Moral Theory*. 2nd ed. Notre Dame, IN: University of Notre Dame Press.

Miller, Vincent. 2015. Resonance as a Social Phenomenon. *Sociological Research Online* 20(2): 58–70.

Moors, Agnes et al. 2013. Appraisal Theories of Emotion: State of the Art and Future Development. *Emotion Review* 5: 119–124.

Nelson, Julie. 2016. An Unnecessary Divorce: Integrating the Study of Affect and Emotion in New Media. *Composition Forum* 34. https://files.eric.ed.gov/fulltext/EJ1113426.pdf. Accessed: 10 September 2023.

Olson, Greta. 2015. Futures of Law and Literature: A Preliminary Overview from a Culturalist Perspective. In *Law and Literature In-Between: Contemporary Inter- and Transdisciplinary Approaches*, ed. Christian Hiebaum, Susanne Knaller, and Doris Pichler, 37–70. Bielefeld: Transcript Verlag.

Papacharissi, Zizi, and Maria de Fatima Oliveira. 2012. Affective News and Networked Publics: The Rhythms of News Storytelling on #Egypt. *Journal of Communication* 62: 266–282.

Papacharissi, Zizi. 2016. Affective Publics and Structures of Storytelling: Sentiment, Events and Mediality. *Information, Communication & Society* 19(3): 307–324.

Penney, Joel. 2015. Social Media and Symbolic Action: Exploring Participation in the Facebook Red Equal Sign Profile Picture Campaign. *Journal of Computer-Mediated Communication* 20(1): 52–66.

Polak, Sara. 2018. Posting the Presidency: Cartoon Politics in a Social Media Landscape. *Media and Arts Law Review* 22: 403–419.

Presser, Lois. 2010. Collecting and Analysing the Stories of Offenders. *Journal of Criminal Justice Education* 21: 431–446.

Pond, Philip, and Jeff Lewis. 2019. Riots and Twitter: Connective Politics, Social Media and Framing Discourses in the Digital Public Sphere. *Information, Communication & Society* 22: 213–231.

Price, Julian. 2021. What Australia Tweeted About in 2020. https://www.9news.com.au/technology/what-australia-was-tweeting-about-in-2020-coronavirus-black-panther-bushfires-nintendo-switch/d4e827ef-711a-482d-8df2-b87ba8175018. Accessed 10 September 2023.

Rambukkana, Nathan. 2015. FCJ-194 From #RaceFail to #Ferguson: The Digital Intimacies of Race-Activist Hashtag Public. *The Fibreculture Journal* 26: 159–188.

Ricoeur, Paul. 1984. *Time and Narrative*, trans. Kathleen McLaughlin and David Pellauer. Chicago: University of Chicago Press.

Robert et al. 2020. *'The Coronavirus and the Great Influenza Pandemic: Lessons from the "Spanish Flu" for the Coronavirus's Potential Effects on Mortality and Economic Activity'*, Working paper, National Bureau of Economic Research.

Robinson, Sue. 2011. "Journalism as a Process": The Organizational Implications of Participatory Online News'. *Journalism & Communication Monographs* 13: 137–210.

Sassen, Saskia. 2006. *Territory, Authority, Rights.* Princeton: Princeton University Press.

Schultz, Alex, and Jay Parikh. 2020. Keeping Our Services Stable and Reliable During the COVID-19 Outbreak. https://about.fb.com/news/2020/03/keeping-our-apps-stable-during-covid-19. Accessed: 1 November 2023.

Schnepf, Julia, and Ursula Christmann. 2022. "It's a War! It's a Battle! It's a Fight!": Do Militaristic Metaphors Increase People's Threat Perceptions and Support for COVID-19 Policies? *International Journal of Psychology*, 57(1): 107–126.

Sharp, Cassandra. 2011. "Represent a Murderer ... I'd Never do That!" How Students use Stories to Link Ethical Development and Identity Construction. In *The Ethics Project in Legal Education*, ed. Michael Robertson et al., 43–61. London: Routledge.

Sharp, Cassandra. 2015. Finding Stories of Justice in the Art of Conversation: Ethnography in Cultural Legal Studies. In *Cultural Legal Studies: Law's Popular Cultures and the Metamorphosis of Law*, ed. Cassandra Sharp and Marett Leiboff. London: Routledge.

Sharp, Cassandra. 2022. *Hashtag Jurisprudence: Terror and Legality on Twitter*. Cheltenham: Edward Elgar.

Shaw, Julia J. A., and Hillary J. Shaw. 2013. From Fact to Feeling: An Explication of the Mimetic Relation Between Law and Emotion. *Liverpool Law Review* 35: 43–64.

Solomon, Robert. 1999. Justice v Vengeance: On Law and the Satisfaction of Emotion. In *The Passions of Law*, ed. Susan Bandes, 121–148. New York: New York University Press 1999.

Steinert, Heinz. 2003. The Indispensable Metaphor of War: On Populist Politics and the Contradictions of the State's Monopoly of Force. *Theoretical Criminology* 7(3): 265–291.

Stieglitz, Stefan, et al. 2014. Social Media Analytics. *Wirtschaftsinformatik* 56(2): 101–109.

Trevor, Thomas, et al. 2020. How the Media Places Responsibility for the COVID-19 Pandemic – An Australian Media Analysis. *Frontiers in Public Health* 8: 1–14.

Van Dijck, José. 2013. *The Culture of Connectivity: A Critical History of Social Media.* Oxford: Oxford University Press.

Volkmer, Ingrid. 2022. Social Media and COVID-19: A Global Study of Digital Crisis Interaction Among Gen Z and Millennials. Key Results of an International Study conducted by Wunderman Thompson, University of Melbourne, Pollfish and WHO. *WHO Coronavirus (COVID-19) Dashboard.* https://covid19.who.int/. Accessed 13 September 2023.

Wurster, Stefan, et al. 2022. Introduction to the Special Issue: The First Year of the COVID-19 Pandemic in Germany. *German Politics*: 1–13.